Appliqué Quiltmaking

Appliqué Quiltmaking

Contemporary Techniques with an Amish Touch

Charlotte Christiansen Bass

ARCO PUBLISHING, INC.
NEW YORK

Published by Arco Publishing, Inc.
215 Park Avenue South, New York, N.Y. 10003

Copyright © 1984 by Charlotte Christiansen Bass

Library of Congress Cataloging in Publication Data

Bass, Charlotte Christiansen.
  Appliqué quiltmaking.

  1. Quilting. 2. Appliqué. I. Title.
TT835.B28   1984   746.9′7   84-346
ISBN 0-668-05873-0 (Cloth Edition)

Printed in the United States of America

10 9 8 7 6 5 4 3 2 1

DEDICATION

To my husband, Ralph, who has been supportive and enthusiastic about my needlework; to our daughters Carla Dee and Claudia Leigh, both fine needleworkers; and to Laura Gae, our daughter who went to heaven.

To my father, Hans Christiansen, from Sarpsborg, Norway, from whom I feel I inherited my sense of color. To my mother, Ruth Price Christiansen, who put a sewing needle in my hand when I was five and whose encouragement to "go forward with positive attitude" I will never forget.

Lastly, to all parents of children who will teach them patience, love, caring, and appreciation by encouraging stitchery.

ACKNOWLEDGMENTS

As a quilter, I have written this book for quilters and anyone who loves fine needlework. All chapter line drawings and several of the detailed drawings with pins and ruffles are mine. H. Dean Golding of Michigan City, Indiana, has rendered invaluable assistance by doing the technical line drawings that appear with the text.

Ed Weiss of Slidecraft, Incorporated, South Bend, Indiana, photographed my Clematis quilt for the cover as well as several others. I'd like to thank him for bringing their colors to life.

A special thanks to the Special Events Department of Marshall Field's, Chicago, Illinois, and to Lyn Kavanaugh for having had faith in my lengthy series of seminars about quilting.

Finally, I'd like to thank the Continuing Education Department of Purdue University, North Central Campus, Westville, Indiana, for having signed me to teach a course, "Quilting at Its Best—And Then Some." The booklets I prepared and distributed weekly to help students understand my theories and techniques were the genesis of the text you are about to read.

CONTENTS

FOREWORD

APPLIQUÉ QUILTING
— THE AMISH WAY

his above all. — To thine own self be true;
And it must follow, as the night the day,
Thou canst not then be false to any man!
William Shakespeare

Life is too short as it is! Demanding perfection in the needle arts is a waste of time, a cause of discouragement, defeat, and dismay. Shakespeare says it all: "To thine own self be true." Do the best you can in whatever you do, and nothing more can be expected. Perfection is a state of mind, not a state of being! Stitchery is for everyone who wants to try it—and the less ripping the better.

Almost-perfection will follow, "as the night the day." Perfection is for the perfectionists, a miserable lot! Not for a quilter! Perfection is not something that should be required of a first-time quilter. It often causes complete abandonment of a project.

Strangely, most persons inspired to try their hand at quilting automatically think *patchwork,* and most teachers teach this method to beginners. Of course, the world is always looking for a better mousetrap and every quilting teacher truly believes that his or her technique is best. This is as it should be! *But. . .* time for a change in thinking. Staying on top of an art is not always easy; as with everything, time marches on. Learning to do original appliqué (original *anything,* for that matter) will not only keep your enthusiasm going, but will also be more likely to produce a truly creative, artistic end result—*regardless* of how fine the stitches are.

It is my sincere hope that when you have read and reread this book it will fill your heart with the joy of quilting and the warmth of sharing and recognizing your own ability to create beauty. Mistakes are not important. This is your beginning in appliqué quilting—and, as I tell everyone, "quilting is making shadows of love with your needle and thread."

You will become daring with the use of color, line, and design, in the mixing of fabrics, and in the use of trapunto (which is nothing more than the stuffing of something). You'll learn to quilt using an easy method taught to me by a very lovely Amish lady, Hazel Bellinger of Walkerton, Indiana. Some of Hazel Bellinger's colorful sayings will be found throughout this book.

Attempting something so large as a quilt is mind-boggling, you think! Not so! One thing at a time, one step at a time, and confidence that *you can do it* is all that it takes.

Before beginning my classes at Purdue University (Westville, Indiana, campus), Marshall Field and Company (Chicago, Illinois), on Public Television Channel 34 (Elkhart, Indiana), as well as in numerous seminars and demonstrations, I have required my students or audience to take a pledge—in jest, of course—and, after they think about the words, in all seriousness:

> I, _____ , promise NOT to strive for perfection in appli-
>   (your name)
> qué/quilting. I will proceed carefully, cautiously, and lovingly.
> There is no such word as 'can't' in my vocabulary. I will not become
> frustrated attempting to seek perfection in my first work, because,
> as Charlotte Bass says: *"No one was born knowing how to quilt!"*

When you shop, you find that it is often impossible to find everything under one roof. You go to one store for fabrics, one store for needles, another for hoops for embroidery or a frame for quilting, and so forth. So it follows with trying to find all the answers in one book. Many books get you to the door and forget to open it. I hope this book will fill the gap.

Imagine yourself on a trip from one major city to another—Chicago to New York, for example. Your road map shows the major highways, but you really need to go to a particular small town . . . and the map doesn't include it! So you founder. It is this way with many books about quilting . . . not this one, however. Good luck and happy appliquéing—happy quilting—happy memories.

Charlotte Bass

PART I

ALL ABOUT APPLIQUÉ

Charlotte's Clematis Quilt (76″ × 112″). Inspired by the gorgeous clematis vines in my garden and the blue sky that framed them! Colors: sky blue background, purple, violet, hot pink, and white flowers. Buds and strip-bars of beige/gray. Trim: white lace over bias beige/gray ruffle. Reverse side all white—including back of ruffle.

CHAPTER 1

IN THE BEGINNING
...THE LAST SHALL BE FIRST

h, don't you remember the babes in the wood,
Who were lost and bewildered and crying for food,
And the robins who found them, thinking them dead,
Covered them over with leaves brilliant red
And russet and orange and silver and gilt?
Well, that was the very first crazy-patch quilt.
—Flo E. Flintjer
*The Romance of the Patchwork
Quilt in America*

Many books save all the mind-teasing ideas until the last chapters. I have elected to reverse this method, thus "the last shall be first."

Color, line, and design are of prime concern in any of the needle arts, including quilting. For your quilt, *your* idea of color. *Your* idea of line. And, of course, *your* idea of design. If you're feeling overwhelmed by all the choices you have to make, help is on the way! The first three chapters of this book will help you plan your quilt.

There is nothing as wonderful as your first quilt, big or small. It is like a first child...it is special. Your heart will always be in your first quilt. Never give it away from the family. It is a work of love—*your* work and *your* emotions.

Where to begin? After taking the "pledge," please begin with a confident approach: "I *can.*" Unlike babes in the wood seeking a way out, you are not lost, not bewildered...just seeking a manner of self-expression via stitchery that will feed your spirit and soothe your innate requirement for fabric arts. Specifically, this manner of expression is appliqué—which is nothing more than applying something onto something else with needle and thread.

First, open your mind to color. Don't be inhibited by what anyone else will think about your selection. Whatever your choice, it should be *all* yours!

Learn to Be Daring with Color

Readers should now close their eyes for just a few seconds. Count to 13. What did you see? Nothing? You "saw" darkness—no color—gray—black—matter. What a phenomenon.

This exercise in "no color" is something I have done in all my seminars and classes. When asked what color they have seen, students have always answered gray/black/darkness. Of course, this is the answer I have anticipated. This is the greatest way in the world to explain color.

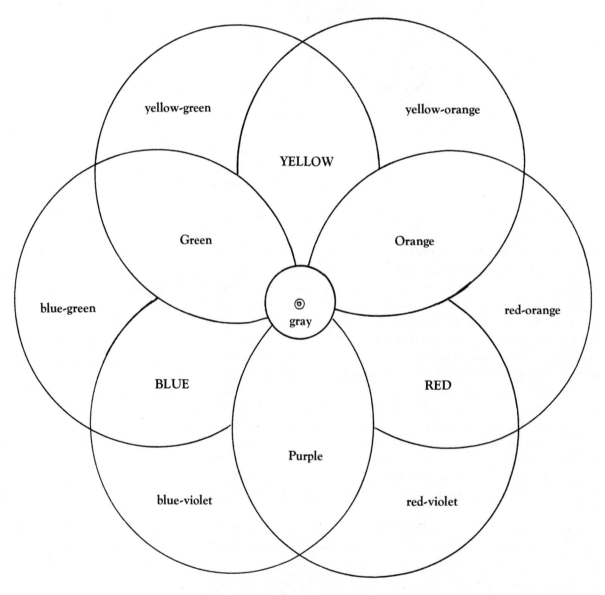

Figure 1.

Color is *light*. Without light, there is no color. Use, enjoy, have, embrace color now, because when you are dead there is no color; besides, it costs no more to have it than not to have it.

Next question: "But what colors should I use in my quilt?"

There are colors that have lain dormant in a person's mind for years, which are to be sought out and used. An entire new personality may emerge with the creation of a quilt! An entire interior of a home can be made to evolve around the new colors. Best of all, excitement is to be found in something besides off-white and beige! Actual color charts are available in fine-art books, but Figure 1 on page 4 will also give you an idea. Do the "Y" test. Pick a favorite and unusual color and use the "V" at the top of the "Y" (Figure 2) to find two other colors that you feel are complementary.

I assume that some of you have no experience in quilting, some have a little, and many a great deal. Whether you have a lot of experience or none, you will benefit by rethinking your ideas about color. Some people claim that the Amish quilts made today lack the sparkle found prior to 1940 and the advent of synthetic fabrics; perhaps the eye of the beholder has changed! Though a return to "natural fibers" is often recommended for quilt making, the Amish stores primarily sell blends of 65% polyester—35% cotton, or 50%—50%. Some, of course, also handle 100% cotton. Nevertheless, it is absolutely untrue that cottons present brighter colors. Blends are very often used in Amish communities.

Colors available in the blends range from the colors created by the rising sun bursting through cloud shadows in the East to the myriad of dusty hues seen on the Western horizon at sunset. Cotton alone does not afford this marvelous choice of hues. The Old-Order Amish, despite their subdued, quiet manner, relish colors and use the entire range of the color wheel—*except* red, bright yellow, and orange. Why not these colors? Because they are considered "too worldly." Although it has been written that white is not used, this is entirely incorrect.

However, it must be stated here that each Amish community across America seems to have different standards, as advocated in individual "Districts." (A District is a community of a certain number of families who meet together without benefit of a formal church site, in individual homes, to practice their religion.) One District edict might prohibit the use of any patterned fabrics whatsoever, while another district might be more lenient and allow calicoes, ginghams, and so forth to be incorporated into the quilts, so long as they are never worn as garments.

Solid colors—including the vibrant pinks, maroons, deep greens, and blues—mellowed with purples, mauves, and black are often found in "purist" Amish quilts. Reflecting back over the 450-year history of the Amish, I think perhaps the availability of dyes was the primary reason for color selection, although the blue probably represents a purist influence, too (indigo dye was also, apparently, readily available). Fabrics once had to be "grown"—from the field to the spinning wheel to the loom—to meet

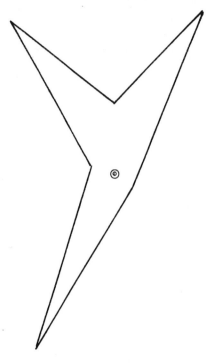

Figure 2. Trace out this "Y" on a piece of paper and place it over the color chart (Figure 1) to find color combinations that please *you*. Place a straight pin through the small dot on the "Y" and match it to the small dot on the color wheel.

a person's apparel needs; then the scraps were put to use in quilts. The Amish felt that quilting was a salvage art. Anything left over from making garments, whatever the color, was saved, as were old garments. These leftovers were then put together, perhaps in the beginning with the feeling that "this is what is available, and, whatever the unusual combinations of colors, I simply must make do." Although this idea is my conjecture, certainly the Amish have salvage instincts well engrained in their heritage.

Home dyeing is not a lost art, but it is certainly not often practiced nowadays. Decades ago, the Amish did a fine job of "setting" the dye colors used in quilts, which still hold their shades. And, remember, they did not make quilts just in cotton in the beginning, because cottons were not readily available. There were linens of fine quality; however, the primary fabric used in quilts then was wool. Surviving the winters would not have been possible with anything but wool or animal skins.

Colors, then, are allowed if they are not too worldly, but prints are prohibited for the most part (except for some of the preprinted small-animal patterns used for children's quilts). However, prints are ordinarily reserved by the Old-Order Amish to make quilts for their famous annual auctions for relief. (The Amish and the Mennonites come together at this time and work hand-in-hand.)

Look to the Amish for great colors. Their color sense is phenomenal—perhaps because they have elected to be known as "the plain people" in dress, and their more vivid quilts give them an avenue to express their love of nature's finest gift—color.

You've raced across town to see a quilt show, where you viewed someone else's quilt and wished your work could be as exciting. A rush of ideas comes . . . and goes just as quickly. Chances are, when actually selecting colors for a quilt, you will be firmly entrenched in the same dull scheme you have used for years in your home, your dress . . . *only because you have been afraid to branch out.* Emulate the Amish; find your colors in nature. The inside of an orchid embraces a multitude of colors: salmon pink/yellow throat, with outside petals of soft violet/pink; or salmon pink outside with a blush yellow throat tipped with maroon. Look at hyacinths or violets wih their yellow throats. A simple clematis flower has its loud roar of fuchsia/lavender/purple/white/pink, set off by mottled gray stems.

And remember: green is not "just" green. Each plant in nature has a different hue to its leaf and stem structure. Attempt to match the particular green to the particular flower—*nature's* way. The green of a violet leaf is deeper than the green of a hollyhock leaf, and so forth.

Other sources of color ideas? Look at birds on the wing: the robin with its beautiful breast of orange/brown crowned by its black/gray/brown body and its yellow beak; or a red-headed woodpecker proudly combining black and white to complement his head. More subtle is the magnificent bluebird, sporting an elegant, muted royal blue, burnished orange and white, with some brown and black.

Do not discount vegetables; their interior and exterior colors have unexpected beauty. Cut an orange crosswise, and several colors jump up to please your eye. Try a pumpkin, a green pepper, lima beans; don't forget their blossoms. What about nuts? The black walnut with its green hull soon turns to a gray/black with the interior meat a soft beige/brown.

Perhaps the *pièce de résistance* often ignored in thinking about color is the sky. Magnificent magentas, purples, peaches, reds, oranges, blues, grays, yellows emanate from the burning ball of gold sun, going down behind clouds to make a new day on the other side of the world. Use them.

Sunrise and sunset are equally breathtaking. It is nature's way of opening your eyes to color with the beginning of a new day or with its closing finale. Enjoy this gift and translate it into your world of quilting.

There is more! What about the silhouettes of trees, mountains, hills, bushes, animals on the horizon—colors of black/gray fenced up to the sunrise or sunset? This is not to expound the use of these objects especially, but to expand color use.

Visualize a beautiful flower in a garden. The backdrop is the lovely blue sky. Perhaps clouds are caressing the atmosphere in their billowy whites and grays. There is no color code in nature: it juxtaposes such colors and combinations; why can't you? This is a polychromatic color revolution! Put some of the colors that nature has seen fit to wed together into a quilt: this is where your own originality can be liberated. You will be free from fixed ideas. Be different, using nature's example.

All within reason, of course, select three to five shades for one quilt and carry one of the main theme colors to use as the backing. Down with quilt backs sold by the package! They are dull—and unlikely to match your original color scheme.

Scores of colors, the *polychromatic* approach to color, might please your color sense. However, there is also the opposite way to use one color, radiating like ripples in water from light to dark to darker. This is called a *monochromatic* color scheme. Do not mistake this for *monotonous*: it is anything but. Lilacs, pinks, yellows, peaches, even whites used as a single color in various shades can be magnificent. Pink, pink, pinkerrrrr.

"Will I be able to live with this color combination?" you ask yourself. "What happens if I run out and purchase all that fabric and then when I get home I can't stand it?"

Have you thought of colored paper? Water colors? Sample swatches? Paint chips? Purchasing one eighth of a yard of fabric? That's how you survive the night. Then go back the next morning and purchase the bulk of fabric needed . . . *that's* how to learn to live with it. Live with the colors a while before you jump in with both feet. But if you have the fever, watch out. Find a balance between common sense and striking while the iron is hot.

If all else fails and the ideas already propounded do nothing for you, look at a favorite picture in your home, in a book, or in a gallery. Steal three colors from it and proceed in the same manner. Even wallpaper will lend itself to ideas. Choose something from within your environment that will please *you*. You'll spend many hours making your quilt and many more living with and enjoying it.

If you garner nothing else from this chapter, perhaps it will inspire you to try a new color—or colors—in your world. If you have lived with beige for decades, it is time to try something new.

Beige sometimes turns people beige in their thinking. It is a "safe" color. Beige cars or brown, beige clothing or brown, beige interiors—all these produce a "beige coma." There are, however, thrilling ways to use beige. There is nothing the matter with it—except when used too predictably. Bringing a swatch of orange, green, or lime to beige will brighten up your entire world. Addiction to beige can be broken; just try it.

Perhaps you have been using traditional patterns. Frankly, making the so-called traditional patterns can be an utter bore. They've been done so many times before. Canned colors, canned patterns that have been accomplished by others for years, and the same old quilting lines: it is no wonder you are not satisfied. America is a land of originality—the land of the free—and needlework should reflect everything we hold dear, in my opinion. It is the unusual, the flamboyant, the unique that brings big money in the arts—the glamorous, not the dull, drab, and dismal. Do the extraordinary when selecting colors for your quilt. It will positively amaze you how this color explosion can change not only your home but maybe even your personality and entire outlook on life! Be flamboyant—color costs no more in the marketplace. You are *alive* . . . so use color and be happy!

CHAPTER 2

COME LINE, COME DESIGN, BE MINE!

et up, get up for shame: the blooming morn
Upon her wings presents the God unshorn;
See how Aurora throws her fair
Fresh-quilted colours through the air . . .
—Herrick
"Corinna's Going A-Maying"

Everyone knows that design is something that fills space. In creating a quilt, you automatically become a designer, a fabric sculptor. It is imperative to reacquaint your mind with basic grammar-school mathematics. Learn to draw inch-mark measurements with a ruler. Keep that pencil sharp. And, if patchwork is your forte and you have an innate desire to do something more daring than a traditional pattern, then applying patchwork to the world of appliqué can create for you a whole new concept of design.

So, "get up, get up for shame" some blooming morning, dig out those boxes of pieced squares, and apply them to the world of appliqué. Design is everywhere, not just in "cutsie" animal cutouts seen at the marketplace for quilters. All this time in the bottom drawer has resided "Aunt Hattie's" pieced work, which never quite made it into a completed project. Create a flower garden of a quilt by thinking *space* first . . . a solid piece of fabric . . . then drop a few of the squares here and there as if they were petals on the water and see what kind of motion your fabric imitates. "Fresh-quilted colors through the air . . ."

You say, "ridiculous." Absolutely not—not if the growing world of art can embrace people dipping hair braids into wild colors or rolling various color-soaked balls across canvas. You, too, can create by "letting fall" fabric on fabric.

Auctions across the world produce boxes of pieced work, cherished but never made into a completed quilt top for a frame or bed. This is where old-time art can find a new beginning. Most of the fabric is cotton, since the world of polyester-anything did not exist until recently. But be certain

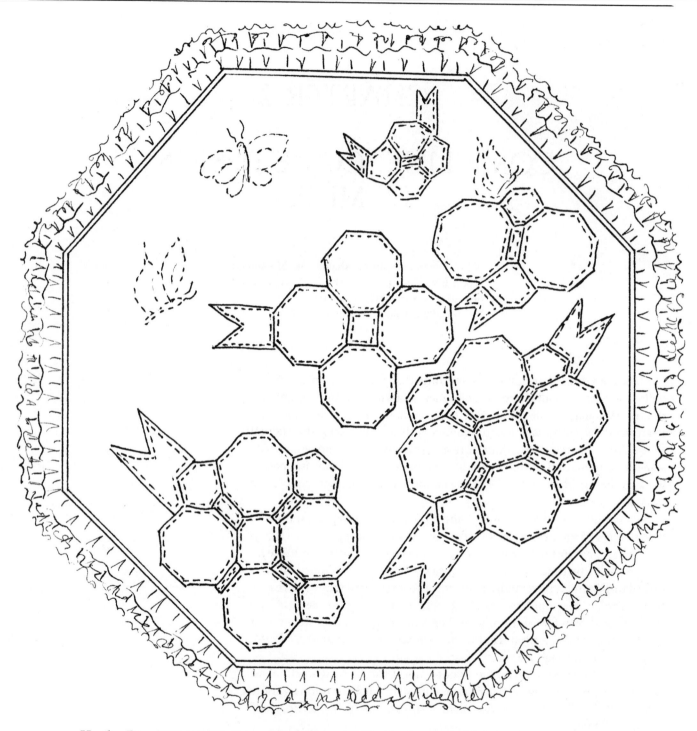

Heather Rose (98″ × 98″). *Colors:* Heather (grayish lilac) background with "roses" in three shades of peach and leaves a sea-mist green. Ruffle of heather bordered with green and crowned with 3-inch white chantilly lace. Back of ruffle is medium peach, bordered with green; back of entire quilt is "winter white." Quilt fits twin-size bed with dramatic effect.

you use polyester/cotton blends when thinking of creating this new garden in which "colors will fly."

If there is an octagonal shape in your block, make the entire quilt eight-sided. (Chapter 2 opens with a fine example of an octagonal quilt that will fit a twin-size bed or serve as a throw on a king-size bed. It is called "Heather Rose.") Tradition need not be adhered to at all. Remember? It is your quilt. You can do what *you* want. Do not be handicapped by—to use that Victorian expression—*convention.* Color will excite you when you look to nature, and line or design will do the same *if you open your mind to it.*

Suppose you have a gorgeous piece of old chintz with a wonderful flower spray in the center. Try using the strongest color as a potential background. Pick out a subordinate color or two for borders for your overall design. Later, lift one of the flowers, enlarge it on paper, and use this for the quilting pattern; draw straight lines between leaves, flowers and stems to join one "statement" to another. This is nothing more than tying the designs together, using the empty space, and giving continuity to the overall look. Quilting those straight lines is much easier than quilting an intricate feather design, for example, which would break up the "statement" of the flower spray anyway.

Enlarging a design is easy (see Figure 3). Use the spray at center front. Lay black thread over it making lines that divide up the design to be enlarged into sections. Criss-cross the threads, since they will be no more than guides to enlarge the work. Then you can transfer it by eye onto paper on which you've already drawn lines criss-crossed in the same pattern as your threads.

Your enlarged transference need not be perfect—nature is not perfect! "Lift" background lines and use them as quilting motifs later. If you do not have a very large piece of paper handy (for example, the wrong side of a piece of wallpaper is useful, or a large paper grocery bag), use a dark felt-tip marker to transfer your design to newspaper using the same technique. Pencil lines will not be strong enough on newspaper, which is why you'll need the darker medium.

Look beyond your piece of chintz (or whatever). See where nature has laid the flower petals one next to another; see the veins of a leaf (don't add too many), and the stems. Use just the major lines. Don't forget the stamen (center) of the flower. If it has a long stamen (hollyhock, hibiscus) or a flat, buttonlike stamen (poppy, clematis), make allowances for something long or something buttony to show nature's diversity. The use of embroidered French knots adds dimension; so does even a simple line of embroidery stitches. But let us note here that all this should be thought about *now,* while you're planning—*before* the quilt top is on the quilting frame. Then it is too late. Also, be certain to consider stuffing for added dimension. (You will often hear the Italian word *trapunto;* translated for homespun stitchery buffs, this is just plain *stuffing.*)

A few thoughts on trapunto. First, do not *over*-stuff anything if it is intended to be quilted. Using a quilt batting with extra loft makes your

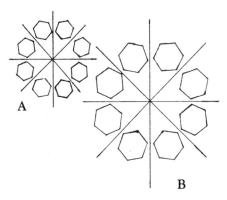

Figure 3.

A. **If the design you wish to enlarge is on paper, draw pencil lines very lightly through it, dividing it up into sections. If the design is on fabric, overlay dark threads in the same fashion.**

B. **Look at a section of the design A and transfer it, by drawing freehand, to the same location in your enlarged version B. Be as exact as you can. The closer together your dividing lines are, the easier it will be to do this. If your reproduced drawing does not look quite smooth, go over the lines again; apply more pressure on your pencil until the lines connect smoothly.**

material difficult to handle. Secondly, use the same stuffing as you will use for your quilt to obtain uniform washing and drying.

Rule of thumb: Determine how much stuffing you think will be necessary to give added dimension . . . then plan on using one half this amount. It will be just right!

Designs Are Everywhere

You won't only find designs in the old patchwork box. A child's drawing can be interpreted in a quilt or wall hanging; so can a favorite family sport (football, tennis, baseball, golf, basketball, bowling). Sports offer a wide variety of appliqué opportunities. Here are some examples:

Football: goalposts, helmets, shoulder pads, water bucket, shoes, socks

Baseball: caps, bats, balls, base markers, umpire's mask

Tennis: net, judge's chair, rackets, balls, scoreboard

Occupations offer unlimited and fun-to-do design possibilities—for example,

Computer science: the machine parts of a computer screen, a satellite, etc.

Physician: symbols, stethoscope, microscope, telephone, baby

Nurseryman: flowers, bushes, shovel, rake, seeds, trees

Design is wherever we are. The kind of design, the reason for it, and the number of ideas to incorporate into one item are the important decisions to make. Originality is within everyone's grasp. Simply *think original* and it will come. There is nothing more dull than a class in stitchery in which everyone is required to do the same design!

There is no such word as *can't* in my vocabulary . . . and there should be no such word in yours. (Once you've taken *the pledge,* there shouldn't be!)

A design idea may come to you by way of a greeting card, wallpaper in your home, a lovely piece of fabric, even an advertisement in a newspaper or magazine. There are designs and lines everywhere. Coloring books are full of ideas. If you borrow a small picture from a fairy-tale book and render it large, this is certainly not being a copy-cat. It might be the only quilt design like this in the world . . . and you made it. Whereas there are millions of Bearpaw, Double Wedding Ring, Around the World, and other traditional designs, there will be only one of yours. Open your eyes and think about line, design . . . and add a pinch of Chapter 1, now that you can appreciate color with a new eye.

Should true appliqué not appeal to you, there is always *counterpane,* which is nothing more than three layers of anything put together with small stitches in a line design. The word is frightening, but if this word were better defined to students, counterpanes would be made more frequently. I like to combine the technique with appliqué, adding large pieces of fabric to larger pieces of fabric, particularly to create beautiful baby quilts. Even some old-timers are afraid of counterpane because they simply don't know what it means, yet they have been doing a form of it all their lives! Look at the back side of a completed quilt. It is counterpane you are seeing. If this stitchery design on one piece of fabric were on both sides, without embellishments, the work quite simply would be all counterpane. (The term *counterpane* is often misused.)

Line and design go hand in hand. Take pencil in hand *now* (a medium lead pencil is all I ever use). Put a piece of paper in front of you. This is how to begin. Sketch what you think you want; be certain to include some kind of border, and decide how wide the border should be in relation to the overall design. Even include ideas about quilting lines at this time. Do not dismiss simple ray lines (like sunshine lines), which can emanate from some central object. This line is simple and makes a strong statement. Rays focus the eye on the main subject.

Do not be misled into thinking that appliqué is difficult. It is not. In fact, it is the best route for a new quilter. Appliqué is the answer to frustration: more projects are completed; certain accomplishment is the reward. *Appliqué grows faster than patchwork.* Patchwork can be a frenzy of matching corners and copy-cat work. Be original: do your own interpretation of something you admire. Line and design are *yours and yours alone,* just for the taking.

Big Top (56'' × 70''). *Colors:* **The background of this quilt is forest green; the big top is of various colors and the train is in preprinted circus fabric. The border is white, hit with hot pink patchwork insets and bound with hot pink bias and white eyelet lace. The reverse side is all hot pink with white eyelet showing. Four black yarn tassels and one large black pom-pom decorate the big top.**

CHAPTER 3

PLANNING YOUR MASTERPIECE

hou mystic thing, all beautiful!
What mind conceived thee, what intelligence began
And out of chaos thy rare shape designed,
Thou delicate and perfect work of man?

—Thaxter
"To a Violin"

"What 'mystic thing' shall I make? An infant's quilt, a large quilt, a wall hanging, a throw?" Ask yourself this question. And in your answer, include this: "I will complete whatever I begin, I promise. . . . I'll do something within my reach!" Fine! You have already come a long way.

Wonderfully, the thing you did *not* say is *pillow*. You may not agree, but my personal feeling is that creating a pillow is a waste of time, energy, and money. The end result is nothing but a . . . pillow. Though this may not be an important factor to you, pillows have no value on the auction block or the marketplace. Moreover, they very often find their way to a dark spot in the closet. Copycat counters are full of pillow kits. What a waste, when original work is so easy to do! To add insult to injury, the chances of winning anything in competition are nil, unless there is a separate category for pillows. When you have completed your work (having been disciplined by this book), you will certainly have work worthy of entering into competition with your peers—as well as a potential heirloom.

Remember this! However fine your stitchery, however fine your design, if this is your first work, in some ways it is your best. It is the best you can do *now*. Of course, you will get better. Be brightly proud of your quilt, and, as already remarked, never part with it, except to family. To repeat myself here: "No one was born knowing how to quilt, appliqué, or anything else, for that matter; the only natural instinct is to survive, and that is, to nurse."

Choosing Quilt Size

Will you be making a baby or crib quilt, a carriage robe, a christening comforter, a youth-bed quilt, a twin-queen-king sized quilt? Or consider a fireplace cover to be mounted on board to keep drafts away. Perhaps you prefer the perennial wall hanging—much larger than a pillow top, please. Think about a bell pull in appliqué with just a bit of quilting; then use the same colors and design in a bedspread quilt. If you have a set of pieced squares from Aunt Hattie, create your own design by appliquéing them on fabric—perhaps off-center, perhaps with a leaf (or ten) in proportion to the squares....I would say you are on your way to becoming addicted! And quilting can be an addicting, wonderful event in your life.

You can have the best of all worlds in your quilting. Creating original items will keep your work artistically interesting after that of your peers has faded. Why? Perhaps because your peers stayed in the world of imitation and became bored to tears.

The size of your project should be determined by need first, practicality next, and the cost factor last. Don't bite off more than you can chew! Don't be too ambitious if you are short of time or money. Try to do one thing that is necessary for all good planners—quilters included: visualize it first.

Here are approximate bed measurements with their probable yardage requirements, using 44''–45'' fabrics.

Bed Measurements (vary in size from one manufacturer to the next)	Mattress	Quilt (with 12'' drop)	Yardage
King-size/dual	76'' × 80''	100'' × 104''	20[3]
Queen	60'' × 80''	84'' × 104''	16
Full	54'' × 75''	77'' × 99''	15
Twin	39'' × 75''	63'' × 99''	10
Youth[1]	33'' × 66''	45'' × 78''	7
Crib[2]	28'' × 52''	36'' × 50''	5
Cradle[2]	16'' × 32''	22'' × 34''	3½

[1]With drop.
[2]No drop allowed.
[3]Nine yards of this is for the back without piecing strips.

Also take into consideration how many other quilts you have on your bed during the winter to figure out how much "drop" you desire. The 12-inch drop allowed should cover the mattress and only a bit of the boxspring underneath.

Yardsticks are better than tape measures when computing for a quilt—they are flat and stay put. Two yardsticks make it easier! The figures given for the quilts include "over the pillow." There are other variables to consider. For example, if you believe in "pulling" your quilting stitches (I do), your finished quilt will be a bit smaller than the dimensions given; it also makes a difference whether you will use a hoop or a floor frame to do your quilting on. An important consideration is the kind of batting to be used, which we'll discuss later. If you'd like a heavy batt, the quilt will obviously be shorter all around because of the loft! If you allow an extra two inches when using a heavy batting, you will be safe.

After checking the possible sizes, decide on your size and stick to it! This, of course, is after you have tentatively sketched out your design. Do yourself a favor and do not change your mind once you have decided on a quilt size.

Planning on Paper

It is easier to correct mistakes made on paper than those made on fabric! Planning time is time well spent. When you are finished with the original paper plan, your work will look like an architectural drawing. But it will be *your* plan! I usually make two drawings. When my mind is free, designs flash through it, and I jot them down. Here is a planning sequence:

1. Determine the exact size of your quilt. Draw an approximate shape.
2. Remembering that most fabric is 43 to 44 inches wide (after the selvage has been trimmed), it is usually a good idea to have a center panel no more than 42 to 43 inches wide. (You must remember that you have to allow for seam allowance on both sides, 1 inch total. If your quilt size is to be large, planning side panels, additional borders or wider borders, etc., is preferable to piecing the center panel.) A good rule of thumb is to make your center one third again as long as it is wide. This comes to a center panel 43″ × 65″ or 44″ × 66″.
3. Supposing that your quilt will be full size (77″ × 99″), center the 43″ × 65″ panel inside this full measurement. You have, then, a difference of 34 inches on the length and 34 inches on the width. Divided in half for top and bottom, right and left side, this is 17 inches all around the center panel.
4. Next, with this measurement jotted down on paper, decide how wide the strips or borders you are going to build around the center panel will be. You may wish to use the 17-inch measure as a frame for the center panel. Divide the 17-inch figure into the number of border strips you'd like to use. For example, three border strips in complementary colors can be very satisfying visually; think, then, in increments of three different widths, say, 9″ + 5″ + 3″, which together total 17 inches. Widths will, of course, vary with border size: I suggest 7″ + 5″ + 3″

for a 15-inch border, 6″ + 4″ + 2″ for a 12-inch border, and so on. You will want to vary the widths of your strips, using proportions like these. Take plenty of time to plan your layout and play with it.

5. If the arrangement you've come up with pleases you, make a more exact drawing. Some teachers suggest that quilt plans be drawn on graph paper, but I think this is unnecessary. You can read numbers and draw lines—and think.

If your color selection is monochromatic (combinations of shades of one color), think light, dark, darker for your border strips.

After making your drawing and adding in the measurements for the actual or finished size you want (see Figure 4), put another number beside each of these measurements. Add ½-inch to each side of each piece mentally, and record this in your second figure. If a strip is actually to measure 6 inches across in your finished quilt, add one full inch (½-inch for each side); write this figure next to 6″ and put it in parentheses (7″). (If for some reason you must piece your strips, remember to add in the seam allowances for the piecing as well.)

The next step in quilt planning is to transfer your findings to a cutting chart. This chart will save you hours of heartache caused by cut strips that are too short, border strips that are overlooked until it is too late to cut them without having to piece, and so forth. Projects need not be abandoned nor money wasted because of poor planning.

Figure 4 shows the finished paper plan for a full-sized (77″ × 99″) quilt. The dimensions shown in Figure 4 have been transferred to a cutting layout chart in Figure 5. The cutting chart includes seam allowance: the dimensions transferred are those you have put in parentheses. Note that the corners of our sample quilt in Figure 4 are inset squares rather than mitred strips. In transferring the dimensions of the quilt (with seam allowance), I have decided on a hypothetical color scheme. Before you do a cutting layout, you too will have to figure out which colors you want to use in which portions of the quilt.

When you plan your cutting layout, be certain that you anticipate the "grain" of the fabric—lengthwise or crosswise. Unless you make a special decision *not* to, you will want to keep the fabric grain consistent in the whole background fabric of your quilt: center panel, side panels, borders; blocks if you use them. If your quilt is very large and your fabric has no obvious *nap* (see page 21 for more about nap), you may want to disregard this aspect of planning, but it is best to cut with grain in mind whenever possible. When you sew, you do not want to seam crosswise grain to lengthwise grain if you can avoid it. "Avoidance" in this case means planning in advance. When you transfer border strips or whatever from your paper plan to your cutting layout chart, look at the position of the strips on your plan and determine which way the grain should run. Long side strips will usually run on the straight of grain, and top and bottom strips will have to run crosswise (across the straight of the grain), for

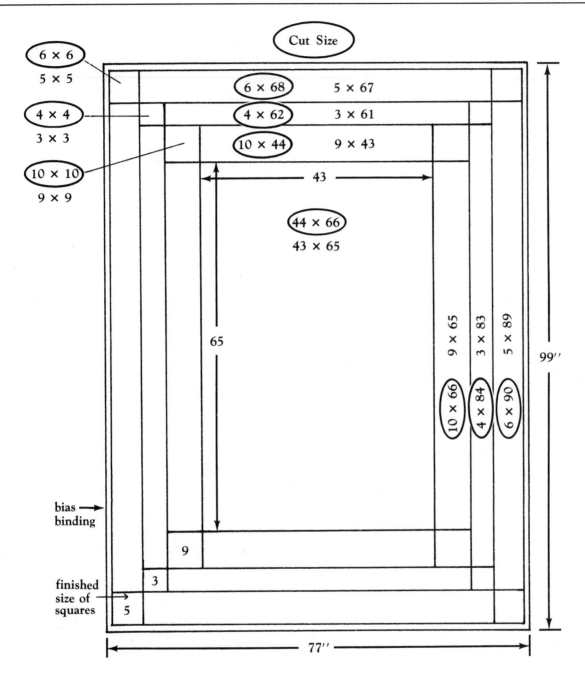

Figure 4. Final version of a paper plan for a sample quilt, 77″ × 99″.

example. You may find it helpful to indicate the straight of the grain on all the pieces in your paper plan by means of a small arrow to minimize the chance of error when you transfer the dimensions to your cutting layout.

The measurements for our sample quilt from Figure 4 are quite large, and, assuming that the fabric hypothetically chosen has no obvious nap, I have made a cutting layout chart (Figure 5) with everything placed on the straight of grain. The next step is to list every piece to be cut out of each color of fabric, with cutting dimensions, taken from the numbers in parentheses on your paper plan (which also appear on your layout chart). Refer to Figure 5 as you examine the following list:

Ice Pink	Cut	For Finished Size
1 center panel	44'' × 66''	43'' × 65''
2 side panels	4'' × 84''	3'' × 83''
2 panels for top and bottom	4'' × 62''	3'' × 61''
4 corner blocks	6'' × 6''	5'' × 5''

Backing layout:

2 18'' × 109'' for sides of quilt back   }   Extra fabric allowed here for "crawl"! Do *not* cut

1 44'' × 109'' for center of quilt back   }   back fabric to exact measure: *always* allow extra!

Medium Pink	Cut	For Finished Size
2 side panels	10'' × 66''	9'' × 65''
2 panels for top and bottom	10'' × 44''	9'' × 43''
4 corner blocks	4'' × 4''	3'' × 3''

Hot Pink	Cut	For Finished Size
2 side panels	6'' × 90''	5'' × 89''
2 panels for top and bottom	6'' × 68''	5'' × 67''
4 corner blocks	10'' × 10''	9'' × 9''

I myself never cut the back of my quilt until the top is finished. Why? Because I just might change my mind about something—it is my prerogative, isn't it?—and if the back is cut, I am committed! After getting involved in the quilt and doing the appliqué, you may have a change of heart as to what color you choose for your back. This does not mean, however, that you can neglect to think of the back until your top is finished. As has been stressed before, it is very important to think everything concerning your quilt out beforehand, including the colors you mean to use. You really must purchase all needed fabric of one color at the same time to be sure of it all being from the same dyevat. I usually allow myself some splurging at the fabric-buying stage: I do enough quilting and other sewing to be sure that extra fabric will not be wasted. But fabric is expensive, so consider carefully.

Now that you have made your cutting layout chart, it is time to compute the fabric yardage you will need. Look at the chart and figure the length of each of the colors that is required, then add about ¼ yard for your quilt's posterity: later you may want to add a perky bow or add decorative touches that coordinate your quilt with other items in the room it is intended for, and so forth.

Yardage

Medium pink	3 yards
Hot pink	2½ yards
Ice pink	9 yards: this includes 6 yards for backing, 1½ yards for center front, and 1½ yards for bias binding.

I always buy about a yard more of the backing fabric than I have figured in place of the ¼ yard "posterity" length; the extra fabric will go in part to the making of a sleeve for the quilt. Therefore, in this case, I would actually purchase 10 yards of the ice pink.

About the sleeve: almost without exception, quilt shows require that a 4-inch sleeve be attached to the top of a quilt for hanging purposes. If such a sleeve has not been attached, the quilt may be disqualified from competition. Most of my quilts have a built-in sleeve, which is nothing more than additional quilt-back fabric that I have turned under and hemmed into the bias binding instead of cutting off. If you are interested in showing your work in competition, this complementary sleeve gives a more professional look to your finished product; you should consider adding it. When the quilt is "retired" from competition or exhibition, the sleeve can be removed with no damage to the quilt.

The sleeve will require a full 8 inches across the top of the quilt, to be folded in half across the width. The end result will be a tube or sleeve about 4 inches deep. This relieves you of the necessity of sewing anything else onto your quilt for hanging. Most important, the stress of weight is very evenly divided across the quilt to protect your fine quilting stitches and appliqué lines, which may be inclined to pop or even—horrors—break if too much stress is placed on them.

For our hypothetical quilt (Figure 4), yardage requirements for all colors except the ice pink can be reduced by about ½-yard if all strips are cut on the length of the fabric. (The length of the fabric is parallel to the selvage.) This subject introduces a slight complication. Some fabrics (not all) have *nap*: a slight variation of shade when the fabric is seen widthwise as opposed to lengthwise. Think of how different velvet can look when seen from two different angles. If you are a beginner, I advise you to avoid fabrics with nap; as you become more experienced, you will find them easier to work with. If you *must* work with nap, however, you will have to work and plan with the nap in mind. This means that you'll have to cut the strips for the border width on the width of your fabric. Cut the lengthwise strips on the length of the fabric, as already mentioned. Obviously, if you are working with fabric that is the standard 44″–45″ wide, you are going to have to piece those widthwise strips. If piecing *is* necessary, be sure to figure in the necessary seam allowances on your cutting chart.

If you desire to mitre your corners instead of using the squares shown in our hypothetical quilt (Figure 4), your yardage requirements increase by 1 yard per color for the border colors. Your cutting chart will also need adjusting. If you prefer to mitre, try to use fabrics without nap; you can then cut all strips on the length of the fabric and avoid seaming. If you must seam, be sure that the seam is nowhere near your mitre: even if you can execute the mitre properly, the seam will detract enormously from the mitre's appearance.

The technique of mitring is explained elsewhere, but figures are provided here to assist you in your planning. A simple way to think about mitres is this: "I begin with the center panel and add a border; now I have a larger panel. To this larger panel I have another border to be added, and now I have an even larger panel." For example, say one side of your quilt's center panel is 63 inches long and you want to add a first strip 4 inches wide, as for layout B in Figure 6. The top is 42 inches wide, and the strip you will add there will also be 4 inches wide. This means that your new center measures 50″ × 71″. (These measurements are *finished* size, i.e., they do not include seam allowances.) Successive strips work in exactly the same way. Here is what the figures look like for the mitred quilt shown in Figure 6B.

Vertical (Length)	Horizontal (Width)
63″ + 8″ + 8″ = 79″	42″ + 8″ + 8″ = 58″
79″ + 4″ + 4″ = 87″	58″ + 4″ + 4″ = 66″
87″ + 6″ + 6″ = 99″	66″ + 6″ + 6″ = 78″

Your quilt top diagram will look like Diagram B in Figure 6. Your cutting chart will look similar to that shown in Figure 5.

Since the art of making a mitred corner is so exacting, and machine stitching is inclined to draw up stitches and distort exact measurements, I recommend that 3 inches be added to the measurements for the lengths of side and top and bottom border strips, as a "fudge-factor."

I would like to mention here that you should not attempt to handle the long seams on your quilt with only ¼-inch allowance, or even ⅜ inch. There is simply not enough to play with in the event that a seam is put in ever so slightly crooked. For dressmaking and appliqué seam allowance, ¼ inch is usually fine. However, for piecing your top you truly need ½ inch. (Patchwork piecing is not what I mean by "piecing your top"; I am referring to piecing background and border strips for your glorious appliqué only.)

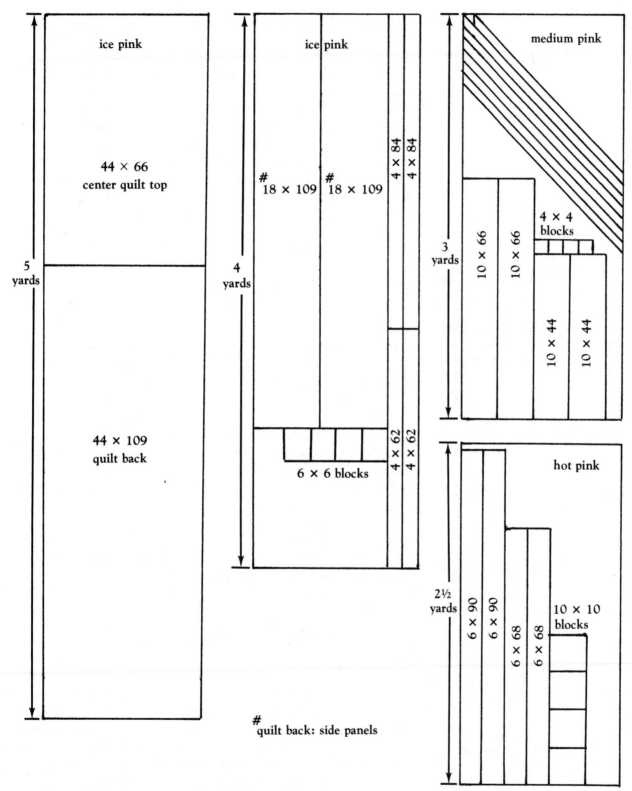

5 yards

ice pink

44 × 66
center quilt top

44 × 109
quilt back

4 yards

ice pink

18 × 109   # 18 × 109

4 × 84   4 × 84

6 × 6 blocks

4 × 62   4 × 62

quilt back: side panels

3 yards

medium pink

4 × 4 blocks

10 × 66   10 × 66

10 × 44   10 × 44

2½ yards

hot pink

6 × 90   6 × 90

6 × 68   6 × 68

10 × 10 blocks

Figure 5. Here is a cutting chart for the sample quilt in Figure 4 (77″ × 99″).

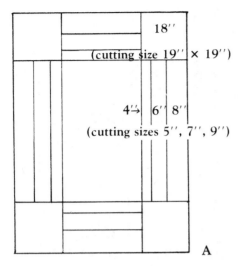

Figure 6. These diagrams show two more ways to handle the corners of your quilt (compare Figure 4, page 19).

A. This may be the easiest way of handling corners. The diagram shows border strips of 4″, 6″, and 8″ (cutting sizes 5″, 7″, and 9″). For an 18″ corner block, any combination of numbers that adds up to 18 will do. Please your eye—and consider your center panel design.

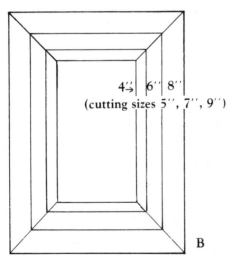

B. This layout has mitred corners. The border strip measurements are the same as for A in width, but you will, obviously, have to cut all of the strips *longer*.

An aside here about the mitred corner. You may be interested to know that the Amish do *not* generally mitre their corners. Usually they either blank-end the bias and leave a blunt end at the corners, or they use the technique I will teach you later of pulling the corners around with two little tucks. The inset square corner is also common. Amish quilts, handed down from generation to generation, are priceless (if they are not all worn out); no one is going to quibble: "But they don't have mitred corners." If you prefer not to make a mitred corner—don't!

For a first quilt—or for an Amish touch—you may find it easier to use large square blocks for your corners that cut across the border strips, as in Diagram A of Figure 6. This layout keeps the border strips to 43 inches on the width, so you know you will not have to piece them. Another tip: if you attempt either a mitred corner or the kind of smaller block corners shown in Figure 4 and you find you have miscalculated somehow (either in planning or in execution) you can resort to the large block corner very easily.

Words of Wisdom About Appliqué Planning

Much rhetoric has been put forward regarding planning on paper all the steps of making your quilt. What this world would do without paper is beyond me. When I have finally struck upon an appliqué design to go on my top, however humble it may be, I cut it out of either newspaper or colored paper and lay it out on the fabric I have purchased. Getting an idea of how the design will look "life-size" can be very revealing. Perhaps your appliqué design is impractical or not as effective as you thought.

Think about a wreath of small flowers and large flowers to be placed in the center of your quilt. Cut the designs out of newspaper—*not* cloth. Cut out all the designs that you intend to use, and place them on the fabric. Is the design too busy, or not busy enough? Perhaps you ought to consider using only the large flowers for the appliqué and the small flowers as a quilting design. Or, if both flowers please you—*and that is what this is all about*—maybe you could quilt in leaves to complement the flowers, or vary your arrangement a bit. Consider using a butterfly in your quilting design: this adds grace and charm to lines that might otherwise look too hard or sharp. A fine example of how this can work is my Heather Rose quilt (layout on page 10). The hard octagonal lines, the octagonal shape of the entire quilt, needed *something*—as your quilt might. Three butterflies in flight were my solution. There are 25 yards of lace on a 15-yard ruffle to further soften this original work, which began its life as a pieced top. I detest piecing and found it difficult to even think about it, but think I did.

When working on the machine with the pieces, I accidentally put a piece in the wrong place, and I found that it looked like a small blossom. Therefore, instead of continuing with the idea of an entire pieced top, I followed the advice I've already given you. I went to my fabric supply closet, pulled out some colors, and literally threw the pieces on the fabric, which I had spread out on the floor. The pattern made itself. Then I got out my trusty newspaper, clipped a few sharp-lined leaves, and played with the arrangement for a day or so, laying it first one way, then another . . . looking at it during the daytime and at night while passing the living room. Finally, I decided which way to go, and I did. To date, this is one of my favorite quilts.

The point is this: the possibilities are endless. When you plan your masterpiece, keep the door open for originality and self-expression. A dormant spark of creativity may be blown into a fire if you allow yourself to vary your original idea. Be prudent, as we've discussed previously, but do not be trapped or inhibited by what anyone else is going to think or say. Express *yourself* in this wonderful fabric art.

Heirborne II, from the collection of Dr. and Mrs. Clement Elshout, La Porte, Indiana (Designed and made by author) *Colors:* three shades of peach and blush white. There are peach/beige satin bows on the four corners. The quilt is edged with 3-inch snow-white chantilly lace. The center is ice peach; a loose bias of deep peach next to blush white follows, then another loose bias of ice peach next to deep peach. On the top, the border is medium (peach with lace). The reverse side is entirely blush white, bound with snow-white bias to complement lace.

CHAPTER 4

NOW COME FABRIC, BATTING, AND OTHER SUPPLIES

*M*atrons and maidens sat in snow-white caps and
in kirtles
Scarlet and blue and green, with distaffs spinning
the golden flax for the gossipping looms, whose
noisy shuttles within doors
Mingle their sound with the whir of the wheels and
the songs of the maidens.

—Longfellow
"Evangeline"

Homespun fabrics have become heirlooms. No longer need we rely upon the busy spinning wheel to provide thread or the home loom to provide fabric. No longer need we worry about too much shrinkage of fabrics or running of dyes. Yet selectivity in purchasing fabric is imperative.

"Matrons and maidens" *do* sit behind quilting frames and hoops today and do stitch with such enthusiasm and quickness that tomorrow's heirlooms are being produced at an amazing rate.

In days of yore . . . the crowned heads of Europe controlled the weavers' trade. Only the elite were allowed to wear certain royal colors; particular fabrics (such as velvets) were only for the royal families; and women were never allowed to weave anything. Their deft fingers were limited to fancy stitchery on tapestries, oftentimes using golden needles. Strangely enough, needles were not introduced in England until about 1560, during the reign of Queen Elizabeth.

Mary, Queen of Scots prepared beautiful tapestries for her cousin, Elizabeth I, in hopes her "needle" would persuade Elizabeth to spare her head! Alas, to no avail. Fortunately, Mary's needlework remains. But an untimely end could come to your needlework if you purchase fabrics that are not just right.

Natural fibers are the best: silk, wool, cotton. In my decades of sewing, the idea of using synthetic fabrics (such as the polyester knits, jersey, and cotton-like synthetics) has been alien to my thinking—and my fabric collection. Although I appreciate the ease of caring for these fabrics, I lean toward clothing solely in natural fibers.

However, as for all rules, there is an exception. Contrary to most quilting authorities, I absolutely do not recommend the use of cotton fabrics for quilts. Not 100-percent cotton, that is. A blend of 65 percent polyester/35 percent cotton is the best choice. Or 50 percent polyester/50 percent cotton, at the most. (The general name for this kind of fabric is *broadcloth*.)

Why no cotton? Because by the time a new quilter—or an old hand, for that matter—completes the project, the fabric looks as though it has been slept in for years. Cotton is too expensive for what you don't get! It wrinkles too much. Want evidence of this? How about those shirts of 100-percent cotton that say "little or no ironing"? What folly! I'll take the polyester blend with cotton that I don't have to iron every inch of. More work ironing means less time for quilting! (When I mentioned "cotton-like" synthetics above, I was referring to heavy fabrics—*not* broadcloth, which is the fabric used for quilting in general.) Blends lend themselves better to handling in the long run, and they also hold dye more effectively. Blends have a certain kind of luster which enhances a quilt that plain cotton does not have. Cotton looks old before its time. The best reason of all for using blends is their economy over 100-percent cotton. Therefore, do not think pure cotton when considering fabrics for a quilt!

Heirlooms must, of course, endure for many years; therefore, your work and time are better spent on solid colors. Using quaint calico prints does make for old-time charm, but their fading properties are astounding over the long run. If your project is a baby's quilt that will be used daily and washed regularly, do not even think of calico. Old-fashioned checked gingham is a good choice if you must use something other than solid tones. (This kind of fabric also offers built-in quilting lines.)

Broadcloth has a smooth face and close texture, similar to bed sheets but not as closely woven. It is often used in men's dress shirts or in Victorian-style undergarments. Broadcloth was one of the first utilitarian fabrics made on wide looms, thus its name.

Fabric shops can offer certain obstacles to the quilter. It is unfortunate that many clerks are poorly qualified: never having quilted anything, they are nevertheless placed in the position of having to give advice. Lack of knowledge often costs the customer money. Worse, it absolutely discourages new quilters at the outset when materials sold as "being just right for quilting" don't work out.

Quilters should beware of the measuring machine used by many stores. The lovely unwrinkled fabric is pulled through its iron jaws haphazardly; the cutter is depressed after the measure; the sales clerk then tears your fabric off the bolt. The next procedure is to fold the fabric into oblivion and jam it into a too-small bag! By the time it is carried home, the fabric is a disaster and needs to be ironed. If you are lucky, all the wrinkles will come out.

Do your best to avoid extra work. Request that your quilting fabric (or any fabric, for that matter) be carefully measured by ruler or yardstick, carefully cut or torn, and carefully folded. The ideal is that it be wrapped around an unused or discarded bolt board. This way you take home nice, new, fresh, unmangled fabric.

In addition, fabric is frequently cut very crookedly, and even the "torn" edge is rarely straight. Never purchase exactly what you need but at least ¼-yard more . . . for insurance.

So you were taught to pull a thread from yardage to straighten the end of a piece of fabric. Nonsense. A simple way to straighten your future quilt fabric is to take a piece of newspaper (which provides perfectly squared-off corners most of the time—if you are really fastidious a piece of construction paper or board may be used) and place the edge of the paper against the edge of the fabric. Smooth the paper out across the folded fabric (you have, of course, seen to it that the selvages are even), and you now have a straight line across the fabric end. With a yardstick as a steady guide, draw a pencil line to even it up. Then cut! How easy. Otherwise your measurements might not be true and you will make unnecessary trouble for yourself.

The reason you "square off" the folded fabric is merely to obtain a straight line with which to begin. Store personnel do not necessarily cut straight and fabric is always distorted when torn. It has a straight line—but not for quilt measuring. It is imperative that this method be practiced to save headaches! It is not until all of this is accomplished that you begin measuring anything for your quilt.

> "Straight to begin will make a happy ending."
> —Charlotte Bass

After the fabric has been straightened, it is time to cut off the selvage of the fabric. *Selvage* is that tightly woven strip along each side of your fabric, usually about ¼-inch wide. If your fabric is 44 or 45 inches wide, figure on it becoming 43 or 44 inches wide (approximately). Often you'll want to use that extra half-inch on each side, but do yourself a favor and *do not use it*. Why? Because it is impossible to quilt through selvage. It is too tightly woven. Furthermore, in the washing process selvage has a tendency to shrink up. Do yourself a favor and never get into the habit of leaving on the selvage. There is only one exception here: your quilt back, which will be discussed later.

Wash your fabric? Almost everything printed about quilting these days will say, "Wash and iron your fabric before using." This is not necessary. There are no better quilters in America than the Amish and most of them do not wash their fabric first. These fine folk have no electricity for hot water or irons. Do you really think they go through the agony of this extra work? They trust in the manufacturer's word at the end of the bolt: "Less than 1% shrinkage." The frugal upbringing of the Amish does not allow them to waste money foolishly, either, and so I am inclined to adopt their method.

As a matter of fact, after years of haute-couture sewing and using fine, expensive fabrics, I have yet to wash mine first. Shrinkage is more likely with wool; thus I would steam-iron it lightly. That is all.

One exception to the rule about water. Should your color selection include deep green, black, red, navy blue, deep purple, or brown, you might snip a piece of fabric and boil it with soap and water combined with an equal-sized piece of an old white sheet. If the dye is going to run, this is a good way to find out. Then—and only then—it is up to you to decide whether the fabric needs a total bath. Otherwise, if you are bound to use water, jump into the bathtub yourself . . . leave your fabric alone! In any case, even after one washing or a cold-water soaking (which is sometimes advocated by teachers), there will still be dye left to run.

Weights of Fabric

There are many weights of broadcloth. Some are too closely woven to be good for quilting. Most difficult is the weave similar to that of a percale sheet. The thread count is too close; wiggling your quilting needle through your prepared quilt top, batting, and backing is hard work.

Thread count varies from fabric to fabric. Think about a light piece of wool, where every fiber of the warp and every single fiber of the woof is visible . . . this, of course, is an exaggerated example. But if the warp and woof mesh too tightly, quilting is next to impossible. The finest percale sheet is the worst for quilting. "200 count per inch" is a common notation on sheets . . . and this is to be avoided. Of course, there will be times when you are tempted to use a muslin sheet—either plain or printed—for the back of the quilt, but don't do it.

In every seminar I recommend broadcloth—broadcloth with a blend of polyester and cotton is just right. Sheets are for sleeping between, not for any part of a quilt.

Generally, three weights are available in broadcloth: thin, medium, and heavy. You can choose the heavy weight; it is actually less heavy than a percale sheet. (The word *heavy* is not really fair here.) Think of a fine piece of broadcloth in a dress shirt. Although your fabric will not be as closely woven, this is what you should approximate.

With experience, your fingers will "feel" fabric quality. Look determines your particular conception of how the quilt will appear as a finished product. Some broadcloths, particularly cotton, have a rather rough finish which looks like it's screaming to have an iron with it always; the blends, on the other hand, have a consistently crispy look.

Often, when fabric is being taken off the bolt you will detect flaws. There is no need for you to pay "top dollar" for the marred fabric; there should be an adjustment, either by allowing an extra quarter- or half-yard or a reduced price. Most Amish stores will make such an allowance for a flaw. Remember, though, that the cloth is no bargain if the flaw will be visible in the middle of your quilt.

Most important, the price of a piece of broadcloth does not determine its quality! In the purchasing of quilting fabrics, the adage "You get what you pay for" never has applied. Don't take it for granted that more expensive fabric is necessarily of better quality. Many shopping facilities jack up their prices to what the trade will bear. Sad, but true.

One tip you might consider when purchasing fabrics: look carefully at the selvage. It should be tightly woven for quilting. If you can see the warp and woof, the fabric is too loose. However, if the selvage is so tight that the fabric next to it is actually puckered, this suggests another problem. Check the end of the bolts for shrinkage percentages, quantity of blend, manufacturer's name. If you find a fabric store that handles a particular brand you really like, keep using it.

Be careful about unknowledgeable salespeople. Don't be misled into buying batiste (a very fine weight of broadcloth-like fabric that can be seen through) because the color is just what you need. Batiste is no good for quilting. Take fabrics to the door and see if you like them in the daylight. I seldom buy fabrics in the evening or on a cloudy day.

Discounting your own knowledge about fabrics might be your worst mistake. If you have sewn anything over the years, you have some knowledge about what you like—what wears well, and so forth. When all else fails, talk to someone older than yourself, someone whose sewing ability you respect. Then do what pleases *you!* At least you have the benefit of their knowledge and can use it as a guideline.

How do I purchase fabrics? I shop primarily in the Amish community. However, when I want something other than the polyester-cotton blends, I go to the finest fabric stores to find luxury velvets, lamés, satins. I once did public relations work for G Street Couture Fabrics in Rockville, MD (formerly Washington, D. C.), through which I had access to perhaps the finest fabrics in America. I've had excellent experience with the shops in Chicago, particularly Marshall Field and Company, to whom I send interested persons for "something different."

I purchase the top of the line in Amish shops. There are usually three grades of fabric among the blends. Very rarely do I go to the second quality, unless I am strapped for a specific color (and this has happened). I like the extra-smooth texture, finish, and color reflections of the best-quality blends. Sometimes I am asked, "Is your quilt made from silk?"

All the techniques discussed in this book may be adapted to the use of wools or silks. If you are an experienced quilter, try these fabrics for a marvelous experience in luxury. Of course, plan carefully.

How Much Fabric to Purchase?

As already noted, to avoid unnecessary work quilts should be planned the same way that moving furniture into a new home should be planned—on paper.

Determine the quilt size. Figure the yardage carefully, following the directions in Chapter 3. And never let anyone sell you a precut quilt back. (Precuts do have the virtue of being unseamed—perhaps their only virtue.)

Ordinarily, the fabric in a precut back is inferior to what you have purchased for the top of your quilt. Fabric textures in a quilt should match, if possible. The cost of a precut is *not* inexpensive; often it is *not* the correct size—and if it is too small you may end up cropping or distorting your original top design to accommodate the back. There is not enough difference in price between a precut back and purchasing the fabric to coordinate with the quilt top to make the risk worthwhile.

Don't slight the quilt in your planning. Figure extra yardage of a matching (or complementary) color from the quilt top for a more beautiful coordinated effect.

A quilt back is where the quilt's hidden beauty lies. Anyone will love the top, but a quilter's heart springs with joy when someone admires the back; so, use a sophisticated color there—not always white or some basically uninteresting "cutesy" print. What a waste! Another strike against precut backs is that they are usually available only in white. As for prints, too often quilt backs using a print have absolutely no connection whatsoever with the top design. Horrors!

Allow a double length of fabric for a quilt back if the quilt is wider than 43 inches wide. Slit the fabric in half, crosswise, join the long sides together, and sew. See Figure 40, page 90. This is the only time when I do not trim the selvage off immediately; I wait until I am ready to trim that back seam to ¼-inch. If the selvage is left on, it serves as a guide for a straight line—along with the ½-inch seam guide I tape onto my sewing machine. (More about these matters later.) After the seam has been sewn, press according to the instructions on page 80).

Planning ahead in fabric purchase is important. Perhaps a coordinated dust ruffle might add charm, or a dressing-table skirt, or lampshades to match. Buy the fabric all at one time so that the dye is all from the same vat and the fabric is exactly the same color. Colors vary from bolt to bolt of fabric, as they do with yarn. Don't *wish,* too late, that you had purchased enough.

Deal with a reputable store that will stand behind its merchandise. You have made no bargain if you discover something wrong with your fabric after all your work is expended. Be selective.

Something Besides Cotton/Polyester?

Do not automatically discount using silk because it is so perishable. If you want a silk quilt, make one. There are certain things to know about silk that will make your life easier. For example, silk scorches quickly. Finger-pressing works well: run your fingers along the seams to press. (However, it snags on rough fingers.) Silk is airy to handle; the use of tissue paper (cut to whatever size you're sewing and including seam allowance) will make handling easier. Simply tear away the tissue when done. A certain test to identify silk: put a small piece in an ashtray and light it with a match. If the ash stays in one piece and burns rather slowly, it is silk; if it goes *poof,* it is a synthetic look-alike.

Making carriage robes out of China silk was the vogue in Victorian days. Little or no surface design was used except embroidery. Occasionally, pure counterpane work was done. (Once again: *counterpane* is nothing more than something quilted all over with no embellishment of appliqué or patchwork; it is pure quilting. A counterpane looks like the back of a completed quilt, only on both sides.)

Sad, but true, silk does not stand time well. It rots more quickly than any other fabric. The elegance garnered, however, makes it worthwhile to use this wonderful fabric despite the number of drawbacks. On the subject of luxury, do not hesitate to use velvet or velveteen; just be certain that the grain is running up for more color depth. When the grain runs down, there is a shadow of gray.

Remember—do what *you* want to do, not what someone else has talked you into or out of. It is your quilt, no one else's.

Bat . . . Batt . . . Batting

No matter how it is spelled in the dictionary, bat, batt, batting . . . is the filling used to create a quilt. What kind to use? Here again, price is not the critical factor; expensive does *not* equal good. Knowledge about "care and feeding" before and after selecting a batt is imperative.

Feeling batting might become habit-forming for you, although most packages are taped closed. Some batts are sold off a roll. They will fit large quilt sizes perfectly, but most of the time they are too wiry. I looked for the price in the beginning, not knowing any better way to judge. I used "off the roll" batting not unsatisfactorily, but ignorance is bliss! I was lucky and there has been no bearding.

I want a soft batt with loft—which means batting that will stay puffed and not crush down to flat, even when washed. Some batts work their way out of the fabric on the top and bottom of your quilt in the form of a "beard," which is nothing more than the tiny fibers poking through. I look for a batting that is soft, but substantial, and bonded. At the moment, I recommend to my students (and now use exclusively) Stearns and Foster's Mountain Mist® Fatt Batt.

"Care and feeding?" you say. Yes. *Feeding* is letting the poor batt rest and "feed" on space. Most quilters prepare their top and then run out to purchase a batting. It is always a disaster of wrinkles if purchased in a package. You must plan ahead. Purchase the batt early on (about a week before you really need it), lay the batt out, and let it rest. You need not open it all the way out: just take it out of the bag, lay it across the foot of a bed—unrolled just once—and let it rise like yeast. When you use it a week later all those awful wrinkles will be almost gone. Because of the wrinkles, you may be led to purchase your batting off the roll because it looks better; however, batting on a roll is usually not of as good quality as the packaged kind.

I prefer bonded batting for easier handling. There are many brands on the market. Most "off the roll" brands are used for reupholstering furniture; this batting has too many bristles and should be avoided. Some very wide and less wiry materials *are* available off the roll of which salespersons might say, "Of course you can use this for a quilt batt"; but chances are these salespeople have never made a quilt in their lives. Use your own good judgment. Purchase a well known, tested brand. Improvements are being made in batt brands all the time.

Cotton Batt or Polyester/Dacron?

Cotton or 100-percent polyester or dacron batting for your quilt? Old-timers swear by cotton: "My stitches can be much smaller." Not only *can* they be, they *must* be. Those old-timers never left more than one square inch unquilted . . . and they had more time to devote to quilting than you are likely to have. If you use cotton batt but do not quilt very closely, the batting will ball up when your quilt is washed. Cotton has no warmth to it—another factor to consider, unless you live in a warm climate and warmth is not a prerequisite. Cotton breathes because it is a natural fiber. If both quilt top and bottom are of cotton fabric and the batt is cotton, your quilt will not hold the heat.

However, fabric blends do retain heat. If you use a cotton batting with polyester blends it will not breathe as freely and therefore be as cool as a cotton quilt. Natural fibers all breathe—silk, wool, linen, cotton—but if you blend them with any of the synthetics some of the 100-percent breathing capability is always lost.

Dacron or polyester batts, because of their "airy" content, allow some air to pass through the fibers. Thus if your quilt top and bottom have a certain amount of cotton in them, the entire quilt will have a breathing capability; the quilted layers will breathe to a degree but not too much. A great combination!

Polyester/dacron battings come in various weights. Some come by area measure, some by pound weight. You may have been told never to use those heavy batts (probably because your source has not tried one). I strongly recommend the "fatt batt" weight. It creates lovely shadows and is well worth the extra money for the extra loft; besides, it is relatively light in weight in proportion to the warmth it gives to those snuggling beneath it.

Thin, normal batt weight is all right, but in many ways it leaves a lot to be desired. The fatter the batting, the fewer stitches to the inch in quilting is possible . . . but who cares?

Making Shadows of Love . . .
Carefully planned impressions via needle and thread
Pivoted into uniquely created quilt—coverlet—bedspread.
Stitch—by—stitch, carefully guided by a wisdom above
Yes, everyone knows that quilting is . . . making shadows of love!
—Charlotte Bass

Shadows of love with each stitch into top/batting/bottom is what you create when you make a quilt. It is the play of light and dark. The fatter the batt, the deeper the ravines and crevices, the more drama, the more warmth, the more elegance.

You will fit perhaps six to seven quilting stitches per inch with the loftier batt. This is plenty. "But," you say, "I was told to have twenty." This formula was true when grandmother (more likely great-grandmother) was a girl; then, batting was thin and fragile and time was no problem. But six to seven stitches per inch is just fine today. Life is too short to demand of a quilter so many stitches to the inch. Using heavy batting, if you have a steady, even-paced stitch (and this is putting on about three stitches per needleful), you will have a magnificent end-product and can be proud of your work.

There are those who put the needle up and down, moving it completely in and out of the fabric. I wiggle mine! Use whichever method is most comfortable for you. Quilting is joining three things together with fine stitches . . . and, I must add, giving your thread a pull as you go. Many quilting teachers advocate not pulling. This is nothing more than a glorified basting stitch—not quilting. I love the shadows that pulling helps create; the heavy batting does even more justice to my romantic theory of quilting.

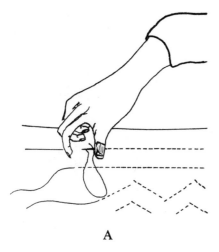

A

Figure 7.
Use the "P" method of quilting to become a quicker quilter!
A. *Plant* the needle, straight down; as soon as it hits your finger beneath the quilt, *Push* it up again.

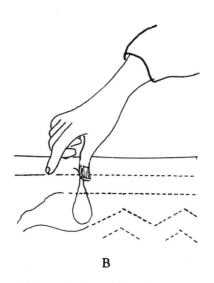

B

B. *Pick* up stitches and *Pile* them on, usually 3 to 5 per needle. (Use the No. 7 or No. 8 crewel embroidery needle as recommended.)

As you know, bearding comes from batts that are too wiry for a quilt. Over a period of time, coarse fibers will rise above the top or bottom fabric and actually scratch the skin. Some of my students have actually found angel-hair components in the fibers of quilt batts. In this respect, you get what you pay for in quilt batting. Buy wisely and without *too* much frugality.

Like a Needle in a Haystack

Next, alas, you are told to purchase quilting needles. I say *no*. For alternatives, there are in existence some 250 varieties of needles for every kind of work, from fine silk embroidery needles to the heavy industrial needles used to sew canvas, leathers, and so forth.

History records that it was the Chinese who originated the steel needles, perhaps to accommodate the minutely fine silk threads used in their luxurious embroideries. From China needles were brought West by the Moors. It is said that it wasn't until the time of Queen Elizabeth I in the mid-sixteenth century that the needle was introduced to England.

Methods of making the needles often died with their secretive keepers. General knowledge about the trade was not made available until the mid-seventeenth century. It is said that ladies of the courts used golden needles for their fine embroideries; however, golden and silver needles were not necessarily limited to royalty. As time went on it was found that the precious metals did not rust, and in tropical areas gold and silver needles were quite commonly used. Today England and Germany are perhaps the prime needle manufacturers. Sizing does not vary.

When you go looking for that needle in the haystack (the "bottle of hay" in Shakespeare's *Midsummer Night's Dream*), be certain you select a needle to suit you—not what someone else suggested because of what has always been. I absolutely do not recommend the quilting needle for quilting! I use a No. 7 or No. 8 crewel embroidery needle. This question of needle selection is crucial to a beginning quilter and is true for any other kind of stitchery as well. Which for quilting? Which for appliqué?

I repeat, my only needle for quilting *and* appliqué (and general sewing) is the No. 7 or 8 crewel embroidery needle. Reason? The needle usually used for quilting is a lethal weapon. It is too small, its eye is too small, its top is too sharp, and its shank is too short. Crewel embroidery needles have a longer shank on which to *throw* stitches. The needle eyes are longer for easier sight-threading; and the top is smooth, should it go amiss and plunge into your flesh. When selecting a needle bear this in mind. Often I have broken needles on quilts because of stress caused by my "wiggle" stitch. This is okay . . . there are more needles where that came from. Do yourself a big favor and open your mind to my needle idea. You will be happier, especially if you use the lofty batt in quilting. Quilting goes faster, too. Threading that long No. 7 or 8 eye is so easy—with or without glasses.

Thimble, Thimble, Who Has the Thimble?

Fear not, my spouse! said Vulcan, ne'er again,
Never shall any needle give you pain.
With that the charming goddess he embraced,
Then a shell of brass her finger cased.
—Allan Ramsay
"Thimble"

Plastic, steel, porcelain, brass, silver, gold, and leather thimbles for milady. All except the leather thimble are fine for a collector's showcase, but not for rapidity in appliqué or quilting. Why? They provide no traction for the needle in those little crevices on top. Leather does, with its graining and natural animal oils. Figure 7 demonstrates the thimble technique.

"I simply cannot stand to wear a thimble." "I feel trapped, like the Man in the Iron Mask, with one of those terrible things on." "My finger becomes too warm." These are just a few of the comments I have received from women to whom I've suggested using a thimble. Fool yourself not . . . to quilt comfortably, you must wear a thimble.

One student, Carol Ruzic of Beverly Shores, Indiana, completed an entire quilt without a thimble, throwing one stitch at a time, up and down. The quilt is magnificent, the stitches are small—but, according to her testimony: "I spent more time on the floor threading that darned needle than I care to tell." Using a thimble even reduces wear on your thread. It is possible to quilt without a thimble, but who has that kind of time? Not me!

A leather thimble breathes. A pattern to make one of your own is included here (Figure 8), as well as instruction on how to use it effectively and efficiently (see Figure 46 on pages 96–97). If you prefer an easier method: cut off about the top third of a finger of an old leather glove; then cut off another of the same size. Fit one "finger" over the other, inserting a piece of metal between the two; put a few stitches through the leather fingers to hold the metal in place. The easiest piece of metal to use is the end of a pull-*out* tab from a soft-drink can, although these are becoming more and more scarce. Your "thimble" is then two leather fingers, one over the other with the metal in between.

There are other metal-reinforced leather thimbles on the market (and some without metal) that might be available to you at stores with a good selection of quilting supplies or through ads in quilting magazines.

Figure 7 (continued)

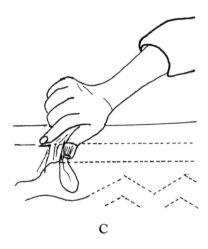

C

C. *Pinch* all the stitches together to *Pucker* the fabrics.

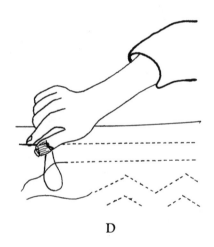

D

D. *Pull* the needle and thread through top/batt/back of quilt until taut, then release and begin next set of stitches.
PLANT, PUSH, PICK UP, PILE, PINCH, PUCKER, AND PULL!

One of my students, H. Dean Golding of Michigan City, Indiana, who is also an inventor, has improved upon my thimble line-drawing. (Dean has done many of the technical illustrations in this book.) He has developed and patented a thimble that out-thimbles all thimbles, in my estimation. His thimble has increased my quilting speed 100 percent—and I was fairly quick to begin with, with all my years of sewing experience. This thimble will outlast anything on the market, as well as the homemade versions I've described above. The thimble is called "Finger's Friend,"[1] and it can be used on any finger or thumb. I spend as much time with it on my thumb as on my middle finger. (See Figure 9.) When I place it on my finger, I usually criss-cross the ends at an angle. I can then quickly flip it onto my thumb when changing work direction on the quilting frame.

Possibly the main advantage of using a thimble is that the pivot of the needle simply rests on the thimble; it isn't held with the fingers. Another helpful feature is the added traction in pulling the needle out of the fabric. So be a quicker quilter . . . try a leather thimble.

Threads to Use

As with pure cotton fabric or batting, I do not recommend the use of all-cotton thread for the actual quilting; however, I do recommend the use of mercerized thread for appliqué because it does not knot so easily. "Mercerized" thread was developed by John Mercer in 1866. Mercer was an English calico printer who came upon a method (using caustic soda) to give cotton thread more lustre, strength, and color retention than had previously been available.

All-cotton quilting thread does not take the tension that I feel is needed to "pull up" the shadows in quilting. But mercerized thread, which is cotton and used for general sewing, is ideal for appliqué work. The thread does not untwist and knot all the time. Think about a single-strand embroidery floss and how wonderfully it handles. It does not knot—it is similar to mercerized thread. Alas, however, I am often forced to use polyester thread nowadays as my supply of old-time mercerized is all but exhausted and it is sometimes difficult to find.

If mercerized thread is not available to you and you must use polyester (cotton-covered 50 weight dual duty, which sews all fabrics), be certain to use short lengths. And, most important, immediately knot the end being cut off the spool. This minimizes knots and kinks, since you then do not go against the spun grain of the thread. Mercerized thread can be knotted at either end. Many quilting shops are beginning to stock a supply of mer-

[1]Distributed by Risdon Corporation. See page 123.

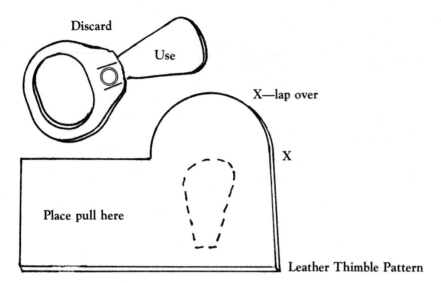

Discard

Use

X—lap over

X

Place pull here

Leather Thimble Pattern

Figure 8. Leather thimble: leather from the top of an old glove, soft and pliable, should be used. Cut pattern as given; wrap it around your finger to ascertain proper size. Stitch sides up, then stitch the curved flap to close circle-hole. Insert the tear-shaped portion of a soft-drink can opener beneath curve, near the bottom edge of finger-thimble; stitch in place. Or, take one third of finger section from glove, insert inside your homemade thimble, and stitch metal tab in place.

cerized thread; it is still more expensive than it should be, but it is worth the extra money.

Cotton quilting thread is a disaster! It kinks when it comes off the spool because it is so curly. To avoid this problem, unroll it as you would rope off a roller . . . moisten with a bit of saliva . . . if you must use it!

Etcetera

> See a pin, pick it up,
> All the day you'll have good luck.
> —Mother Goose

Straight pins at least one inch long are good for quilting. Of course, pins come in all sizes and you should choose your pins for the job you have in mind. Using fatt batt requires more length and strength. Pins to be used for appliqué should be fine so that unnecessarily large holes are not left in the fabric. Pins are meant to *hold* things in place temporarily. Whichever you choose, purchase only rust-proof pins. Never use pins purchased in an office supply store; they are often dirty.

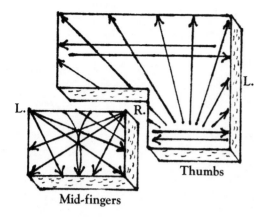

L.

Thumbs

Mid-fingers

A medium-lead pencil, a clean eraser, newspaper, brown paper bags, brown or white wrapping paper, plastic milk cartons, lightweight cardboard, sandpaper . . . these are other items you will find useful in quilt making. I use newspaper and cardboard to make pattern pieces; fine sandpaper and the other listed items are possibilities. One thing *not* needed are the expensive templates being sold primarily to novice quilters. Two straight yardsticks are a must!

Wait to spend your money on expensive items. Wait until you are certain what you are about. And notice that missing on the list above is that "disappearing quilt marker." No one knows for certain what that chemical will do to quilts fifty years from now. I care; so should you . . . so don't use it.

Figure 9. Quilter's Cake—Quilting with a leather thimble increases your range on the quilt frame. The small rectangle represents the mid-finger and the territory it can cover; the other three fourths of the sketch represent the "space travel" that can be accomplished by using a thimble on your thumb—which I do—a *thumble thimble*!

Think of this broken rectangle as a cake. By wearing a leather thimble on your *thumb*, instead of getting just a *piece* of cake you can have the whole thing—in cooperation with your middle finger!

CHAPTER 5

STITCH THAT APPLIQUÉ!

No walls so fair are those our fancies build—
No views so bright as those our visions gild!
"The School Boy"
Oliver Wendell Holmes

How many times have you gasped with delight on seeing a beautiful quilt? Walking up to examine it closely, though, has perhaps proved that it was not perfect by any means; you've said to yourself, "I can do as well as that—I'm going to try it!" Exactly. This chapter shows you how to appliqué and notes many of the pitfalls to be avoided. A whole catalog of do-and-don't suggestions follows. It is all well and good to give you directions to make particular quilts in 1-2-3 easy steps—and I shall do this later. First, though, I'd like to offer the basics: general guidelines and explanations.

The instructions for preparing your top that follow pertain to quilts having a center panel with pieced side panels on which the appliqué work is to be done. If you choose to construct your quilt top using individual blocks (as I've done, for example, with my Marsh Marigold quilt (see page 104 for the layout), you will eventually be using the dot method of joining described below, but not until your appliqué is complete. Therefore, you will want to mark your dots now, but you will not actually be sewing blocks together till later: see "Building a Quilt," page 83. For now, you should concentrate on doing your appliqué.

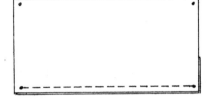

Figure 10.

How to Begin

Suppose you have elected to do the Clematis quilt, for example (pattern given on page 126). After you have cut out your border strips, measure ½-inch square into the corners of each of your strips and your center panel. Put a small pencil dot at the inner corner. *Each* corner! This mark will assist you in making a straight seam (with the help of the marker on the seam

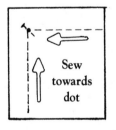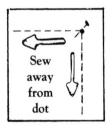

Rule: Sew up to dots and stop, sometimes!
Sew away from dots and continue!

Figure 11.

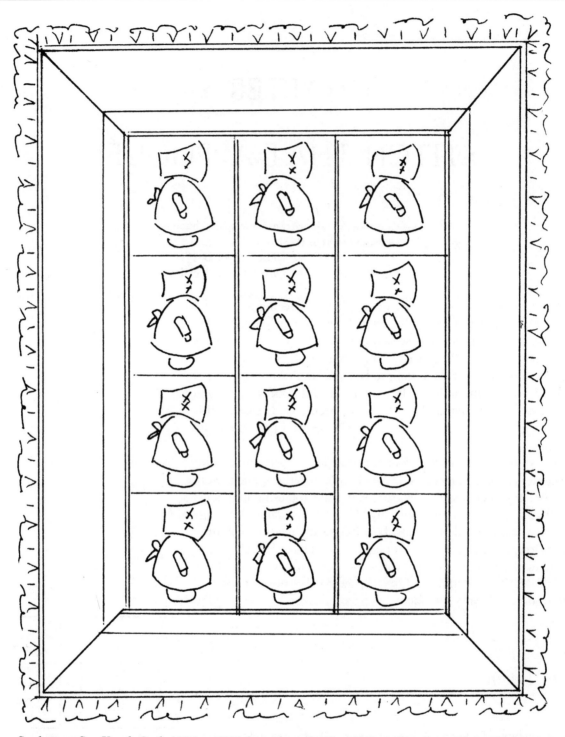

Sunbonnet Sue Youth Quilt (60″ × 62″) from the collection of Carla Dee Bass. These blocks were made in 1935 by the author and pieced into a quilt, but it was never completed until 1983. *Colors:* Dolls are on a white background, bordered in bright orange and bright "Irish" green; corners are soft meadow green. A white 3-inch bias ruffle is bordered in orange. On the back, a white ruffle is bordered in soft meadow green and "Irish" green full reverse.

guide ½ inch from the needle of your sewing machine), and especially to signal the end of a seam. Dots are frequently used in constructing garments (in putting in a dart, for example); dots can also save you miserable hours of ripping when you are quilting. They show you where to stop and where to begin from. The mitre technique really requires the use of the dot, especially when joining that first strip to the center section. Sew that strip *only* to the dot. (See Figure 10.) You must leave this ½-inch seam free in order to get to the point in the center where the rest of your side strips are sewn on. (When sewing long seams like this, do not "lock" your seam with a final backstitch—you may need to work out puckers later. See page 90.) Mastering this technique will also pay off for patchwork, especially when delinquent corners to be matched refuse to cooperate. Sometimes, beginning a seam at the dot and sewing away from it (Figure 11) is the only way to keep control of your work.

Use a straight pin pushed through one dot on one piece of fabric to find the dot on a second piece of fabric. Stitch and remove the pin.

If you are working with a lot of small patches to be pieced together, especially if they are not square or rectangular patches, you may find it easiest to mark your dots if you use your template as a guide. If you've used a template in actual finished size (without the seam allowance), simply center the template on the cut piece and mark the corner dots. If you've made a template that includes seam allowance, cut away ½-inch all around and then follow the same procedure.

Do not try to sew over the dots to get a point; it doesn't work. Using the dot system is the way to get all those lovely corners to come to a sharp point.

Figure 12. Flowers (or leaves) laid out with a template and drawn on fabric with medium pencil. The solid line indicates a template edge where the pencil has marked; the broken line is the ¼-inch seam allowance you will leave when cutting. *It is not necessary to mark fabric with broken lines;* this is only given as a guide for you to see the space necessary for the seam allowance.

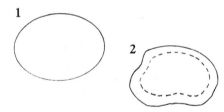

Machine stay-stitch distorted

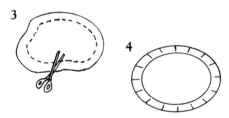

Stitch clipped and pressed to almost original shape.

Figure 13.

Preparing Appliqué Pieces

Once the background of your top is ready, proceed to the appliqué. The Clematis quilt design will require a lot of tracing on fabric for all of those bright flowers (remember to allow for ¼-inch seams all around). See Figure 12. I did not stay-stitch around the flowers for this quilt because they are so small. Sometimes, however, you will find this step necessary. If you decide to do the Hollyhock Heaven throw, you will need to stitch around the entire huge center hollyhock, leaving just less than ½-inch seam. (For larger pieces, you will want to leave a larger seam allowance than the usual ¼-inch.) Use a medium sewing stitch. Stay-stitching usually complicates matters (it is an extra step, among other things), but there is one major exception to this rule. *All* large curves should have a machine stay-stitch around them. This is done *before* the appliqué design is cut out of the whole

Figure 14. When you have leaves or petals that overlap each other, it is necessary to plan ahead to avoid unnecessary ripping and additional sewing. Parts of some petals and leaves may be hidden underneath each other, and there is no need to turn in that ¼-inch; just *ease* and lap (over or under, whichever case it may be), and you will have a smoother appliqué. It might be necessary to clip off a bit of the leaf or petal to make it lie smoothly.

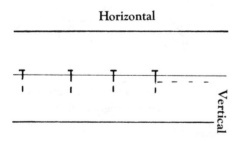

Figure 15. Pin-basting is so much easier when you place pins vertical to a horizontal line ... you don't get stuck so often!

fabric, for all pieces requiring a stay-stitch. Why? It is easier to handle; also, your hand stitching (and therefore the shape of your design) is not distorted. Later you can clip a stitch here and there if the curve is too taut or too curved; these stay-stitches will be buried under your handwork stitching. (See Figure 13.)

Many books correctly instruct the reader to clip into corners and curves to the line of stay-stitches, but they read as though this were a task to do at cutting time. This is incorrect. If you trim your corners and clip your curves too soon, the few threads left may fray a bit and the pattern you originally planned so perfectly will shrink. Only trim and clip when you are actually ready to appliqué—not before.

The Clematis quilt is easy because it is pure appliqué with little complication in adding strips to the sides. Cut out all the flowers needed in various colors; also cut out the center pieces. Never use pinking shears: you do not want a "picket fence" look on the front of your finished quilt, and you do not want your appliqué to wear unevenly. Both of these things are possible with the notches left by pinking shears. Getting down to the appliqué takes plenty of cutting time first. (It also takes quite a bit of fabric, perhaps more than you imagine.) Some instructors propound the idea of cutting pieces to be appliquéd to exact size—that is, leaving no seam allowance, and then using a buttonhole stitch to appliqué the shapes down. This would perhaps work if your buttonhole stitch were absolutely perfect and minute: no raw edge of the appliqué would show at all. Another approach is to do a buttonhole stitch around the edge of a design shape and then to cut off excess fabric. This can be beautiful, but it is too much work; moreover, the result—especially for a beginner—might be heartrending instead of heartwarming. There is no way with this method to do trapunto until *after* the appliqué is complete; then you must open up the material from the back, stuff it, and join the edges together using a turkey stitch.

For both the Clematis and the Hollyhock patterns, the following instructions will hold. As described in the chapter on design, place the cut flower fabrics on the background fabric in the color combinations you desire with the approximate spacing you have in mind. Work as nature does, at random. The cascade of flowers at the lower portion of the Clematis quilt may be more heavily blossomed; the same holds for the small area over the pillow. It is for you to decide.

Pin a few of the flowers in place at the top, being certain to leave open space beneath a petal if you'll want a leaf coming out from under it. This way, you need only turn under the outer section of the leaf and not the entire leaf. (See Figure 14.) Later, as you sew, you might find it judicious to move the flowers around a bit—turning in the ¼-inch seam allowance as you go will give your quilt a different look, and perhaps too much space around the flowers for your taste. This is why you should not necessarily place all of the flowers on the background fabric at once. Later, you can add flowers freely.

Only if it will help you, you might draw on the background fabric exactly where you want each flower and leaf to go. Use a very light pencil mark. Remember, if you try this method, that the pencil mark is on the fabric and may not come off too easily. (Please do not use the "disappearing marker," for the reason given earlier.) I do not recommend this technique, but you may use it if it makes you feel more secure.

There is no need to thread-baste anything following my technique. Many books tell you to baste the ¼-inch seam under, but pin-basting is faster. If you are not comfortable just pin-basting, I suggest that you baste through the middle of the piece you are working on, making an "X" if the piece is rather large but leaving the edges free. Thread-basting through the middle will keep the work from shifting too much; you can pin-baste the edges as you go. I usually pin-baste about 3 inches ahead of where I am working.

Pin-basting can be hazardous for some, since the threads of hand sewing can become entangled in the pins. Be certain to place your pins vertical to a horizontal line: you'll be "stuck" less frequently and have more space to sew. For every 5 inches, you really need only about 4 pins. (See Figure 15.)

Use an embroidery hoop (the kind with the screw, not the spring-loaded kind) to do your appliqué work. Your work will not get too pinched, and you can control the tautness. A 9-inch oval or a 6-inch round hoop is best (I prefer the oval). You think, "That's too small." No! This size of hoop allows more room to manipulate, and the appliqué goes faster. Your piece needs to be rather loose: then you can make a "hill" with your finger underneath in order to pick into the fabric. The fabric should be "bounce-able"; your finger underneath, feeling the needle pierce the fabric, can make an uphill indention on top of the fabric, and the finger on top can make an indention downhill. (This could be called a "Hill and Vale" technique.) Wiggling the needle in quilting is very much faster than making one stitch at a time: you can carry several stitches through on a single needle pull. For appliqué, however, one stitch at a time is the rule. One stitch at a time is the only way to do my Amish back-stitch (see Figure 16). For both quilting and appliqué stitching, the less needle showing through on the top when piercing, the smaller the stitch or stitches taken.

All the time you are sewing on the appliqué, there is no problem with your foundation fabric being "missewn": the hoop will save you hours of problems with lumpy, bumpy, gathered-up stitches on the wrong side.

When it comes time to stitch down the flowers, match your thread color to the piece you are appliquéing as closely as is feasible. The finished look will be more professional. Do not use too long a length of thread; about 12 inches will give better control, the thread will not knot up as much.

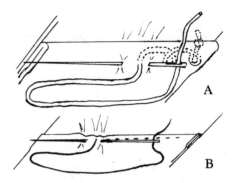

Figure 16. Charlotte's Amish Back-stitch

A. This is an enlarged view of the backstitch showing how I move my needle (I am righthanded). The diagram shows three stitches; the third is just being completed. Lefthanded persons should turn the book upside down or use a mirror to see how the stitch is done. Dash lines show the thread *beneath* the layers of fabric.

B. This diagram shows a line of backstitches done by a righthanded quilter.

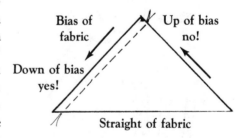

Figure 17. Machine stay-stitch a bias if you are going to handle it frequently. This will prevent it from stretching out of proportion. Always sew *down* a bias direction: *never* sew against the stretch. (This rule applies to *all* sewing.) Sew *down* a bias—not up! Should the other section beyond the stay-stitch become puffy and saggy—press it carefully back into shape with a steam iron.

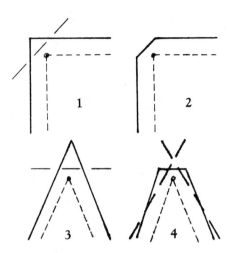

Figure 18.

1 and 2 show the squared corner, before and after cutting.

3 and 4 show a sharp-angled corner, before and after cutting.

Figure 19. It is easy to stuff (trapunto) each flower very gently by using a small stick or your scissors. The appliqué work should be in a hoop when you are stuffing—this makes it easy to create a smooth trapunto. *Do not overstuff* and make the appliqué bumpy!

Appliqué Stitching

Sew down the flowers, leaves, and buds, using Charlotte's Amish Backstitch (Figure 16). This is really nothing more than a backstitch pulled taut. The stitch will secure those appliqué pieces once and for all; you will not have to worry about feather or hem stitches wearing out or becoming snapped or snagged on someone's ring or a hook on clothing. I have developed and applied this wonderful backstitch to all of my appliqué. All the extra thread is on the back of the fabric on which you are sewing; only the smallest indention shows where the needle went through the appliqué. To begin, I use a traditional spit knot, placed under the petal. If you prefer, leave your knot on the back of the quilt top. My ending-off is done on the back; I run about one inch of thread into the flower between the layers of fabric to leave a tail, just in case undue stress is placed on my quilt someday and the knot wants to pop out to the front again. This backstitch is worked from the top; there is no need to take your needle through and reposition it for each stitch.

Turning down those little ¼-inch seams is not difficult, though it may seem so at first. If you have stay-stitched your flowers, you must clip into the machine stitch, stopping just short of the line of thread. Only clip—do *not* cut out notches, even though some books tell you to do so in order to eliminate bulk on curves. Don't do it. Why? Because if the fabric being appliquéd is a bit lighter than the background fabric in color, you will find these notches looking out at you when your quilt is finished, right through the appliquéd petal (or whatever). Although they'll be muted, they'll bother your eye. If you merely clip, a continuous ¼-inch seam line will be visible—if anything. One way to overcome this "shadow" problem altogether is to use two layers of appliqué fabric to strengthen its color and keep the background color from showing through. Another method is to use a small amount of stuffing to hide the "shadow seam."

Stay-stitching and clipping curves will give you better control of a curve, and the stitch line can actually be a guide on which you roll that ¼-inch seam under. The procedure can complicate your job on tiny flowers, but it works wonders on broad curves and circles.

I sometimes use stay-stitching and clipping on a long bias edge to keep it from stretching out of shape (see Figure 17). If you do not use stay-stitching on a bias edge and the fabric stretches, steam ironing will bring it back to its original size—if you know what that is, or made a note of it when you were first planning your quilt.

Too much fabric bulk on the corners can be an appliquéer's bane. Clipping off is the answer to this problem (see Figure 18). Make a backstitch on either side of your dot to secure your stay-stitches (if you've used them). It is your needle that will help you turn a corner, *not* a lot of basting (which will only make your job more difficult), and not a lot of pins, because there will be no room to sew the corner down and the fabric will be full of pinholes. I usually trim the corner just above the dot (if your work is all hand-done, it is probably better to clip a bit further from the dot); then I trim each side of the dot at an angle (see Figure 18). Don't be afraid to clip, but go gently at first. Next, I fold the tip under a little bit (to the dot if it is visible), and with my needle I carefully fold in one side of the corner at a time and stitch. It is a good idea to give the tip of your corner an extra stitch—a tiny one. This precaution makes the corner more secure. Use of a hoop makes this procedure very much easier.

When three quarters of the flower has been sewn down, think about putting a little batting into the area between the appliqué and the background fabric. This is trapunto . . . stuffing! And, as mentioned earlier, use only half the amount you think is necessary, just enough to give the petals a little rise. This will give the finished quilt a three-dimensional look. Do not overstuff. Push the stuffing in with a popsicle stick or the end of your scissors (see Figure 19), not as you would stuff a toy, but just laying it in gently. (More will be said on the subject of trapunto later.) Once the stuffing is laid in, complete the last petal.

What about the stamens (centers) of flowers? These are handled differently, following nature's shape and design for each kind of flower. For the Clematis quilt, for example, I advise that you count up the number of flowers you are using. Then draw or trace the stamen pattern on the color fabric you've selected (again allowing for a quarter-inch seam), and do your embroidery of French knots in the inner circle before doing any cutting out (see Figure 20). I use two strands of matching embroidery floss (that is, two of the usual six) and make about nine knots. Then I gather a one-inch circle around the French knots, pull to puff up (leaving the thread and needle in), and stuff the little puff with batting. This time I use a good bit of batt to give the stamen loft (as opposed to a little rise). Then, on the back, I take my needle and do a couple of criss-cross stitches to lock the stuffing in place. Finally, I knot off the floss and cut. Another needle and thread—this time sewing thread, not floss—is used to make another circle of running stitches around the remaining area of the small stamen (see Figure 20), leaving the thread loose. Then pull up the line of running stitches in order to give the circle a curve; the little ¼-inch seam will pook under all by itself, and there will really be no need to clip it at all. Sew the stamen to the center of the flower; just before you close it up, add some more stuffing to give another layer of loft. Then finish closing up. Now the stamen is stuffed twice and sewn down to the blossom. For a finishing touch, run some long stitches from the edge of the stamen in to the center edge where the first line of gathering stitches was sewn, using a single strand of embroidery floss. (See Figure 21.)

All of the stamens can be worked with French knots on one large piece of fabric instead of starting and completing one stamen at a time: it is easier to handle and control a larger piece of fabric. It takes about 45 minutes to

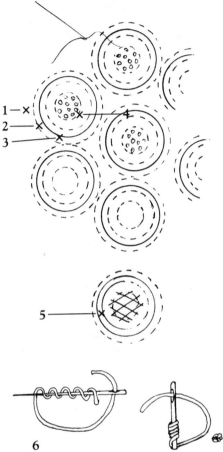

Figure 20. Stamen being embroidered with French knots.
1. Cutting edge.
2. Template drawing edge.
3. Gathering edge (gathering to be done *after* French knots).
4. Gathering edge for first stuffing, also done *after* French knots.
5. Reverse side, after cutting out stamen and stuffing has been added. Use "turkey" stitches (shown) to hold in batting.
6. How to execute a French knot (right to left).

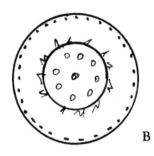

Figure 21. Stamen
A. This diagram shows a side view of a finished stamen.
B. This diagram is a top view of the stamen *before* the final embroidery stitches have been applied. At this point, the stamen has been sewn to the center of the flower (which is already appliquéd and stuffed, if desired).

an hour to make each one of these little stamens from start to finish, but the finished product closely resembles the dimensions of the flower as nature made it.

The rest of the quilt is done in the same manner. You may prefer to stuff just the flower and the stamen, or you may stuff both of these plus the leaf. It is your choice; you may decide not to stuff any of it. I recommend that at least the stamen be stuffed. It *does* need that dimension or it lies too flat on top of the blossom. (This kind of stamen can also be used on "Magnolia Elizabeth" pattern on page 140).

In the center of my Hollyhock Heaven throw, I elected to put a small tassel, drapery style, and a button. You may prefer simply a small circle. It is your quilt—so please yourself.

The Clematis quilt does not have any stems, but should you choose a design for your quilt with curved stems in it, there is a simple way of making them that will save you a lot of headaches. (See Figure 22.) Decide how wide you want your stems to be. Do not make them too thin—quilts need strength of design, and skinny stems will not pull their weight. Cut the shape you need out of cardboard. Depending on the width of the stem, allow ¼-inch seam allowance on each side. Cut the fabric you've chosen for the stem *on the bias* to this width and the proper length. *Bias curves.* Next, on the ironing board and using a steam iron, center the cardboard template you made on the bias length of fabric. You will have to wiggle the bias piece to fit the curve of the stem, but it *will* fit. Press the seam allowance over the cardboard template. Magic! You have a curved stem. Be careful not to handle your new stem too much; it will lose its shape. Of course, you can re-press it if this happens.

"Why can't I just make that stem on a straight piece of cardboard and twist the fabric afterwards?" you ask in dismay. Because the curve will "go" into the bias with pressing—and if you use a straight template it will be difficult to make the curve work. This is one of the tips that will make your experience with appliqué much easier.

Should you find that you really *do* need an ever-so-tiny stem and you do not wish to appliqué a bias strip to represent this piece of nature's work, I recommend that you embroider that stem in place; when it comes time to quilt, remember to quilt on *both* sides of the stem (if there is room). For your embroidery, use any decorative stitch you like: chain stitch, running stitch, or even a simple backstitch are all candidates.

Another tip: if you have a small circle to make, turning under the usual ¼-inch seam is *not* the way to do it. Gather circles up to about one inch across with hand stitching, using regular sewing thread. Pull the thread as tight as you want it (the looser the thread, the larger your finished circle) and knot it. Then wiggle the piece into a circle and appliqué it down. Consider trapunto before you draw that last stitch that finishes the appliqué (Figure 23).

If you are joining a number of flower petals one by one, use the dot method—and *stop* at the dot to make your job easier. If you are cutting a lot of flowers for appliqué and you are not going to stay-stitch, I recommend that you snip in on the curves to about ⅛-inch (Figure 24). The curve will turn more easily and will be less likely to fall in points. Snip *in*—but do *not* snip out; avoid unsightly notches (see page 44).

Most of my appliqué has some trapunto treatment. About the only pressing I do on appliqué with trapunto is with a steam iron lightly on the edge of the appliqué. If your iron is old and apt to make a water mark, it is best to go out and get a new one! The dollar cost will be infinitely less than what your work and time is worth. A handful of fancy stamens would cover the cost if you look at your work in terms of dollars per hour.

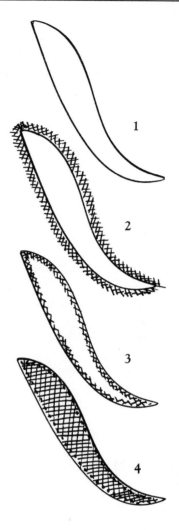

Figure 22.
Making a narrow bias curve for a stem, basket, etc.
1. Cardboard template.
2. Cut bias ¼-inch larger than the template on both sides.
3. With a steam iron press bias over the edges of the template.
4. Remove the template. Handle bias as little as possible; place where needed and stitch.

GENERAL RULES OF THUMB FOR APPLIQUÉ

The ''Do'' Side of the Ledger

- Do stay-stitch all curved items and *then* trim back to ¼-inch seam allowance. If stay-stitch tends to distort appliqué line, simply cut or break thread here and there and proceed. These pieces should then be pressed to ease out the bulge . . . they will then lie flat.
- Do plan ahead on using small leaves, flowers, and the like, drawing them all at one time and leaving enough room in between to allow a seam allowance of ¼-inch when cutting.
- Do stay-stitch *before* cutting out small items if you feel it necessary. This will save time and trouble.
- Do clip into stay-stitching and *stop* just before you near the machine stitch.
- Do unroll your quilt batt at least one week before using. This will allow it to 'rest,' and it will 'rise!' Most wrinkles will disappear.
- Do use tissue paper to act as backing on very fine fabrics if you decide to use them. Tear tissue away after stay-stitching is complete. Tissue can also be used at any time in sewing to increase machine tension and give better control of fabrics.
- Do use two layers of fabric if one is too sheer and background color bleeds through to the eye of the beholder; handle as one fabric. Or, you can use a small amount of stuffing to hide shadow seams.
- Do use cardboard templates (patterns). Other materials are all right, but cardboard works fine. If you are in a hurry, just newspaper works!
- Do use matching thread for appliqué work. Any color may be used for stay-stitching—it won't show anyway since it will be turned under.
- Do use mercerized thread for appliqué if available: it does not know how to curl and knot! Polyester/cotton thread is difficult to use in appliqué unless used in short lengths.
- Do consider using two needles in appliquéing. Stitch as far as possible. Move hoop and continue. This saves eyes from extra threading—also fewer endings.
- Do use a regular "spit" knot when appliqué is being done. Hide the knot under the appliqué or background fabric upon which the appliqué is

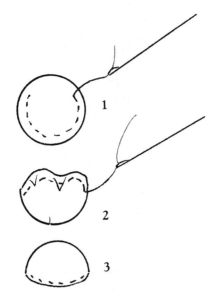

Figure 23.   How to make a small circle ready for appliqué.
1. **Hand-gather ¼-inch in from edge.**
2. **Pull thread to gather and pucker circle underneath to desired size.**
3. **Press down with fingers to appliqué (diagram shows that stuffing has been added). Stuffing will make the overall circle smaller.** *Experiment first.*

being sewn, or under the piece being sewn down.

- Do use a knot tied by hand for quilting. Don't use a "spit" knot, which is too large to be pulled through the top fabric to begin quilting stitches.
- Do appliqué *very* close to the edge of your fabric, using Charlotte's Amish Backstitch.
- Do plan on doing 6–8 *stitches per inch* in quilting, especially if you are using a fatt batt. This is "sane" quilting. There is no need to try for that old standard of 20 stitches to the inch!
- Do use an embroidery hoop to appliqué, either a 9-inch oval or a 6-inch round. Either plastic or wood will do, but be certain the hoop is the screw kind.
- Do use a curved piece of cardboard to make those thin stems needed for so many appliqué designs. Use a bias fabric ¼-inch larger on both sides of template; press with iron. Handle gently, because bias stretches easily.
- Do avoid designing with too many tiny pieces.
- Do lay out appliqué pieces; if some are lapped over others there is no need to turn under the part of the ¼-inch seam that is buried beneath another piece.
- Do avoid "fighting" colors. Use your color chart for verification of complementary hues—but use a lot of color.
- Do keep small pattern pieces in separate envelopes for each shape, or else run one thread through all the pieces of one shape with a huge knot at the back end but left unknotted on top. Take one piece off at a time as needed.
- Do run your needle through your hair while sewing should it become sticky; the natural oil will make sewing easier.
- Do cut through a piece of wax paper to help ease sticky scissors— "chop–chop–chop." Then, discard the paper.
- Do let your imagination run wild when thinking design, line, and quilting. Often follow your first inclination, which is usually correct.
- Do have a balloon (burst or uninflated) handy when quilting to help in your pulling of the needle. Otherwise, you can go the leather thimble route.

- Do use the dot method in all of your sewing.
- Do think about the "mother-father-sister-brother" method of joining pieced work and finishing up your appliquéd quilt. (See Figure 38 on page 84.)
- Do use a pencil—medium—with not too sharp a point.
- Do try using a clean eraser if you make a mistake with the pencil; sometimes the pencil mark will come out.
- Do use your own saliva to remove any blood spots from needle pricks on your work. Put a piece of your quilting thread into your mouth, saturate it with saliva (if you have lip coloring on, be careful not to get that color on the moistened thread), and use the thread to rub on the blood spot. It

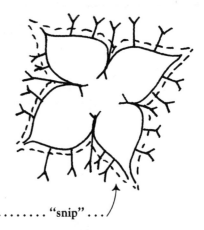

.... "snip" ...

Figure 24. Whether you stay-stitch flowers to be appliquéd or not, it is always necessary to "snip" a curve to about ⅛-inch to make turning easier. If there is a deep crevice, snip into it deeply to form the proper shape of the flower. . . . *don't be afraid!*

will disappear . . . no need to do anything further. It must be *your* saliva for *your* blood.

- Do use club soda to remove other small stains (coffee, for instance) that may show up on your work. Moisten a piece of clean cloth and pat the spot gently. You may want to test this on a piece of leftover fabric first to be sure the color does not run. This works best with fresh stains.
- Do use only polyester-cotton-wrapped thread for quilting—*never* cotton! Cotton thread for quilting breaks too easily.
- Do give your quilting stitches a "pull" to make shadows; otherwise you do not have quilting, just glorified basting!
- Do use No. 7 or No. 8 crewel embroidery needles for of your work in appliqué as well as for quilting. Never use quilting needles—they are too short and too sharp, and the eyes are too small!
- Do make a quilt or wall hanging—not pillows!
- Do purchase enough fabric in the beginning—later is usually too late to obtain the same dye-vat color.
- Do remember that "expensive" is not necessarily "best" in anything!
- Do figure the dollars and cents of how much a quilt will cost before beginning. This might frighten you out of too large a project for your first attempt, which is *good.* Do work on something you are capable of completing!
- Do stick to your original measurements when your quilt is planned.
- Do allow ½-inch seams on all seams, except appliqué pieces, for which ¼-inch is used. Very large appliqué pieces may require ½-inch seams. But these will be stay-stitched and trimmed to ¼ inch for final appliqué turning under.
- Do always wait until you have pressed your entire quilt top *before* trimming any seam.
- Do press on both sides of a seam before opening it up to press. Then, when all adjustments have been made, press on the right side of the seam, *after* seams have been trimmed to ¼-inch.
- Do work with the mitred corner technique; it solves all kinds of problems.
- Do clip bias curves in to the stay-stitching, but not through it. *Never, never* clip out small pieces on curves.
- Do experiment with luxury fabrics. Velvet is a joy to quilt. Silk will require silk thread for appliqué (short strands). Remember when pressing silk that it scorches faster than any fabric made.
- Do boil dark-colored swatches in soap and water with a piece of white fabric. If the dye is running too badly, do not use the fabric. One single washing will *not* remove excess dye or prevent running.
- Do use polyester/cotton fabrics for traditional quilting. Cotton wrinkles too easily and does not stay "perky" with a lot of handling.
- Do trust the manufacturer's statement at the end of the fabric bolt (e.g., "Shrinkage less than 1%.") Washing and ironing of fabrics is *not* necessary in most instances.
- Do be flamboyant with colors.

- Do avoid the "patchwork syndrome" for beginning quilting.
- Do think appliqué.
- Do think positive. In fact, that is the only way to think when thinking quilting! PROCEED—go forward with needle and thread.

The "Don't" Side of the Ledger

- Do not press appliqué pieces unless they are long, straight pieces. They should be pressed over a clean piece of brown paper bag to get a straight line. Some appliqué pieces are so minute that they cause burning fingers and incorrect corners when pressed. Use your needle to roll the ¼-inch under.
- Do not baste the edges of your appliqué down before you stitch it onto your background fabric. If you have a large item, you can "X" baste it *in the middle only* to hold it secure, *if* pins will not do the job too satisfactorily for you.
- Do not clip wedges or notches out of your appliqué pieces. If the fabric is not dark, the right side will look like Tom Sawyer's picket fence to the discriminating eye.
- Do not use what is commonly known as the "appliqué stitch." There is too much thread revealed on the sides of the work and it could conceivably be pulled out with a ring or hook on clothing. My Amish stitch is hidden and all excess thread is *underneath*, out of harm's way. Avoid using the buttonhole stitch; it is even worse than the appliqué stitch, unless worked very close together.
- Do not be afraid to cut off excess fabric when turning a corner, no matter how sharp. Use my method. Remember, too much bulk is difficult to handle and it looks unprofessional. And you are going to be *very* professional—even if you don't think so now!
- Do not forget to learn the "uphill-downhill" (or "Hill and Vale") method of appliqué and quilting.
- Do not think negative . . . there is no such work as "can't" in *our* vocabulary.

These are details about appliqué work you may never have dreamt of—answers to questions never asked. These are the *why's* explaining what you may have been told to do by someone else or that you may have read about somewhere.

Appliqué can express so many things, as my friend William L. Durant writes:

> Those scraps of memory from your life
> Will live again through appliqué.
> Having read this chapter, now proceed
> To record your history in this novel way.

"9" (Cloud 9) (42″ × 57″).   *Colors:* Cloud-white background. A preprinted lamb is appliquéd on a hot pink cloud; other clouds are soft blush peach. The quilt is bound in hot pink with peach eyelet lace edging. Satin ribbon is tied around the lamb's neck and may be untied for ironing. The reverse side is hot pink . . . with eyelet showing. Trapunto and tying (knotting) are used in addition to normal quilting.

CHAPTER 6

APPLIQUÉ THE EASY WAY
—MORE ABOUT QUILT TOPS

... *H*alf finished? Tis the motto of the world!
We spin vain threads, and strive and die,
With sillier things than spindles on our hands!
—Robert Bloomfield
"To His Mother's Spindle"

Even if this is your first try with appliqué, there is no need to do something so mediocre that it is no challenge. Do something with *some* challenge, but don't use too many small pieces of appliqué or too many colors in the beginning. Perhaps when you think of appliqué, you think of the tiny vines and flowers on those heirloom quilts displayed in museums. I love them, too. But the needlewomen who made them were pros with years and years of quilting experience behind their needles. Do what you can, and do the best you can. If you are not satisfied with your first attempt at appliqué, you can depend on improving with time and practice.

Most important, when you begin something, finish it! Are you half-finished with a patchwork quilt? Appliqué what you have already accomplished onto a colorful background. Don't waste those hours of work. "With sillier things . . . on our hands"—half-finished anythings! Don't let this be *your* motto.

I must confess that I, too, have my white elephant. Of all the quilts I have begun, there is one that I have not finished and probably will not, a Hawaiian quilt of deep orange and deep purple. It plagues me every time I go into the closet. Do you have something like that hiding on a back shelf? Drag it out and use it.

Patchwork is not the only needlework that lies dormant in a hidden place (put there so that you don't have to think about it). What about those squares of actual appliqué once begun and never completed, or those six or eight prestamped square embroidered pieces that you never got around to doing anything about? Now is your chance to accomplish that task put off for years. Don't forget that tablecloth you embroidered and never used. Now is the time to reincarnate items of this kind. You are half-finished with a quilt and don't realize it!

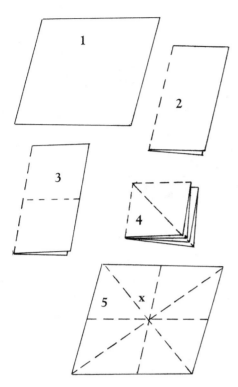

Figure 25. To find the center of a piece of fabric, use these diagrams and the directions in the text.

Using Preprinted Items

I created "9" (Chapter 6, opening page) as a teaching instrument, because some beginners are afraid to tackle altogether original work. It *is* possible to take some "canned" ideas and broaden them to create appliqué with some originality. This is how "9" came to life: I began with a little lamb, one of the many readily available preprinted needlework items that can be purchased at any fabric counter. Many of these charming animals have both a front and a back, or a side view to be sewn on the back. When the work is turned over, there, in all its glory, is the "rear end"—it is fun! I thought of little lambs to be counted, and this train of thought brought to mind—what else—clouds, stars, a moon. I stay-stitched the lamb all round so that I could turn the curves easily, and I left only ¼-inch seam allowance to turn under. The instructions for many of these canned items recommend that you turn under ½-inch or even more. *Don't do it.* Very few of the canned designs will have the sort of very long curves that require more than ¼-inch seam allowance.

Appliqué does not always have to be centered on a quilt. It can be quite as effective (and perhaps more so) placed off-center or to the bottom, as I did with "9." I built the rest of my appliqué composition above the lamb. To find the center of your top—or any piece of fabric—to aid in positioning appliqué, fold the fabric in half, in half again (now you have quarters), and, if you have anything very detailed to place, in half *again*, but this time diagonally. (See Figure 25.) Finger-press along each fold line. Do *not* iron! Opened up, the fabric will show eight lines. Then you can take your motif, fold it in quarters, and match centers. Use a pin if you wish to position your motif dead center; if not, the finger-pressed lines will help you keep your pieces straight.

To prepare the lamb for this positioning process, I appliquéd the lamb to a cloud (placing it a little off-center because the front end of the lamb shape was larger than the tail end and I did not want the lamb to appear "front-heavy.") Then I folded the piece in quarters and marked the center spot with a pin—just on the front of the lamb, leaving the cloud behind it free. I wanted to stuff my lamb; I thought it would be difficult to do this in the usual manner, because of the little legs and tail, the wool bulges, and so on. So, I slit a hole in the back of the cloud *behind* the lamb, leaving the lamb itself intact. Then I stuffed it from behind, as shown in Figure 26. (I tore my batting to almost the shape of the lamb—and put it in whole—one layer only.) After that, I closed up my slit with a turkey whip-stitch. Finally, I used my center marker to position the whole piece on my background fabric and appliquéd it down. I used trapunto on my other clouds as well, again stuffing from the back. To keep the stuffing from shifting in the washing process, I knotted the clouds and lamb in various places, using the kind of knot described on page 102 in the chapter on finishing techniques. I also put a ribbon around the lamb's neck—this can be done either before or after appliquéing.

Combining knotting with appliqué is a lovely way to dress up a quilt quickly. You can also incorporate quilting lines, as I did with the stars and moon in this project; I also quilted in a few more clouds. I edged "9" with eyelet lace (the commercial kind already gathered on a strip) and two strips of bias. I think the result is charming.

Combining Embroidery Blocks with Appliqué

Look at my "Les Fleurettes Violetta" cross-stitch-appliqué-trapunto quilt (see the color photographs following page 116 and the line drawing on page 78). This was an exercise using "canned" embroidery blocks. I do a great deal of my needlework while riding from one place to another in our car—when it is not my turn to drive—and my husband and I travel a great deal, so I found myself once with sixteen squares of embroidered violets.

My entire life's color is lilac. My father adored it; he used to say, "Paint anything lilac and a fly won't sit on it!" (It's true!) No color pleases me more. I use shades of purple, lavender, lilac, and complementary colors in much of my work. The canned package instructions had recommended fuschia and purple for these cross-stitched violets. I thought that this would perhaps be too much of one thing, so I researched the various violets to find out what colors they really were. I came up with the sixteen different colors that I eventually used in my sixteen squares. I departed from the canned instructions still further by making the frame stitching (the area around the violets) an off-white, almost ecru color that resembles lace from far away. I knew that the sixteen squares of cross-stitch were more likely to be seen from far away than close up.

My final innovation in completing the embroidery was to use two strands of embroidery thread instead of the 3 or 4 usually recommended. This required less thread and the result is more delicate-looking.

Once the cross-stitch was finished (many car trips later), it was time to assemble the squares. I found that the thought of joining the squares in the conventional manner with blocks and strips (which I refer to as the "father-mother-sister-brother" method of building a quilt—see page 83), made me cringe. So I put them on the floor, and happenstance intervened. We have lilac carpeting in our home. While I was placing the squares, before all of them were put in place, the lilac carpeting caught my eye. I thought, "Why not make an inset and place the squares around it?" I did. In fact, not being satisfied to leave it at that, I set about building a

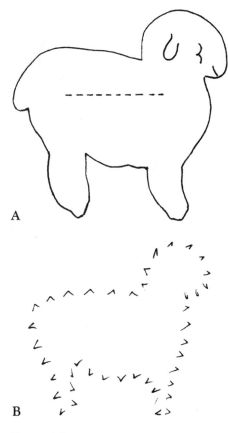

Figure 26.

A. This diagram shows the *reverse* side of the lamb, already appliquéd onto a cloud. Cut back as indicated—it is the cloud only that you are cutting, *not* the lamb.

B. Tear batting to fit the approximate shape of the lamb. Do not bunch the batting. Make a hole large enough so that you can gently push the filling into place by hand.

picture in the center of the squares. One thing led to another, and I wound up doing trapunto under appliquéd flowers. I cut the pattern for the flowers "by guess and by gosh," using all the muted shades from the violets that I could gather: peach, lilac, lavender, violet, and so forth. I picked up the greens for the leaves and built the center "out of air," thus completing the picture of the border blocks. Just joining the center to the blocks did not give enough dimension, so I built a frame around my centerpiece, using the mitre method. And instead of using the conventional lattice stripping, I simply joined my cross-stitch blocks together.

POSTSCRIPT: everything was going so beautifully that I got overconfident. Thinking "I was so smart," I trimmed my seams along the squares too soon after joining. *After* I had my top completed, I found that I had two blocks *upside down*. Horrors! But there was not enough seam to correct my error; in fact, to ease one place I had clipped it! There was no way on earth that I could turn those squares over. No one is perfect. It is at times like this that I say to myself, "Fifty years from now, who will care!"

This quilt has an unusual corner, for which I used the same techniques as for the center instead of the usual corner square.

I'm not certain how accurate my French is in this instance, but the back is embroidered "Les Fleurettes Violetta"—the little violets—or whatever!

An important point I'd like to make here is that if you have blocks of anything, there is no rule saying that you must use the conventional block-bar joining. Do it if you like; if you prefer, do something different.

The size of your background block is important to consider when doing appliqué. Do not crowd your appliqué pieces. Once again, a sample block should be cut and the appliqué-to-be should be placed on it to see how it will look. If it is too crowded, perhaps you should use a larger block. Otherwise, you can change your mind about the appliqué. It is best, however, to find your overall quilt size in the planning process and work your design out on paper, not in cloth. In general, it will be better to stick to your original plan. Nothing dictates to you the size of your squares, but you want to make this decision in the planning stage to avoid wasting effort and materials. As a rule, play with ideas at the planning stage.

Another note on the subject of planning: if you'd like to do any embroidery—and note that this includes the all-important signing and dating of your quilt—it should be done before your quilt top is joined to the batting and backing. Otherwise, it will be difficult to execute without catching on the other side, showing, or pulling the quilt unattractively. Plan ahead. If you want to add another leaf or give another thought to the appliqué because there is a spot that suddenly looks bare to you, do it *before* the quilt is put on the frame. I usually let my quilts-to-be alone for a couple of days before they go on the frame, spread out so that I can see them—just in case there is something else I'll wish to add. This is a fine rule to follow. Haste makes waste—or at least it can breed disappointment.

More Appliqué from Printed Fabric Panels

Although my Big Top quilt (see Chapter 3, opening page) was difficult to quilt because of the heavy weight of the printed fabric, it was still fun to do. However, I must warn you here to be careful about which printed fabrics you decide to adapt to appliqué. Some canned patterns are too heavy to appliqué and quilt.

So you have a print with circus wagons, an elephant, lions, and giraffes (my favorite zoo animals). What to do? I detest using someone else's thinking, so to personalize my quilt from such a print I purchased two sets of the wagons. Once again, I stay-stitched around the curved sections. Of course, when you appliqué the stay-stitched edges down, you can push those machine stitches out of sight, never to be seen again. (The needle is a wonderful invention.)

I always play with colors when I am planning a new quilt. For Big Top, I looked through my scraps for various shades of orange, pink, red, and blue, all picked up from the wagon colors. Nothing pleased me until I came to a great piece of forest green broadcloth (similar to percale but not as tightly woven). But, for shame . . . it had a corner cut off where I had used it for cutting a bias binding. There I was with a just-right piece of fabric, the color was perfect—and it had only three corners. Of course, it was Sunday, and the stores were all closed . . . and I was really ready to work on this quilt. What to do? I cut off the other three corners! Innovation is the name of the game. Make do—at least when you are pulling fabric from the scraps and pieces you have been hoarding up.

Now that I have four corners cut off, I had to do something about extending the edge; thus leftover white fabric from another quilt came into play. Then I had to fill those vacant angles (see the layout on page 14), so I cut out hot pink angles and filled in these spots—using the dot method, of course (I hate to piece). But what about the center of this big piece of green? A circus parade called for a big top. So, with newspaper folded again and again to make the necessary points and shape, I used scrap fabrics to make my big top. Yarn tassels at the corners, and a pom-pom on the big top, also seemed necessary. I added them—but I also quilted an extra tassel at the point of each tent corner, knowing how frequently tassels get taken off.

Trying to keep in sync with the circus wagons, I quilted in a sort of chain between the wagons and the animals. This is really a happy quilt. I give this detailed account to inspire you to use what you have, innovate when you can—and be daring with ideas. Make mistakes (if you've made any) work for you. And don't tell anyone about your mistakes—tell people you

Figure 26 (continued)

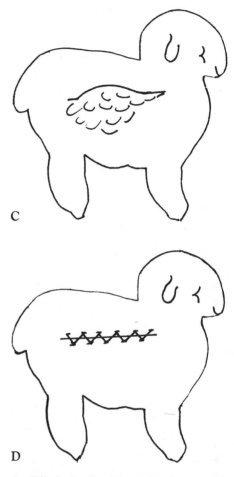

C. Fill the lamb with gentle shoves and pushes—by hand.
D. Close up the incision with turkey stitches. Remember, it is the cloud that you've cut—and it is the cloud you sew up, very loosely. Your stitches should not catch the lamb.

planned it all along! There is an adage that quilters always plan a mistake—a "God's Eye"—in a quilt so that it isn't perfect. I don't need to plan one . . . they manage to happen all by themselves!

Serendipity

Ideally, you plan out your quilt in detail, in advance. Sometimes, though, it doesn't happen out this way. Sometimes you have a flash of inspiration, and the rest of the pieces fall into place only later. (This is not so likely to happen if you are a beginner; if it does, you will wisely consider the idea of resisting impulse, or at least of channeling it a bit before you rush for your scissors.) Here is my favorite example of playing with a quilt:

My abstract Calendula quilt began with one large square, a 26″ × 26″ design. Where did such a design in such an unusual size originate? In a painting. While visiting friends in Washington, D.C., Major General and Mrs. Jack E. Thomas, USAF, Ret., I saw and was very taken with General Thomas's oil painting "A Study in Black and White." I immediately visualized a quilt top. He allowed me to trace the pattern. I had fabric left from my Marigold quilt (a pattern that appeared in the July/August 1980 issue of DECORATING & CRAFT IDEAS magazine). Therefore, I used the fabric on hand to make up the design. (See the color photograph following page 116).

Cutting out the many pattern pieces in cardboard was nothing compared with cutting out the fabric: over one thousand pieces, literally, before I was finished.

I had no idea in the world what I wanted to do after the original block. Then I decided that another block with the colors rearranged would be nice. I made it. What about more? During a half-sleeping, half-waking state, it occurred to me to break up the original pattern. Thus the quilt has many facets of the original design broken up over the balance of the quilt. Of all my quilts to date, this is the one that captures the "ahs" of beholders. It pleases me, too. This quilt won the only Blue Ribbon at Ball State University's Yesterday, Today, and Tomorrow Exhibition (Muncie, Indiana). As a professional, I do not enter competitions, this was a People's Favorite Choice!

Dedicating yourself to finding just the right pattern before you begin may turn out to be folly; you may have, say, a picture around the house with a perfect pattern for the centerpiece of a quilt all along. Just be sure not to commit too much of your time and your materials to a project that you have not thought out thoroughly. Serendipity is wonderful, but there is a fine balance of creativity, discipline, and sense that allows serendipity to occur.

Seek and ye shall find . . .

CHAPTER 7

REVERSE APPLIQUÉ

*W*ith her neeld [needle] composes Nature's own shape of bud, bird, branch or berry."

—William Shakespeare
Pericles

Many people who have done lovely appliqué work are afraid to tackle reverse appliqué because they think it is particularly complicated and difficult. You think you know yourself better than anyone else; but perhaps you have already accomplished this supposedly difficult feat and do not know it. Think!

Do you recall having put a patch behind "John's old trouser knee," whipping the fabric from the pant top under to cover the frayed edges? "Why, yes," you reply, "is that reverse appliqué?" Yes, sure 'tis! That's what it is all about!

Devoting an entire chapter to reverse appliqué is a joy. It will perhaps convince you to try this fascinating method of appliqué. So many different effects can be achieved using reverse appliqué. But, first, some background on this unique method of stitchery.

Kuna Reverse Appliqué

The origin of reverse appliqué cannot be attributed to any one country; there are many variations of the work. My first acquaintance with the technique was made while we lived in Panama. There we saw the Kuna Indians of the San Blas Islands, not too far from the Isthmus of Panama. Their magnificent reverse appliqué work is known worldwide and the Kuna (the most common name given to the tribe) are credited with its origination by some historians. However, the Hmong people of Laos have their own method of reverse appliqué that may rival the Kuna method in age. The two peoples are, obviously, far removed geographically from each other, which rules out the question of influence.

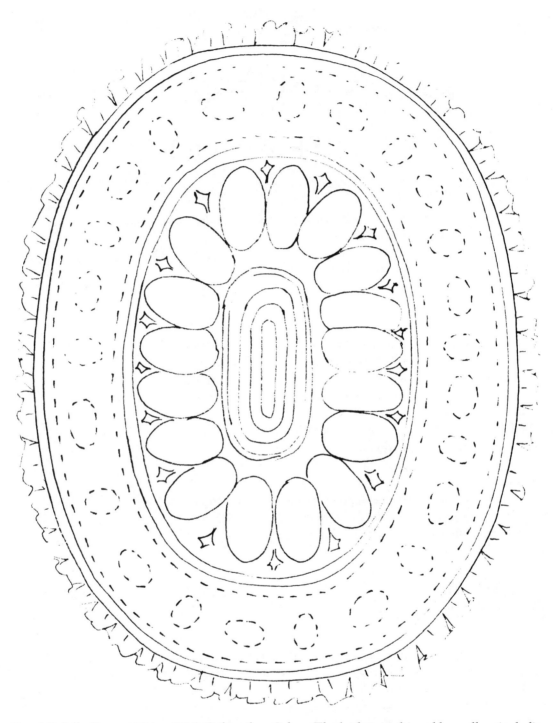

Ronald's Jelly Beans (46″ × 56″) Crib quilt. *Colors:* **The background is golden yellow including small diamonds and center yellow reverse appliqué to expose this color. Other "jelly beans" are appliquéd in multicolor — purple, orange, pink, green, turquoise, and other related shades. The center has a free bias of lilac next to purple, then hot pink, off-white, and finally yellow. The quilt is bound in lilac bias with a 2-inch bias ruffle. Reverse side is soft green, with yellow bias trim next to the lilac ruffle.**

The women of the Kuna tribe are the bosses! When the Kuna came to shop in Panama, the men, dressed in fine white shirts, black trousers, and hats, were required to walk behind their women by many paces. The women wore colorful skirts and white blouses or colored blouses (not their molas, as their needlework is called). The thing that really attracted attention in the marketplace was their jewelry. It was pure gold! Gold necklaces around their necks, rings through their noses, and so forth. They possessed such dignity that they were almost like royalty on parade. The San Blas Indians have kept their bloodlines pure over the centuries. They are an independent people and resist foreigners penetrating their communities.

This independence is reflected in Kuna needlework, which is characterized by pure, strong color, outstanding and seldom-seen combinations of fabrics, and in general by completely original designs depicting San Blas culture. Many of the molas are made especially to depict carnival time in Panama—the season just before the beginning of Lent, comparable to Mardi Gras in Louisiana. There are no "canned" patterns; the women "do what comes naturally" with their scissors, needles, and thread. All work is done by hand. Often there are as many as 25 separate colors in one small mola about 18″ × 20″; if a blouselike garment is made in the mola style, each side affords different designs and colors—thus sometimes doubling the number of colors.

Even thinking about that many colors and textures on one article is mind-boggling, and all of the colors are tied together by the use of red, orange, and black. However, each color is not given a whole separate layer as one would think: weight alone would make such an item impractical. The mola is layered in sections and then stitched. For example, one section of a mola might show blue satin with hot pink and yellow fabrics topped with red. To make this, the pieces would be laid onto the black background (which may be thought of as the lining of the mola); then a shape would be open and its edges pushed away and sewn under with minute stitches. This process would then be repeated, and carefully cut away, one piece at a time per color.

Kuna stitchery is often framed and hung purely as art. It is seldom used as clothing. Prices of molas vary from a few dollars to hundreds, depending upon the intricacy of the design, the colors, and the size. It pains me to see molas put together in one quilt top and "tied" into oblivion. Too often, the makers think they have created a masterpiece. Horrible! A mola or work like it should stand alone to be appreciated, looked at, and saved for posterity. Should you have a mola in your collection and want to make a quilt out of it, I would suggest that it be the focal point of a medallion design, placed in the center. The outer edges beginning from the initial foundation cloth could be made in a series of mitred frames (see quilt layout B shown in Figure 6, page 24). But a good piece really deserves to stand by itself. Another thrilling piece of needlework can thus be saved from oblivion by becoming a wall hanging or a tapestry in its own right.

Hmong Needlework

That women from other parts of the world are so proficient with needle and thread has been a revelation to America. We have learned much from immigrants and refugees from war-torn countries of the world. When the Hmong refugees came from Laos, their exciting and original textiles quickly attracted attention; exhibits of their work have now traveled the length and breadth of this land. Their textiles are so unique that at first glance it appears that the fabric has been printed to perfection; upon closer examination, one finds that various colors have been appliquéd or reverse appliquéd in astounding detail.

Commissions have been given to Hmong refugees to create huge wall tapestries for many leading banks, hotels, and other establishments, particularly in the Minnesota Twin-City area. The Hmong language was not a written language until the end of the 1970's, but their self-expression in needle arts "spoke" in color, with breath-taking emotion.

The Hmong (Mung) people are originally from China. In the course of their history, they have been split into groups, and they became known to the Chinese by the color of their garments: Striped Hmong, Flowery Hmong, White Hmong, Blue Hmong, and (even) Chocolate Hmong. Like the Yao-Iu Mien people of Southeast Asia, who were also forced to flee their homeland, the Hmong found their way to Laos. During the Vietnam War, they assisted American troops in various ways. Because of this assistance, entire Hmong villages were destroyed once the Communists took control of Laos, by use of deadly bio-chemical toxins in the form of "rain": yellow, blue-green, red, and white (these colors now appear frequently in their needlework).

In their magnificent needlework, the Hmong employ appliqué, cross-stitch, and fine embroidery; reverse appliqué, counted satin stitch, and other surface stitches are included, with breathtaking results. Hmong needleworkers use even-weave fabrics and needles so tiny it boggles the mind—less than an inch long! (Consider, however, that these people have very small, fine bone structure and their hands are comparatively tiny. Therefore, handling such a small needle is not so difficult for them, especially because Hmong women are taught to wield a needle when only three years old.) Their stitches are not merely minute—they are all but invisible. The kind of thread they prefer to use is made in the Orient. When they are unable to obtain it, they simply unwind our usual sewing thread and use a single strand. When they are unable to find an exact color match for a particular piece of cloth, they unravel an edge and use one of the threads from the cloth. The Mien women work their cross-stitch from the back because they find this easier, but Hmong women work theirs from the front. As many as 22 stitches are made to the inch in some of their work.

Both the Hmong and the Yao-Iu Mien use American fabrics almost exclusively now, both cotton and cotton-polyester blends such as I recommend. Our fabrics have a wider weave than the fabrics traditionally used in the Hmong homeland, and the difference in weave makes the stitch-count lower. But the effect of Hmong fold-clip-and-tuck-under technique is so magnificent it is hard to fathom that such handwork is done at all.

Perhaps the most familiar of Hmong designs is the "snail" pattern. The "snail" is no more than a circle cut into a long strip having the same width its entire length. Think of peeling an apple in one continuous peel—when you remove the peeler, it falls back into a circular shape, though it has really been cut into a spiral. The snail can be done in all sizes, from tiny, coin-size to large renditions. (My simplified version of the "snail," Hmong Tulip Circle, is an adaptation of the traditional Hmong "snail" using concentric circles: see page 172.) Once the circle is cut out of a piece of fabric, it is laid onto a background fabric, very carefully pinned into position, and then appliquéd down. If you attempt my version or your own version of the "snail," it is advisable to follow the example of the Hmong and sew a backing to the bottom layer of fabric. This will give you your appliqué on top, a background fabric, and a soft backing fabric underneath—I suggest a soft batiste. The batiste layer will provide stability: it will help keep the shape of the appliqué and will later make the whole piece easier to handle. This backing is particularly important for traditional Hmong work, which is not quilted.

Hmong and Yao-Iu Mien women do not use patchwork as we know it, although some of their work looks as though triangles have been pieced into place. A solid strip of fabric, for example, is laid out with triangles; once these triangles are appliquéd down, the strip looks pieced, as in Figure 27. All sizes of triangles are used, from minute pieces half the size of a mosaic tile to much larger ones.

Hmong work in reverse appliqué is particularly remarkable. It makes a very subtle statement. Often it is "hit" with minute embroidery so that it appears to be printed fabric. (The Hmong in America have access to beautiful prints, and some of these fabrics are finding their way into Hmong masterpieces.)

Here is one point of comparison between the Hmong and the Plain People, the Amish. At first, the Amish had wool only. Then they had cotton, which was more reasonably priced than wool, and so they used cotton. Then they blended the dregs of wool and cotton combings and had linsey-woolsey. Along came modern technology with polyester, and for a

Figure 27.

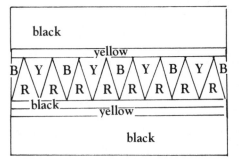

A. Hmong triangle appliqué. Black is the basic background. Yellow strips are appliquéd on, then yellow triangles, red triangles, leaving black triangles on the panel.

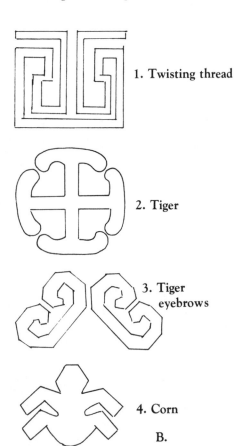

1. Twisting thread

2. Tiger

3. Tiger eyebrows

4. Corn

B.

while the Amish were intrigued with the polyester knits. Then they began to use the polyester-cotton blends. Although many quilting teachers say otherwise, in fact there is *no* set rule with the Amish about what fabric to use—they simply use what is available to them. Hmong women are following this pattern. During ancient times, silk was more plentiful than other fabrics, and their work was accomplished using silks. Today, because of the prohibitive cost of silk, they usually use cottons or blends. "Rules" are for people to break—this is what makes for originality.

Cotton has one advantage for the Hmong: it holds fold and crease lines, which they use as a guide to cut out their patterns. The fold-and-tuck method is their secret. It seems like watching a miracle to see a pattern evolve as the fabric is folded and cut—there are no patterns to start with.

Try the method yourself. Fold a square piece of fabric or paper into a triangle and then in half again; cut a simple shape out of it while it is still folded. Open it up and what do you have? A partially sliced-up piece of fabric, perhaps; if you worked symmetrically, a lovely, lacy design. The "slices" are turned under and reverse appliquéd to make the beautiful Hmong designs. (Clipping is done on corner crevices for "tucking under." Hmong technique differs from that of the San Blas Indians, who usually clip only the straight line and let their slices find their own corners.)

Needlework of the Hmong is known as PA NDAU. Some traditional Hmong (and Yao-Iu Mien) ideas (they can't be called patterns; there are no patterns, as explained above) include Vegetable Blossoms, Maze-like Lines, Corn, Pebble Rock, Paw Marks, Tigers, Tiger Eyebrows, Twisting Threads, Peacock Eyes, Elephant's Foot, and Pumpkin Vines. Figure 27B shows approximate shapes for a few of these. To describe these historic symbols in today's jargon would be impossible. They seem like something that might have come from the tombs of ancient Egyptians: magnificent in detail, accomplished crudely by some and by others with a technique that approaches perfection. Each design has intrinsic meaning, and each needleworker has her own technique within the general outlines of the group methods. The Blue Hmong, for example, use natural dyes in their traditional work, and waxing to protect undyed motifs; their usual background color is blue. This work is then incorporated into circular, pleated skirts, very elegant baby carriers, and so forth. The needlework pieces are embroidered as well as appliquéd by the fold-and-tuck method. The White Hmong are known for their intricate appliqué in reverse, cutting away various layers to reveal other colors, as do the San Blas Indians. Linear puzzles are particularly characteristic of the Yao-Iu Mien. Their designs— some 100 traditional designs—reflect Yao history, legends, and individual status in life. These designs often tell the story of nature, with mountains, sky, rivers, and flowers. Perhaps one of the most amusing is the "enough" design, used on purses to signify "enough children." (It resembles a double Roman key.)

The needle itself is the instrument used to turn under the tiny edges of fabric for appliqué—it is not only used to stitch. And Hmong needles must certainly fly quickly: a major work can be turned out in several months, and smaller pieces may take only days to produce. Few thimbles are worn. The women use their fingernails instead, but note that while their appliqué work is phenomenal, it is *not* quilted! (But this need not deter you and I from adapting Hmong techniques for our own work.)

The Hmong people wear black and dark blue—but any parallel with the Amish use of color stops there; the Hmong use bright, vibrant colors for sashes and collars and for bright pom-poms, which they sew on the hats of small children to ward off evil spirits! (I think this is a charming idea—Hmong children won't ever get lost in a crowd!) When silk was available in Laos—which was not too often—the Hmong rendered their delicate appliqué work in this fabric. Some magnificent patterned silks from Thailand are now used, an example of the culture of a people changing with the times. If Thai silk is used, the Hmong choose bright, clear reds, yellows, greens, and blues.

There are several outlets here in America where the appliqué work of the Hmong is available. These outlets are located primarily in Minnesota (where the largest number of Hmong refugees have gathered); others can be found in Michigan, and some in California and Colorado. In many cases, a woman's fine needlework has saved her family from utter starvation.

In some of their work, the Hmong take one central piece (as I have advised that you do with the molas of the Kuna Indians) and create a frame effect around it. (I have done this for years, without knowing of the Hmong strength of design.) *Mitre* is the word associated with framing; Chapter 9 will explain the techniques. The Hmong take their original square and cut it into shreds with squares, snails, and so forth, and then they reverse appliqué it down onto another piece of fabric. One of their secrets: they add another foundation piece behind the piece being worked, for stability. They use a ruler for measuring, and they crease the fabrics with their fingers to mark cutting lines.

Small borders or frames can be made more simply than by mitring by cutting out a square or oblong of fabric of the size you desire (allowing an extra ¼ inch all around for seam allowance) and whipping the outer edge under. For an 8¾'' × 10¾'' frame, for example, you would cut one piece 8¾'' × 10¾'' and then cut out your centerpiece area from the middle of this piece. Determine how wide a frame you want and add to this width an extra ¼'' for seam allowance. If you want your 8'' × 10'' frame to be 1'' wide, cut all around inside 1¼'' from the outside, whipped edge. Position your frame on the background cloth of your quilt or tapestry (you would be wise to draw in marks for positioning it) and appliqué the frame down, turning under that inner ¼'' seam allowance. If you want to be very, very exact, cut out a cardboard template the exact finished size you want your frame to be, inner and outer edges. Then press the edges of your fabric

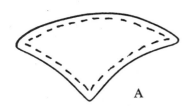

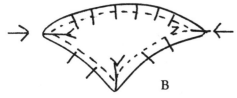

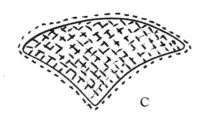

Figure 28.
A. Pencil "dash-dash" line indicating where to cut out fabric using very sharp scissors. Cut . . . allow ¼-inch seam.
B. Clip into corners; if there is a curve, this will make it easier to turn under.
C. Pin-baste down, if you need to; then appliqué, using your needle as you go to turn seam allowance under.

around the cardboard to press in straight edges. (This technique is used to manage the narrow, very symmetrical strips needed to do Celtic patterns in appliqué.)

The color usage of the Kuna Indians and the Hmong (and other peoples the world over) should inspire anyone tied into the "beige world" of no color to try something new.

So Easy to Sew

There are many words used for reverse appliqué. Perhaps "inlaid" describes it for you, perhaps "cut-work"; but try it, whichever term or concept makes sense to you. Abstract, Kuna-style designs are not the only ones that can be worked using this technique. Should you want to make a quilt top with tiny circles for grapes, small buds, accent circles, and so forth, it is far easier to cut a hole in the top fabric, insert the color cloth desired underneath, and then "reverse" or turn under the top fabric (hemming onto the inserted piece) than to fuss with conventional appliqué. (See Figure 28.) This is just one way to do reverse appliqué. The technique is especially useful if you are already dealing with two layers of fabric or more and you want to add other colors.

I recommend that you experiment with scrap fabrics to master the technique. Take two pieces of cloth of the same size but different colors. Draw a small (but not tiny) circle or triangle on one piece. If you wish—and you will probably find it makes your work easier, especially at the beginning—stay-stitch on your outline or just outside it (in the direction of the middle of your shape). Cut out your shape ¼-inch inside your outline so that the cut shape has ¼-inch for the seam allowance, lest your work look like that of an amateur. You are not an amateur, you are a beginner! But we know you will be a fast learner. Pin the top layer of fabric in place over the bottom piece; baste, keeping your pins or basting stitches away from your outline and stay-stitching. You must leave enough room to turn under the seam allowance on the top layer without having the stay-stitching show.

Use my appliqué stitch to appliqué the top piece to the bottom piece. You have accomplished reverse appliqué! Now that your mind is opened and all the cobwebs have been swept away, you know that the technique is easy. You will, I hope, use it in more and more of your stitchery projects. The only difficulty you may encounter is in turning under: if the seam allowance will not lie flat or will not turn easily, snip into the seam allowance—almost to the stay-stitching—as you would for conventional appliqué. Again, do *not* cut out notches; merely snip.

Try another practice exercise: trace the design in Figure 29 onto a piece of fabric. Mark along the dash lines for cutting; then cut out. Appliqué this top piece of fabric onto another, contrasting piece of fabric (that is large enough to fit into an embroidery hoop so that you can get the tension you need to reverse appliqué properly. Outline the inner shape in Figure 29 on the fabric, mark cutting lines, and cut as before. Then baste the two layers with the cut-out shape onto a third, complementary-colored fabric — again the same size as the first piece. Reverse appliqué following Diagram B of Figure 29. Your finished piece will resemble Diagram C of Figure 29.

Here's another idea: if you have a piece of printed fabric with a lovely flower that you would like to see applied onto something, but think it has too many "ins and outs" to appliqué, try putting it under your top fabric and cutting away as explained above . . . appliqué the reverse way.

If you have a small animal design, try this: use gingham beneath a top fabric in a coordinating color. Draw the animal design on the top fabric, cut it out (leaving ¼-inch seam allowance), snip if necessary, and reverse appliqué. You'll find that it is sometimes easier to turn the top under for a small detail (or ten small details) than to do the conventional "laid-on" method of appliqué.

"But now I have a couple of extra layers of fabric to quilt through! Isn't that going to be too heavy? And the gingham checks will show through the top of the quilt—what a mess!" No! The solution is simple and applies to all situations in which you have applied one layer of fabric to another.

Turn the piece over. Very, *very* carefully, leaving a ¼-inch seam, merely cut away the excess fabric from your bottom layer (Figure 30). The checks won't show, the quilting process will be easier, and, when you press your piece, you will have a fine, professional-looking product. You really may be an amateur—but we won't tell anyone!

It is important to learn this trimming technique correctly. Scissors can destroy what you have built; they can also make it more beautiful, lighter-weight, and easier to quilt. Cut away those extra inches of fabric carefully! (See Figure 30.)

Here is an exercise in using *three* layers of fabric. Some effective colors to use are: purple for the top fabric, orange just beneath the purple, and yellow beneath the orange and purple—three colors total. Whichever colors you choose, be sure they have good contrast. Pin the three layers together to begin with; baste around all edges. Be sure to use pieces of fabric large enough to fit into an embroidery hoop.

For the design, I have used a French curve or architect's template. You can use a template of your own or trace off the shape given in Figure 31. Trace whatever shape you use on the top fabric. If a medium-lead pencil

NOTE: Never press seams open on reverse appliqué. You want to avoid the "shadow effect" on reverse appliqué as well as on "laid-on" appliqué.

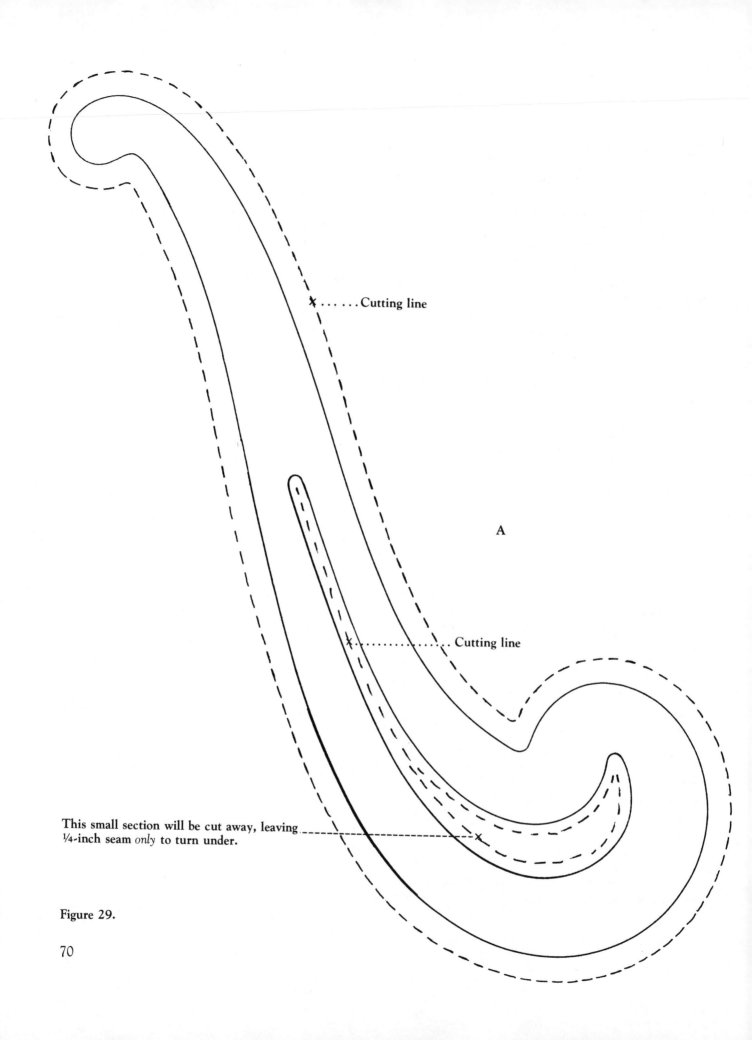

Cutting line

A

Cutting line

This small section will be cut away, leaving
¼-inch seam *only* to turn under.

Figure 29.

70

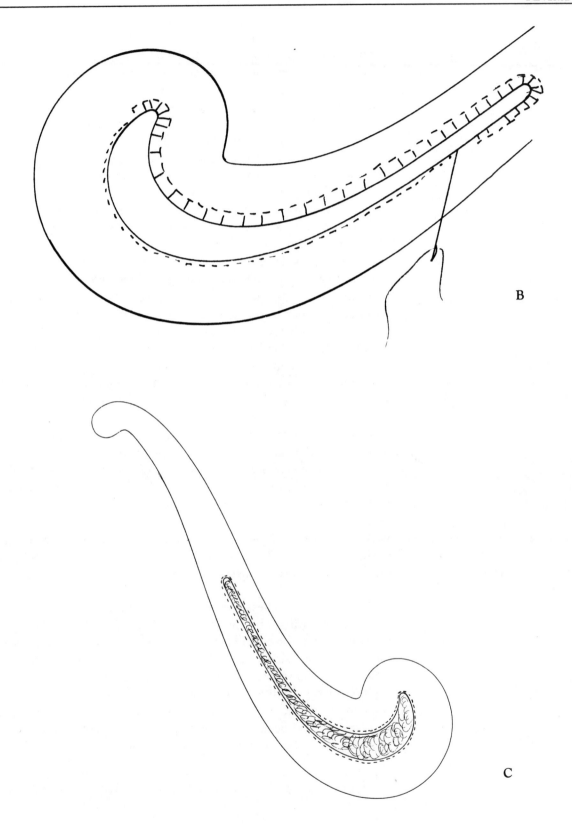

B

C

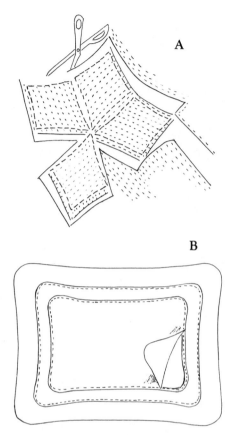

A

B

Figure 30. To avoid "bleeding through" from various prints and colors, cut away excess fabric on reverse side of reverse appliqué. Leave ¼-inch seam allowance. Do *not* press seam open: let it lie flat. Another method of clearing out excess fabric is shown in B. These seams are likewise *not* pressed open.

line does not show, use a white pencil with a fine point. The only outline you need to put on the top fabric is the outside solid line, A in Figure 31. Why? Because after you cut this away and turn under your ¼-inch seam allowance (shown in the drawing), you will then mark the other shapes—four of them on my shape, 1, 2, 3, and 4—on the orange fabric (your second layer). The spaces outlined by these shapes are quite slim and may be difficult for you to turn under; therefore, trim out the excess fabric (allowing a seam allowance, as shown), and snip curves (definitely, for these shapes). Then reverse appliqué these pieces so that yellow shows through. There, you have a sophisticated exercise in reverse appliqué (Figure 32). If you construct your piece carefully, it will be "suitable for framing." Press on a towel, on the *wrong* side. Do not overpress. If you'd like to quilt this piece, trim away excess fabric as described on page 69.

Figure 33 provides a simpler, two-layer version of the above exercise. Try this first if you don't feel quite up to three layers.

If you choose a design for your quilt top or wall hanging that involves a lot of curves, such as the design shown in Figure 34 (Blast Off), reverse appliqué may solve some of your construction problems. For Blast Off, I drew two identical circles on two large squares of fabric, one of sky blue and one of white. Then I drew large cloud shapes on the blue circle and stay-stitched around them. Next, I basted the circles together. The cloud areas could then be cut out and reverse appliquéd to the white circle underneath. When each was cut the open space was, of course, ¼-inch smaller all around than the cloud outline. With a design like this, you will probably want to cut out and reverse appliqué one area at a time to avoid too many loose pieces flapping around. When your reverse appliqué is complete, cut out the two circles, which you are treating as one at this point (be certain to leave ¼ inch seam allowance). Finally, then press. You can appliqué the reverse appliqué piece—in this case, "Earth"—to a background cloth (I used a soft lavender fabric), using conventional appliqué technique. I found I had to baste my circle to its background, much as I hate basting; this huge circle simply demanded extra attention.

Your appliqué stitches, here as always, should be simply the best you can do . . . and you will get better. Mastering all of appliqué is like listening to a symphony—it is the overall picture that will earn you the reward of praise for your special talent. Forget about your crotchety Aunt Hattie, who would criticize anything just for the pleasure of letting the world know that she is (or was) a quilter. Don't listen!

Trying to imitate the San Blas islanders or the Hmong refugees from Laos is a worthwhile goal, as long as you don't set your standards so high that you discourage yourself. Simply tackle what you can handle.

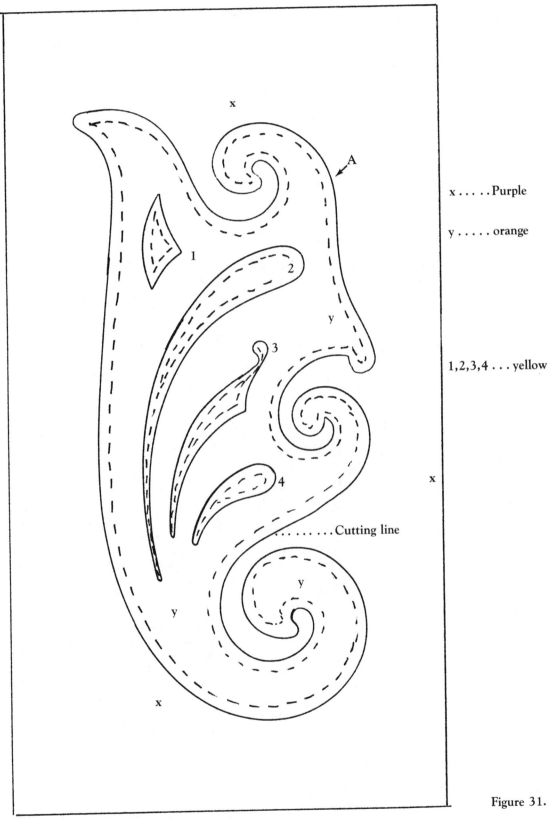

x . . . . . Purple

y . . . . . orange

1,2,3,4 . . . yellow

. . . . Cutting line

Figure 31.

73

Figure 32.

line of appliqué stitches

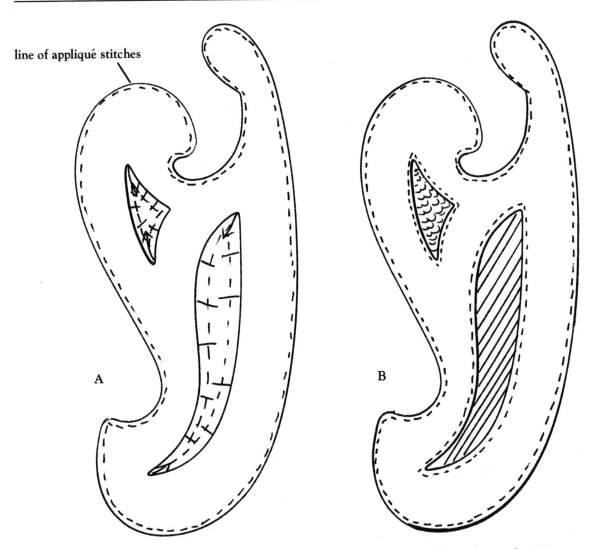

A

B

Figure 33. Follow directions given for Figure 29. Use two separate fabrics here, selecting your own colors.

Figure 34.   Blast Off

CHAPTER 8

ADJUSTING, PRESSING, TRIMMING FOR THE QUILTING FRAME

. . . he heights by great men reached and kept
Were not attained by sudden flight
But they, while their companions slept,
Were toiling upward in the night . . .
—Longfellow
"The Ladder of St. Augustine"

Rome was certainly *not* built in a day, but those who accomplished the gigantic task did not do it in an eight-hour day; they must have "toiled upward in the night." It is the same with quilting, every facet of it. Quilts take time, and patience is important to your success.

Scissors become lethal weapons in the hands of overzealous needleworkers, especially if they want to trim quilt seams *too soon.* According to child psychologists, one common fault of parents is giving a child too much too soon; so it is in stitchery. Using scissors *too much too soon* causes many quilters to abandon projects. Thus quilt tops find their way to dark, dismal attics, to scrap piles, and so forth. If you will remember the TMTS syndrome, many precious hours of work and heartache can be avoided. Your natural inclination is to trim—difficult as it is to fight back, you *must!*

Your quilt top is complete. Perhaps you pressed each block or section as you went along. This is not my style, although in regular garment sewing it is usually done this way. Overpressing may be a needleworker's downfall; those of you who have made garments of wool know that too much pressing can ruin the final product. One of the things looked at by judges at sewing contests is whether a garment is overpressed. If the answer is yes, many points are lost, which can make the difference between winning and not winning. So to return to quilting, the point is the same.

Overpressing is terrible, but underpressing can be just as bad. Those seams must be pressed down, but not until the entire quilt is assembled. There you are with your iron (a steam iron, preferably): you take the fabric

Les Fleurettes Violetta (83″ × 104″). *Colors:* The background squares are white embroidered with violets. The center is white with appliquéd violets (trapunto technique used) laid upon dusty peach, then bordered with a mitre of off-white followed by "Irish" green. After white squares there is another row of off-white, then green edged with off-white. The corners also have trapunto flowers done on a dusty peach background. The entire reverse side is off-white. This was a study in using prestamped pieces in a unique manner instead of the usual "quilt look."

pieces to the ironing board, open the seams and press . . . right? *Wrong.* Many steps are necessary when pressing long seams (or any seam) to avoid puckers on the right side of the fabric.

You have stitched your long seams together *without* using a backstitch at the beginning and end to "lock" them (to prevent separation of seams). When the fabric is out of the machine, run your fingers down the seam toward the open ends to remove any puckers that might have occurred. I often leave both ends open—it depends upon what I am sewing. I lock my stitch when I am sewing *from a dot* if I am sure there is no gapping.

Before any seam is pressed open, it should be pressed *on the wrong side*—on both sides of the seam. This gives any seam a more professional look when you open it out and press it open. *Caution:* there has been no seam trim up to this point. Experiment with this technique. One final step will complete your seam pressing—pressing on top; however, this is not done until *after* you are satisfied that the quilt will lie flat and smooth.

Repeat: Press seams from both angles on the wrong side; then open the seam and press on the wrong side. Turn the piece over and press on the right side *only* after you are certain that the quilt will lie flat. *Then* press the seam on the right side of fabric. All of this is done before any seam is trimmed. What you have put together let no scissor put asunder—until seams are pressed.

Only after the entire quilt top has been assembled and you are satisfied that it lies flat and that is *not* distorted, crooked, short on one end, bulging in the middle, or wider at the top than at the bottom, do you trim your seams.

"But," you protest, "it would be so much easier to trim before I pressed those seams open." This is true—but how are you going to know if the quilt top lies correctly until you have pressed the seams open to have a true picture? It sounds like making extra work, but it is not.

Your glorious ½-inch seam has not been trimmed away. You find that one block does not meld into another; you find four points not meeting; you find a complete distortion of one of the lower corners because your blocks or strips were not perfectly squared in the beginning . . . what do you do? *Adjust the seam.* You can only do this if you have *not* trimmed it away, which was your first inclination. And you thought it would be faster and easier to trim first and then press! Aren't you happy that you followed my suggestion?

Mitre–Miter–Mitring–Mitering

No matter how the word is spelled (and I spell it *mitre*), the definition is "bringing together at an angle without overlapping." To mitre a corner may be the most difficult technique in quilting. That is, until you master

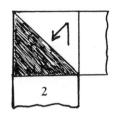

Figure 35.
1. After measuring the 18-inch cardboard square, cut in half, diagonally.
2. Place one half on one side of the portion of fabric to be mitred and fold over fabric;

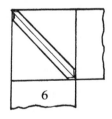 

3. Repeat on the right portion of the piece. Now "wiggle" so lines and seam points match . . . it is bias, be not afraid of it.
4. Both pieces of fabric are now over the cardboard. Press lightly with your iron; remove cardboard.

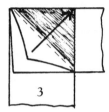 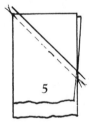

5. Seam carefully, being certain that the cardboard points have matched up with the points (dot) in the center section of the quilt; this step should then be very simple.
6. Press the seam open—*before* you trim, in the event the points do not properly match. If all is well, then trim the seam to ½-inch only. Do not stretch too much as the entire corner will become distorted.

your phobia about it. Luckily, when dealing with mitred corners you are dealing with bias-cut ends. Bias stretches not only to your disadvantage, but also to your advantage. Another factor: there is no way in the world that you can complete a good mitre until your seams are pressed open; that is why the technique has been postponed until this chapter, although measurements and top construction are covered in previous chapters.

Anyone can mitre; it is not only a technique for professionals. Various methods are taught and written about. There are even mitre-measures being sold to quilters (but it takes a Philadelphia lawyer to comprehend the instructions). In reality, the only piece of equipment you need is a square of cardboard.

Of course, you have followed my directions for adding extra fabric to allow for mitring of end and side strips. Measure your border strips from the inner corner of your quilt center panel to the outer edge of all the mitre strips. For example, if the border strips on length and width measure a *total* (finished) of 18 inches across (see Figure 6), you will need a perfect 18-inch cardboard square. Then this square will be cut into two pieces diagonally. (If you have enough cardboard, cut two 18-inch squares, halving one and leaving the other whole. Now you have a perfect mitre template for an 18-inch mitre. How wide your side strips measure will determine the size of your particular mitre pattern. If the strips are 3″ + 5″ + 7″ = 15″ finished measure, you will cut a 15-inch square. Refer to Figure 35 as you read the following instructions.

After pressing open your border strip with seams wrong side up on your ironing board, place the very sharp corners of your triangular cardboard-mitre template (1) at the dot on your center panel so that the long edge (once the diagonal of your square) makes a diagonal line from the dot. One of the short legs of your triangle fits parallel to the outside edge of the border strips and the other short leg crosses the border strips horizontally. Fold the excess fabric on the left side over the cardboard mitre, letting the strip ends hang (2). Repeat on the right side of your corner (3). Now push together the pieces of cardboard to make a square.

Your seams might not match exactly at this first pushing, but this is where bias helps the quilter: simply adjust, push, or pull the fabric so that one seam matches the other (4). Always be certain that the dot in the center piece has the corner of the mitre placed exactly on it.

Do not stretch the fabric or pull it too much around the mitre pattern. That will distort your quilt ends. Let the bias ease help you, and don't be overzealous. You might try this with newspaper over your cardboard pattern to give you some idea of the technique.

After the fabric is folded over the patterns and the edges match, press ever so lightly with your iron, just enough to make an impression on the fabric. Remove the cardboard patterns gently, not distorting what you have just accomplished. The fabrics should be in a perfect mitre. If not, repeat the use of the corner mitre pattern and reshape the fabric.

Knowing now that your corner is square, you might double-check your work by putting the second 18-inch cardboard square over your still unsewn mitre ends to see if the square is perfect. If not, repeat the first process again. If it is perfect, gently open the two flap ends and pin each seam line. Beginning at the inner corner, put a pin through the dot of the center panel and through the two dots on the strips next to the center panel. It is from this point you will begin sewing. Keep pinning, matching dots on each border strip. Then stitch from the center dot to the outer edge of your quilt (5). Be careful when you come to the pins at the strip seams—be sure they match. Remember, that bias works for you; should you need to pull or ease away fabric to match the seam, *do it.*

You may want to baste instead of using the pin method; it might make it easier the first time! Or, if after several tries you cannot make either of these methods work for you, try using the appliqué stitch: barely lap one edge over the other (Figure 36) and work on the right side.

Carefully open up the seam and admire your handiwork. Does the corner lie right? Is it square, matched well at the seams? If not, adjust carefully. If all is well with this mitre, proceed to the other three corners of your quilt. Press the four corners open.

At this point, when you've used a mitred corner design, "flurl" (my term) the entire quilt on the floor and see if there is anything else that needs to be adjusted. It certainly is not uncommon for the mitred corner to pucker in the middle; this does not become apparent until you have the whole top laid out on the floor. A little adjustment will solve the problem. My students use this technique beautifully. Even the beginners have been successful, and so can you! Only now do you trim the mitre seam to ½-inch allowance.

The use of a mitred corner is a beautiful way to complete a work and allows you to avoid that traditional "block in the corner" look if it does not suit your top design. It actually looks like a picture frame for the center work. That is what you have accomplished: making a picture frame for your masterpiece (7).

Satisfaction Guaranteed

After pressing all seams on your quilt carefully, making any adjustments needed to straighten up the top and so forth, and finally after pressing that adjusted seam too and giving the work a final check, *then*, as has been said, you can begin to think about trimming the seams.

There have been times when it has taken me several hours to trim the underside of a quilt top. When I have finished at last, there are threads all over the house! Pieces of fabrics looking like a jumbled rainbow are sitting in my lap, and I have a good feeling about my quilt. How lucky I was to be

Figure 35 (continued)

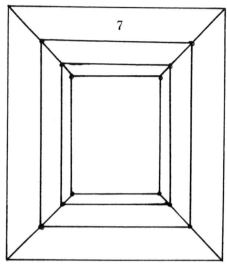

7. This is the outcome of a well-mitred piece. Note the small dots in each of the "picture frame" corners: these are the dots that make it all work so well.

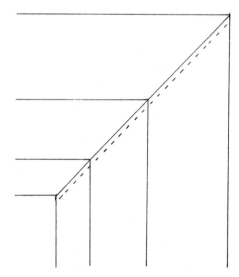

Figure 36. A mitre can be hand-whipped on the right side with my backstitch. Press one side over the other about ⅛-inch and hand-whip down. Tiny stitches are necessary here. Notice how nicely the corners meet.

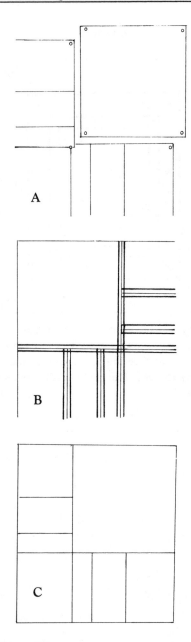

Figure 37.

A. Using the dots on the square to be joined to the top and side of a quilt, match the square for seaming. The quilt corner shows the seam not open so that you can see the dots.

B. Seams have been joined; the reverse side of the quilt is shown.

C. The top side of the quilt is shown; you can see how well the dot system works.

able to wait to trim—because after the ½-inch seam allowance is gone, nothing can bring it back.

Wait to trim. That blessed extra measure is worth its weight in gold. Don't *wish* you had waited to trim: then it is too late to cry over trimmed seams . . . the deed is already done!

Here are a few special tips to help ease a seam or two. Often there is just a little stress at some point on a quilt and a simple, tiny snip of the shears will relieve it. If you are completely certain there is nothing more you can do to ease that "nth" degree of fabric, one last thing can be done: clip the seams just into the stitching, stopping short of the line of machine stitch. However, *never, never* do this until you have explored all other avenues.

After all the seams are clipped, the less you handle the quilt the better. Press one last time now, on the *top* of the quilt, all along those seam lines; then press on the wrong side where your appliqué work is. Give it just a light pressing. At the same time, be certain you have no trailing threads that you forgot to clip. If these are allowed to remain, they might show through to the top of your quilt when you have completed the quilting process, particularly if they are dark in color.

It is entirely possible that you are marvelous at hand appliqué work and yet unable to sew on a machine. Ask for help! Perhaps from a quilting friend, a neighbor, or even your mother-in-law. (It might even salve strained relations to let her know she knows something you don't!) But be certain you have someone who sews well by machine before you entrust your masterpiece to her (or him). Remember, too, that someone else's work on your quilt might take away some of that "made exclusively by me" pride you've rightly developed. Solution? Take a crack at the entire project yourself. Use that sewing machine: you can do it! Your seams may not be just as perfect as you want, but they will all be made by you, no one else. If your seams are crooked as a dog's hind leg, you may find it reasonable to draw ½ inch seams on your fabric and use them as guides as well as the marker on your sewing machine plate I mentioned earlier on.

In the sewing process, dots are not just for sentence endings. You put them there on the ½-inch corners of your quilt (on the wrong side, of course); now remember to use them. They help you avoid a lot of terrible mistakes. Dots make the joining job easier.

If you use a square in the corner of your quilt instead of mitring your corners, you still should follow the dot procedure: it is just as important for the corner-square technique as for mitring. You will want to leave this square out until you have pressed all your seams, as discussed toward the beginning of this chapter. Sometimes the side strips sew in unevenly, especially at the ends of the quilt. You will have to have a true square at your corners. Using a square template will help you to draw a line across those uneven strip-ends in order to seam them off exactly square. Press your seams open (having left a ½-inch seam allowance) and match up the dot on the corner square to the dot on your center panel. (See Figure 37.)

Do not sew from the outer edge *into* the dot; sew *from* the dot to the outer edge. Be certain that you've pinned all seams in place. If you have to trim the seams to square off the side strips, it is advisable to put a couple of backstitches at the end of each border seam; machine stitches have a tendency to ravel otherwise. Repeat this with all remaining corners. Press, as noted earlier in this chapter. "Flurl" the quilt top onto the floor; if adjustment is necessary, do so. Press again after the adjustment has been made. Trim the seam to ½-inch. Look at it again. If all is well, trim at last to ¼-inch. Making perfect corners is a quilting skill of a high order.

However you have handled your corners, one last task remains before your top is complete. After you have pressed and trimmed, find the exact center of each of the four sides of your quilt, and clip in ⅛-inch on the seam allowance of the outermost strip. Later, you will use these markers to line up the three layers of your quilt. (See pages 90– 91.)

Building Your Quilt

Sewing in one direction makes a world of difference in the final product, as does cutting the fabric in one direction. Learning to build a quilt is something I have never seen discussed in print—yes, *building* a quilt. For example, sewing a strip from the top down and then a strip from the bottom up will more than likely result in something that looks like the ragged edge of a carpet. Sew in one direction only, always from the bottom or from the top.

Do not suppose that you build a quilt by sewing all those tiny blocks together with the side-bar strips and then matching the center blocks and their joining bars. It is impossible that everything will fall magically into place—it takes adjusting! I have referred to my method of joining blocks as the mother-father-sister-brother technique. You do not sew all those blocks, strips, and bars together just any which way. The quilt should be built *from the center out.*

If you have designed your appliqué in blocks you should begin with a center block, which I call the "mother." Look, for example, at my sample quilt layout in Figure 38. Sew a side bar (called the "father") to the mother, using the dot-to-dot system, then to the three other side bars. Next sew in the brothers and sisters—the corner squares. Then you join a mother (another appliqué block) to the father bars all around (your work looks like a giant plus [+] sign).
Your next step will be to add a father bar to all of the mothers . . . then add some brothers and sisters. Proceed like this until you have all pieces in place. Please remember, when placing those strips and small blocks, that you must keep them going in the right direction, according to the grain of the fabric. Do not place horizontal (width of fabric) squared pieces incorrectly against the "straight" of the fabric.

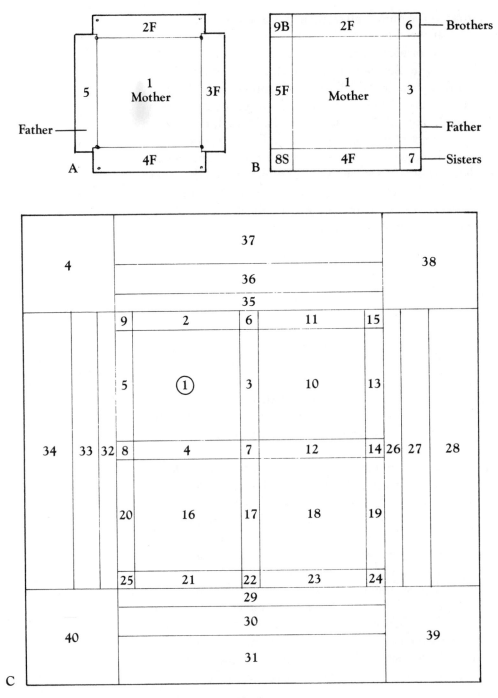

Figure 38. Building a quilt from the "mother" block out.

A. Mother is joined by father four times.

B. Mother and father are now joined by brothers and sisters on all four corners.

C. This diagram might seem like Greek to some, but it is the way to "build a quilt." Each number indicates the order in which strips, blocks, and squares should be sewn to one other. Using the dot system and following this guide, you will have a much finer experience quilting! Try it—I know you will agree!

Repeat: You do not simply sew strips of squares, bars, and blocks together to construct your quilt: you build it from the center out. If you use this method the corners will match, because you've used the match-the-dot technique. You will have to rip less frequently (if at all) to make the pieces match, and the quilt will lie better when completed. Do not be afraid to draw that ½-inch seam line on the wrong side of your fabric as you work with blocks and bars; if you like, sketch an arrow lightly to indicate which blocks and bars should be going in which direction—up or down, whichever the case may be. See Figure 39.

You may have joined quilt blocks before, but remember: there is a chance that you will develop a better technique from having read these ideas. It is possible to join a couple of blocks and strips together without doing one at a time; however, until you have tried this one-at-a-time system—don't do it. This all might seem like a lot of "Mickey-Mousing," but after having gone the other route of sewing it all up at once, I found that this technique was much more sure and accurate and saved time over the long run.

Don't expect perfection the first time, but if you follow the dot your overall job will be easier. Remember, no one was born knowing how to quilt—or sew, for that matter . . . Adam and Eve used leaves! It all takes time, but you are learning; be proud of your accomplishments so far.

Building quilts, adjusting, trimming, pressing are all necessary steps to getting your quilt to the quilting frame in good order, be it a floor frame or a hoop. Necessary, that is, if you want your quilt to look professional, to be the best that you can do. Pressing will become a joy after you have sewn your seams using the dot method. You will not be shocked when you finally "flurl" your quilt top on the floor for that final analysis. You will find it is *not* distorted; it will be just fine. You have come a long way toward enjoying the elegance of appliqué quilting—even patchwork—or whatever medium you choose. My dot system applies to patchwork perhaps even *more* than appliqué quilting, since much more matching of blocks and points is usually required in patchwork. If someone asks you what type of quilt sewing you like best, you might say appliqué; yet all quilting requires "patchwork"—piecing—to join the entire work together. All of the information I have shared with you in this chapter has been garnered from years of experience. Working with very expensive fabrics (some as much as $200 per yard) has taught me—by necessity—valuable lessons in thinking ahead, planning ahead. If something wasn't going just right, I learned to back away and leave it alone for a while and come back to it again later. Patience! Learning new quilting techniques from the Amish has only complemented my past experience. You can reap the benefit of my experience from this book. "Dotting" might take longer . . . but "the heights" really do require some "toiling upward in the night." The results will justify your efforts!

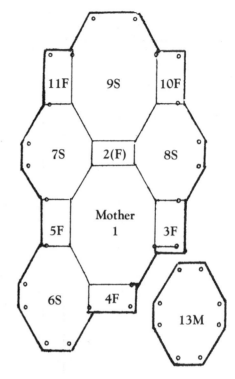

M = Mother
F = Father
S = Sisters and Brothers

Figure 39. Dot joining and building from the middle will simplify your piecing task. Follow the numbers in this patchwork exercise, remembering Mother, Father, Sister, and Brother.

Hawaiian Appliqué (74″ × 84″). Possible colors for this work include gray/aqua, teal blue, and dark aqua, with dark aqua border and teal blue tassels. This quilt resembles one designed by my student Dale Carstens of Beverly Shores, Indiana.

CHAPTER 9

QUILTING AT ITS BEST

o everything there is a season, and a time to
every purpose under heaven.
. . . A time to rend, and a time to sew;
A time to keep silence, and a time to speak.
A time to love, and a time to hate;
A time of war, and a time of peace.

Ecclesiastes 3: 1-8

Your sparkling eyes are set on your lovely quilt top, which you have
prepared with tender, loving hands. The thousands of machine and hand
stitches that you carefully sewed during its creation are now waiting,
finally to become part of a completed quilt.

A quilt, as you know, is three layers joined together with small stitches:
the top, the batt, the bottom. In order to join those three layers, you can
choose between knotting your quilt (which we will get to at the end of the
chapter) and actually "quilting" it. If you choose to quilt your quilt, you
will want to mark your quilting lines before you put the quilt in a frame or
hoop: this is the last step in preparing your top.

Quilting Lines

Without a pattern to show them every step of the way in quilting, many
people become lost. When it comes to deciding what to use as a quilting-
line pattern, ideas evade novices because they think choosing a pattern is
so complicated. It is not. The quilting-line pattern is determined by the
top design of the quilt itself. If it fits your design, plain, pure, unadulter-
ated quilting stitches in a straight line—without benefit of any other

embellishment—is what I recommend. This pattern is all that quilting really is . . . pure joy, if you let it be.

Plan ahead. In designing your quilt in the first place, you should plan on what kind of quilting lines you are going to have. For the beginner, straight lines are the best; radiating lines from the center subject matter are great! To obtain these, measure from corner to corner. Draw a line up to the subject, then across the middle (but not on the subject), then at various evenly spaced angles in between. You might also consider quilting in some motif drawn from the top design that you can trace off from the original and use for a quilting pattern. For example, if the main subject is a flower, trace it off, adapt it to a template (pattern), and use it around the edge of your quilt, being certain to cut slits in the center of the template so you can draw the main inner lines on your quilt for stitching.

Traditional feather designs are gorgeous, but for a beginner they are rough sledding. They are also easily distorted if you mark your design as you go. Feather designs can wind up looking like they came off the broken wing of an eagle.

One item in the quilting world that there is a huge lack of . . . quilting designs that suit the subject of the quilt. Certainly, templates can be purchased from $3 up (and up and up), but to me that route is a pain in the ankle. Often the templates have too many lines included to wear well, not to mention the expense. You can make your own quilting design lines match *your* quilt top by using *your* imagination and perhaps a section of this or that from your quilt top design. For instance, choose a daisy from your pattern and increase its size. Simple butterflies suit many floral designs; butterflies are flying all over my quilts (at least three on each of the flower quilts). Cut whatever design you choose out of cardboard. If there is a design within the design, or some lines you'd like to use for your quilting in the original motif, take a razor blade and trim thin line strips out of your cardboard piece. You can make a nice pattern for your quilt—for free.

Another possibility is to trace a pattern out of coloring books, magazines, wallpaper, newspaper pictures, and so forth. When everything else fails and the thought of using an original design boggles your mind, there are always straight lines, circles (from tea cups), curves (from plates), triangles, and every other conceivable shape.

Make your job easier—have the quilt top all marked with the pencilled-in design *before* you put it on the frame. Very often I have quilting-line markings done before I set squares together . . . if I know that what I am doing will correlate with the overall design.

It is entirely up to you whether or not to draw your design as you go. Many Amish quilters find this method the best, although it actually does not allow for a balance at the top of the quilt . . . but that's the part that gets hidden under the pillow, isn't it? I prefer to know where I am going, so I draw all my designs on before I "flurl" the top onto the floor getting ready for the frame arms. If you wish, you may draw your quilting lines onto your background fabric before you proceed with appliqué.

What to Use to Mark a Design

Use a medium, *almost*-sharp pencil. Too sharp a lead might damage your quilt top. And never, never, never use chemical markers (as mentioned previously). If your fabric is very dark, use a white pencil. These marks will disappear into the quilted valleys and crevices and you will never see them. Don't mark them too hard, just hard enough to see. (Cocoa was once used to mark quilts, but it never stayed. It was used for the mark-as-you-go method, as were flour, cornstarch, talcum powder, or anything handy to make a marking around and through the perforated template.)

Some quilts require no markings at all. Hawaiian quilts, for example, have the benefit of the "echo" design—freehand quilting, like water radiating when a pebble has disturbed its surface. The original outline is stitched over and over again, radiating out from the master design.

Should you have one irregular focal point, perhaps a clown with balloons, consider using the radiating lines. About one inch out—and out and out. Be careful, however, not to *fight* the lines already included in the focal motif (say, balloon strings). Choose where to begin your radiating lines carefully.

Before you draw any lines, lay dark-colored thread (or any color that contrasts with your top) along the radiating lines you are envisioning. It is much easier to move the threads than attempt to erase pencil lines.

Planning ahead and sketching on paper saves time, and, more often than not, your overall design will benefit. Most important, when in doubt what you are doing—*leave it alone*. Let it be. Go back and look at it in a few hours; perhaps an entire new perspective will come. The problem might solve itself. Do not become overly tense; this is not a case of life or death, it is just a quilt. You—not the quilt, not anyone else—are the boss.

A final tip on marking a quilt and seeking patterns. Accordion-folding newspaper—the kind you use to make paperdolls—is a great way to get oblique angles. Measure the width you need, fold the paper, and cut it. This can be done for many original border patterns. Another idea: cut an original design or a design from any source out in cardboard to make a template. Libraries have a selection of line drawings; even dictionaries have illustrations—look at these for ideas. Designs for marking quilting lines are everywhere . . . seek and ye shall find!

Your Quilt Back

Quilt backings are often neglected until the last minute. But you, in your wisdom, planned ahead when you first purchased the fabrics for your top, and you now have sufficient fabric to prepare a beautiful complement

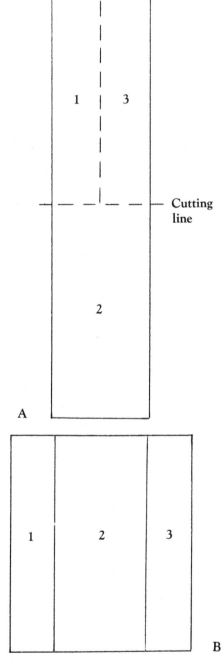

Cutting line

A

B

Figure 40. Making the back of a quilt is simple. A. This indicates the full 6½ yards of fabric, cut in half. B. This indicates 1 and 3 joined to either side of the remaining 2. Stitch, trim the seam, and press. This is the only time you are allowed to trim so soon!

to your quilt top. You will use a coordinating color and the same *kind* of fabric as you have used on the top.

You carefully "guess-timated" how much fabric you would need by planning your entire quilt on paper—first. And you carefully purchased *all* that was needed. To review very briefly, suppose that the quilt is 80″ × 100″. You added 10 inches extra *twice* for the backing length when you bought your fabric, for a total of 220″ of fabric for the back (or approximately 6 yards plus). As advised earlier, extra yardage doesn't cost *that* much more. Better to have extra than *wish* you had it. Thus you've allowed 6½ yards for the back in this instance.

Next, cut the 6½ yards for the back in half, *widthwise*, then one of the two halves in half again, *lengthwise*. See Figure 40. One half of this second cutting is joined to the right side of the large 3¼-yard length; the other half is joined to the left side of this whole length of fabric. When I am piecing the backing it is the *only* time in the entire quilting process when I leave the selvage on the fabric. In case you are wondering, "Why not just sew up that backing in half instead of slitting a section?", answer: there is more stress placed on the center of a quilt, and the seam could conceivably pop years later. Besides, I think it looks more professional!

Sew the seams, leaving a ½-inch allowance. Then trim the selvage off, leaving a ¼-inch seam. Finger-run the seam before pressing to squeeze out any puckers that might have occurred in machine sewing. Press the seam on both sides, then open the seam and press it open. Turn the entire back over and press on the *right* side. "That's a lot of extra work, Charlotte," you say! Nevertheless, it makes for a better end product. I do this with every seam I sew . . . . it's professional.

Snip ⅛ inch at end center top and bottom of back—this is very important—you'll match this with the center of your top very soon.

Some quilters think that you need not open your seams at all for quilting but should merely press them to one side. It is a matter of personal choice. I open my seams in case my quilting stitches from the top later happen to hit one of the double-folded seams on the back. The thickness makes quilting too difficult. Needles don't like to go through too many layers (I asked them!).

The Back Is Ready

I assume that you have (or have improvised) floor space large enough to accommodate your quilt opened out all the way to prepare it for the frame. If you don't, I suggest that you ask a friend or neighbor if you can "borrow" some floor space for a little while. There is *no way* to manage a quilt 80″ × 100″ (or, after the backing has been added, 88″ × 110″) on top of a table, unless you are acquainted with giants who require quite a large one! Your surface must be flat, flat, flat.

I have coined the term *flurl* to express how I throw a quilt onto the floor. My procedure is similar to throwing a sheet on top of a bed. So, flurl your quilt back onto the floor and straighten up the fabric. This can be done by wrapping an end over a yardstick and gently pulling. Repeat this until you get to the end that you are going to call the bottom of the quilt. You will put the fabric "on grain" in this manner and get an even bottom straight across. If you have two yardsticks and a helper so that you can pull both ends at the same time, just a little pull will do the trick for placement of the sleeve—your next task.

The "sleeve" is nothing more than an old sheet casing large enough for the pole of your quilting frame. You will need one sleeve for each end of your frame if you use a floor frame. I am not partial to tacked-on strips; if the wrong pins, tacks, or staples are used, they could rust your work if you take too long to remove your masterpiece from the frame. I make my sleeves as long as the frame poles and about 15 inches wide. Allow a bit more if your floor frame has bulky poles. Some people tape or tack strips onto quilting frames instead of using a sleeve, but this takes too much time as far as I am concerned, and it takes great patience either to baste or to pin the quilt on. I recommend that you either machine-stitch the sleeves to your backing and then flurl it on the floor, or hand-baste the sleeves on while the quilt is on the floor.

Remember that ⅛ inch snip on top, bottoms, and sides I suggested as a center marker? This is where it comes into play. Sleeves and quilt back are joined. You are now going to flurl on your batting, which has had a chance to rest for about a week (remember?). If the batt is just a little too small, give a tug here and there to stretch it out—within reason, of course. If the batting is too large, *tear* off the extra width or length, but *never* as far as the exact edge of the quilt top. (Be *very* sure before you tear. Remember that batts are larger than quilt tops; if you can possibly work with the extra batt, remove the excess later, after you've quilted.) If the batt is way too small lengthwise and you have some extra on the width, then tear some of the extra off and add it to the length. Chances are the length has a blunt end as packaged by the manufacturer. You must tear away this blunt edge before you add any batt. Just a little waste here, but the waste is necessary so that you can *lap* whatever you are adding onto the main batt. This way you have no gap in your quilt where the sharp-cut ends refuse to butt together (Figure 41). Tearing and lapping will keep them together.

Your center marker will help you place the batting and the top, which has also been snipped at the edge to mark the center (no more than ⅛-inch). Placing the batt almost to the bottom end of the back, now flurl your quilt top on top of the two layers, bringing the bottom of the quilt even with the batting. Be careful now. Here comes an Amish saying: "Always begin at the foot of the bed . . . . just in case you make a mis-

Figure 41. Torn batting; once piece is lapped on top of another so that the joining is not visible and it is even in thickness with the rest of the batt.
Yes!

Cut batting, separate although lined up.
No!

**Top end
(Head)**

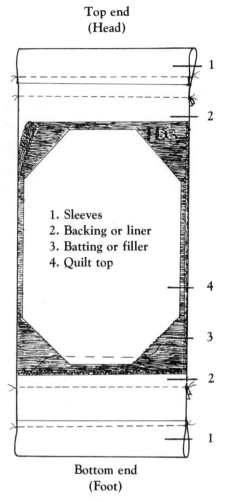

1. Sleeves
2. Backing or liner
3. Batting or filler
4. Quilt top

**Bottom end
(Foot)**

Figure 42. This is what the quilt top will look like before quilting arms are placed in either end. The quilt top shown is an odd shape so that you can see what to do in case you have something other than the typical oblong quilt.

take . . . you can hide it under the pillow." That is why I have you working from the bottom up.

You've placed the bottom of the quilt top at the bottom of the batt and the back; now hand-baste batting and top across on the backing, using quilting thread and long stitches. Be certain that your elegant quilt top's bottom center notch matches that notch on the bottom back. This way the seams on the backing will come out fairly close to the edge on either side when the quilting is complete.

And that is all there is to it (see Figure 42). "But how about all that pinning I was told to do?" "You mean to tell me that is all, no more basting or pinning?" Yes. Of course, this technique is for a floor stand . . . .and I'll tell you about rolling on the poles later in this chapter. However, preparing the quilt for the hoop technique *is* more work.

Even in the world of Amish quilters there are various techniques of putting a quilt on a frame, and most Amish quilters use the floor models. Some, however, use the hoop standing on the floor. I tell my students to go for the oval floor model if they must use a hoop. The hoop technique works well enough, but the backing must be prepared with extra fabric all around to allow "crawling." The quilting process "draws up" fabric; therefore, depending upon your own personal stitch-pull, your technique of framing, and many other things, it is better to have a little extra than to *wish* you did.

Lay all of the materials on the floor as directed earlier in the chapter; allow more at the bottom. Begin to pin, as indicated in Figure 44. After pinning, baste with quilting thread, using long stitches. When this basting is complete, you are ready to hoop-quilt. Many people become discouraged with this technique. (Also, they may have been told that this is the method to use for a floor frame, which is a waste of time.) Sorry, you hoop-quilters, there is no easier way for you if you want to achieve good results.

The extra fabric that you added at the top of your backing will be a lot shorter when your quilt is complete: it crawls! But, if you want to, you can turn it under and bind it as part of the quilt; then you will have a built-in "sleeve" by which to hang your masterpiece in a quilt show. If you don't want it, cut it off! However, read Chapter 11 before you do anything hasty.

Rolling the Quilt on Your Floor Frame

Now that the quilt is ready to be rolled on the floor frame, call in some friends or relations to admire your work—and help! It is much easier if there are two persons working on the project, one at either end of the frame-pole; if the quilt is huge, three persons helping makes it even easier.

Do not be afraid of having wrinkles in the rolling process. Wrinkles come out, especially with the polyester/cotton blend fabrics. If, by chance, you are quilting on velvet, simply do not roll the quilt on quite as tightly.

Begin rolling at the *top end of the quilt* toward the bottom end, where you will begin quilting. (See Figure 43.) This is where I depart from most teachers, because by having your quilt top *on the top roll* it stays looser. The rolling of quilts on the frame poles determines who is in control . . . *you* or *the quilt*! Your extra backing inches give leeway for the "crawling" action of the quilt; do not worry about that. How many of you have cut the backing exactly the same size as the top and found when you go to the end that you were short? This is another reason to begin at the foot and hide the mistake under the pillow.

Rolling the quilt under and over? Over and under? I choose under and over. If you roll both "scrolls" under, there is no room for you to control what happens to the back of the quilt. At the very least, it is more work to control it. The under (in front of you) and over (toward you) method lets you be the master of the quilt's destiny. The top, crawling with the tide of your stitches, can be guided more efficiently.

It will certainly take two people to put the quilt roll into your frame. Hold the handles at the end of the pole until you have the ratchet (the small bar on your quilting frame) securely set near the screw (or cog) on the quilt frame itself. Unlike hoop quilting, with frame-quilting there is nothing to hold the layers of fabric taut on the sides. You need to do this because it allows your needle to work more deftly. Careful, though: *too tight is no good* (remember my lecture about "bounceable" fabric). Therefore, place the sheet strips on either side of the quilt backing and around the frame itself with pins to give some tautness (tightness) to your quilt. During the quilting process, you will find that you are releasing the "side straps," which are strips made out of another old piece of sheet wrapped around the frame itself and pinned at the loose ends on to your quilt top and backing close to where you work. Usually 4 to 6 inches apart is about the spacing needed. Attach 5-inch wide side straps to the quilt on both of the long sides. Now your quilt is attached to the frame at head and foot (bottom) by sleeves and on the sides by strips. Then, at long last, you are ready to sit down to quilt. On an average, full-size quilt about 77″ × 99″, you should be able to go across one full width in about 3–4 hours' time—if you use a leather thimble. There *are* people using metal thimbles who can be quicker-quilters, but I'm not one of them.

Using an embroidery hoop in quilting is different. The clue is *not to have the fabric too taut in the hoop*. Keeping your piece too taut will produce a good case of basted layers of fabric—not quilting. Remember, you need a good pull on the thread to create those shadows of love. I recommend that you use the screw-adjusted hoops in all work requiring a hoop. The fabric must be floppy in the center; quilting will go faster, and it will be *quilting*,

Figure 43. The quilt is being rolled on frame arms after the top, batt, and back have been put into place.

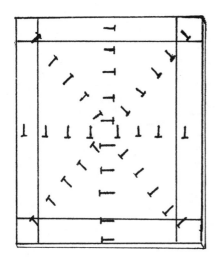

Figure 44.

A. Pin-baste.

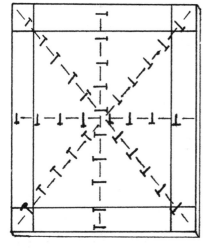

B. Thread-baste, remove pins.

not basting. Also, you need room to wiggle your quilting needle, and you cannot do this on taut fabric.

In fact, if you use your quilting hoop upside down, with the deep channel on top, it seems to give more leverage on the bottom side where your finger and needle meet all the time. It may strike you as odd, but try it.

I recommend a floor-standing long frame above all, if you have room in your home. Otherwise, I suggest you again use a quilting hoop oval with a stand—there is really no place to lean on the large circle hoop for leverage. The larger the quilt, the more difficult you will find using the circle. If you cannot accommodate the large floor-model frame, there is an easy method to follow in attacking the quilt with a hoop. Quilt the center first, then up, down, side to side, and corner to corner of each of the five areas numbered in Figure 44. Another advantage of having that extra fabric on all sides is that it gives your hoop something to grasp when you near the edge. Remember the beginning of the book and my thoughts on having a good road map? Quilting is so much fun, but so much knowledge is assumed by old-timers. No more: now it's in writing . . . here!

Quilting goes back centuries and centuries, and various phrases have been attached to the simple sewing procedure. One in particular pleases my eye and ear: "runnings," which describes the kind of stitching required to quilt. Also, I always invite many students, friends, and would-be quilters to "throw a stitch" on my "anyone-can-quilt" specimen.

Quilting . . . "Throwing a Stitch"

To each beginning there is an ending, I have told my students: you should remember this about anything you decide to make. The ending can be happy—a beautiful quilt of your own—or unhappy—with your unfinished work stuffed away in a drawer. Don't lose heart at the quilting stage. Quilting takes time, but it is not difficult.

The first time I used the expression "throw a stitch" was at a demonstration at Woodlawn Plantation in Mount Vernon, Virginia, a place I associate with fine needlework (among many other things). I put a quilting frame up and invited anyone wishing to "throw a stitch" to do so. Quilting is easy. It does not bite! Anyone can do it and do it easily. Do not be afraid to let someone put in a few stitches when you know they are "itching to try." (If you don't like the stitches afterward, you can always remove them.) It is the fun of trying and sharing that makes quilting such an adventure in friendship. It has been said somewhere that quilters never quilt alone if they can help it, and sharing of knowledge is what this book is all about.

The beginning of a length of quilting stitches and the ending-off when the thread runs *almost* out are the two important moments of quilting. Of course, the "runnings" in the middle are what create the beauty. But if you don't have your initial stitch locked in and the end stitch locked up, you possibly have nothing—except perhaps basting, but for certain no quilting! Believe it or not, a single knot begins a quilt! (See Figure 45.) Do not tie it too tightly. The normal spit knot is unacceptable in quilting, but all right for anything else in the appliqué world. For beginning your quilting, you require a simple, single hand-tied knot, with the "tail" cut off to about ¼-inch. Pull this through the *top fabric only* until you hear the little "pop," then stitch back and forth two or three times on the top fabric *only* to secure the knot. Now, you are ready to run that needle through the three layers—and you are quilting! *You're* secure in the knowledge that the *knot* is secure; this will help you face your task.

Here is a way to begin with a small stitch and continue "runnings" of the same gauge, an Amish technique. Stab your needle straight down through the fabric, barely hit your finger beneath, and immediately "wiggle" it "back to earth," my hill and vale method. Placing the needle at an angle will cause your stitch to be longer. If you place it straight down, it can only come up sooner and closer to the stitch previously set. What goes down must come up. You decide the angle. I know straight is best.

Do not try to take too many stitches on the needle at once. With the No. 7 crewel embroidery needle that I use, I can sometimes fit five stitches. But if you are a beginner, three is fine. You need not get twenty stitches to the inch! Six to eight stitches per inch are plenty. Loose, pliable, limp fabric-sandwiches make the "wiggle" technique possible. (There is no other way to describe the tension for your quilt.) Remember, I do not hold my needle when the wiggle is going on, I merely have it pivoted on my leather thimble (see Figure 46, frame 4).

Speed is not essential in quilting unless you are under a deadline. The Clematis quilt in this book (see front cover) required almost 500 yards of quilting thread. "How long did it take you?" you want to know. . . . "I don't believe it!" It took 100 hours, evenings only, and I had it off the frame in six weeks. The quilt Heather Rose took me eight evenings only. Truly! If you will try the quilting technique I propound, you, too, can be a quicker-quilter. Again, refer to Figure 46.

> Straight down, back up—barely hitting your top finger— and straight down again. Repeat a few times. Then, when there are several stitches on the needle, with your thimble squeeze the stitches back on the needle toward the eye. Grab the needle and pull.

Should you not have a leather thimble, life is easier using a burst or uninflated balloon, an old piece of mason jar ring, or a rubber piece of some kind to help pull that needle through. A tip from the pioneers: running

Figure 44 (continued)

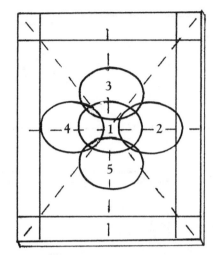

C. These are the numbered steps in quilting with an oval hoop model frame, as well as a round hoop.

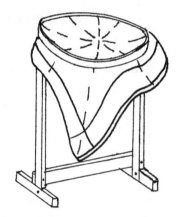

D. Here is an oval quilting hoop on a floor stand.

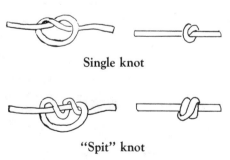

Single knot

"Spit" knot

Figure 45.

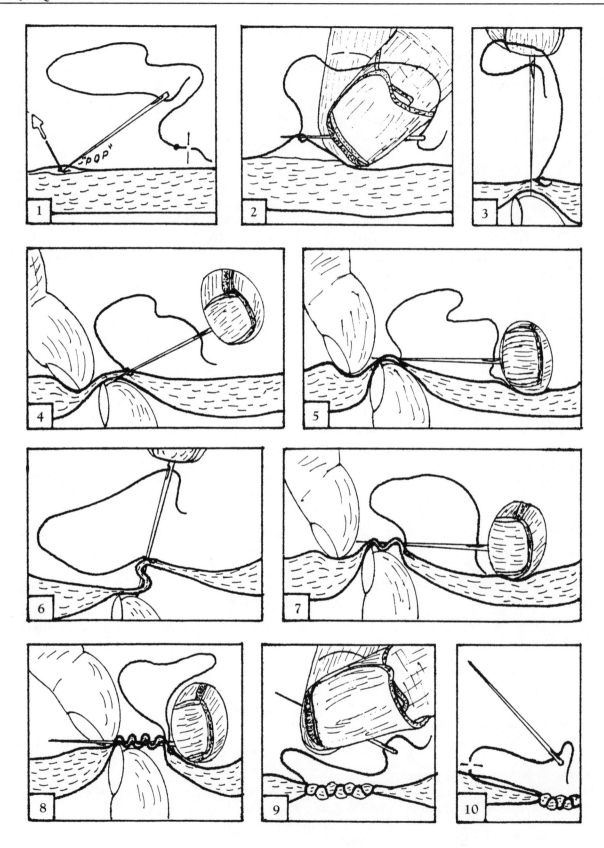

Figure 46. This figure shows how to execute quilting stitches using a leather thimble.

1. Cut excess thread off behind hand-tied quilting knot. Insert the needle under the top layer of the fabric and pull *only* until you hear the little knot "pop." The knot is now buried underneath the top layer, perhaps in the batting.

2. After the tiny knot is buried, a small Amish backstitch is done near the point of thread entry to secure the knot in position so that it will not pull out with normal wear. The less thread showing from the backstitch on the quilt top, the better.

3. The first quilting stitch, the beginning of your new adventure: insert the needle *straight down* until you feel the tip of your needle hit your finger underneath.

4. With your under-finger pushing up and top finger pushing down, you create a "hill" and "valley" in the quilt, through which you push your needle with the thimble until your finger underneath senses the needle touch ever so lightly. Then direct the needle up through the fabric until it barely touches the upper finger.

    Here is the secret of small stitches. The less of the needle you have coming through each time, the smaller your stitch. If you push your needle straight down in the first place, your first stitch is automatically smaller. If you quilt on a slant, your first stitch *has* to be longer, and you are trapped into using larger stitches to keep your stitches even in length.

5. Once the thimble is used to push the needle through to the top *just barely*, you can pivot the needle down to make the next stitch. Using a leather thimble to push gives quick aim and sureness of grip.

6. There is a rocking action—in and out, in and out—just as there is when you do a quick basting stitch. It is imperative that your hoop or frame not be too taut—if it is, you cannot rock your needle, and without that certain wiggle, you do not have any hill-and-vale quilting technique.

7. Repeat steps 5 and 6: you are now putting on or gathering more stitches on your needle. You can put between 5 and 7 of them on a No. 7 or No. 8 crewel embroidery needle.

    All of this is being shown with a fatt batt for a quilt with high loft. With a small quilting needle and a "skinny" batting, I have seen my Amish friends put on 3 or 4 stitches; but with a quilting needle and the fatt batt, putting on even two stitches is difficult.

8. Give your stitches on the needle a "squeeze," allowing you enough of the needle to grasp with your fingers and pull all the way through the quilt. Now pull! Don't forget to keep pushing with the thimble wherever possible—it saves time and fingers.

9. Gripping the needle and pulling it through all the layers is easy.

10. By this time, you have pulled your stitches up to take up the slack thread and make shadows. End off with a backstitch to secure these shadows—that is, the stitches you've pulled up to make them—just as you did at the start, almost in the same place as your last quilting stitch. Make the backstitch as small as possible, as before. Then run your needle just beneath the top layer as far away as you can. Draw your needle out and clip the thread end off, leaving about an inch tail beneath the top fabric.

    Some Amish quilters tie a single knot at the taut part of the thread and let it seek its own place under the top layer because of the tension of the thread.

    Step 9 shows one version of what a cross-section of quilting might look like. You'll want to do about two needles-full of stitches before you give the thread a pull.

Those of you who are left-handed might put these diagrams in front of a mirror for your version!

your needle through your hair will ease the sticky feel . . . and the needle will plunge in and out of the fabric with more ease. If you have an old lamb in the backyard(!), pluck a bit of this wool and enclose it in a small cloth pouch to make a pin cushion: the lanolin makes for easy sewing. (Wool with the natural oils left in *is* sold commercially for knitters of fisherman-knit sweaters, etc., and will serve the same purpose.)

After experimenting with the technique I have suggested here, I hope you'll agree that quilting is fun. Who said you couldn't quilt? Remember, too, to pull your thread, not only to make shadows but to take up the gap of thread which lies between the layers. Without that pull and tightness, you have no quilting, just basting—and there *is* a difference. Vive la différence!

I cannot stress too strongly that you should use a thimble. Amish ladies say, "Take the thimble along, you'll find a use for it." I am one who never used a thimble until the world of quilting opened to me. Now I simply cannot get along without my leather thimble for quilting: However, I still appliqué and sew without a thimble.

Following the quilting lines you placed on the quilt top before you assembled your work on the frame is easy. Run along the lines of design; right up next to the appliqué; "in the ditch"—that is, right on top of the stitches of piecing and appliqué seams. Consider going through the appliqué (where it is necessary to delineate or accent something), and where natural lines of your design live.

Very important: do not forget to pull your quilting stitches. Someday, that gapping thread might become entangled with a ring on someone's finger and be pulled out of your masterpiece. Pull and bury your stitches.

Locking Down the End Stitch

At the end of any particular thread's quilting trail, you must end it all! Stop when the thread becomes too short to proceed or when you have finished a "statement of line." Take a final pull on the thread and, as you did for your beginning "lock," stitch two or three times in the same spot on the top layer *only*. Do not cut the thread yet. Now, take your needle and run it under the top layer only as far as you can. Push up the shank of the needle to the top again and cut off the thread. This way you have an "insurance policy" length if the knottings get loose in the wash, or if someone sits on the quilt. They will, you know. *You* will! You have been wise enough to have a safeguard built in—that extra inch or so of thread floating under the top layer. Practice this technique to perfection. It will save time for you and save the quilt for posterity.

You will notice in some quilt shows (and elsewhere) that old-timers sometimes had their knots "all hanging out." You can, too, if you want to.

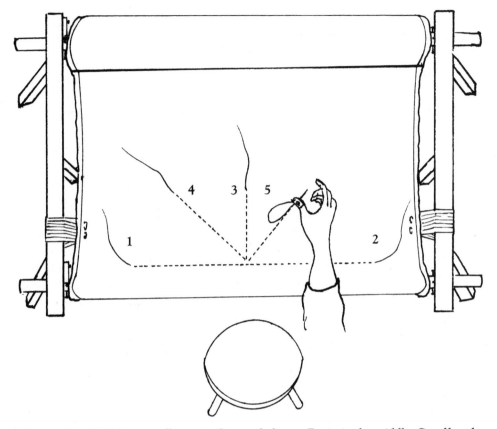

Figure 47. Quilting on a floor-standing quilt frame. Begin in the middle. Go off to the left (1), thence to the right (2), thence up the middle (3). Next, proceed to the left again (4) and then to the right again (5). The idea is to anchor the quilt firmly in the frame at steps 1 and 2. Then, quilt directly up the middle if there is a middle line in your quilting design.

Stitch as far to the right and left, up and down, as your arm will allow before you move your chair and stool. I use a footstool under the quilt frame for my feet—this makes it easier on my back. Quilt away from you, leaving the "tails" to fly once they have been given a slip-stitch to secure the quilting stitches you've already done. That slip-stitch can come out when you have rolled your quilt in the frame and begun your next round of quilting.

That is your decision. However, it only takes a little longer to work this technique and you'll have no unsightly or rough-feeling knots on your quilt surfaces.

I do *not* recommend the method of stringing a 3- or 4-inch tail and just beginning to "quilt." No way. My time and your time is far too valuable for this nonsense—there is no way to "get a pull," which is what makes quilting quilting!

The single-knot method is best, securely anchored. With your patience, you have mastered the technique . . . and you have quilting at its best.

East-West-North-South: Which Direction Is Correct?

I quilt away from myself. Some people quilt toward the body. Toward or away is up to the quilter. I can see no particular advantages to quilting toward myself, but I *can* see some for quilting away. For example, I can leave tails hanging ahead of me when my arm can no longer reach under the frame. I then usually put in a simple, large basting stitch to secure the tension already established, take the thread off my needle, and work somewhere else. Then, when I have finished along the entire section of the frame I am working on, I turn the roller, pick up the thread, remove the basting stitch, rethread my needle, and proceed. This way, my threads are not ending off unattractively all in the same place.

I've already explained the order in which you can proceed using an oval hoop. For frame quilting, begin in the middle. Work sitting at the foot of the quilt. Stitch off to the right, then off to the left (Figure 47). Move your chair and stitch all the way to the right edge; move your chair and stitch all the way to the left edge. Your quilt is securely anchored. Move your chair back to the center and, if there is a line going up the center of your quilt, work on that. Then move a little off to the right following a line, then a little off to the left following a line. Move your chair to the right and work; to the left and work, and so forth. (Or, perhaps I should say "sew forth.") Remember, do not cut your threads unless you have completed a "statement."

My thread is usually no longer than about 20 inches. Of course, if you have one stretch of quilting that is 25 inches and you don't want to have to end off in the middle, allow the 25 inches if you must. There is no harm done, but remember that thread gets worn out and ravels if you try to use it too much—that is, if you subject it to the stress of being pulled through fabric for too long. You have also the tangle factor to consider. Use your judgment.

When the first portion of your quilt is done, remove the side strips, which helped maintain your quilt tension. In the process of quilting you can repin these to adjust tension, and they must be removed when you are getting ready to roll your quilt on the frame to move on to the next section. Before beginning again, repin, adjust the strips: if you don't, your quilt will be too loose. Then set out on a new adventure. I use straight pins as I am working to pull the top fabric taut ahead of me. Control the quilt; do not let it control you.

Quilting in a Hoop

Letting the threads hang loose with a basting stitch will work with hoop quilting as well as for frame quilting, but working away from yourself or toward yourself makes no difference. Some of those original contrasting basting stitches that you put in while the work was on the floor—before it went into hoop or frame—may become a nuisance. Remove them as you go, if you wish . . . but not until you have firmly established the first stitches on the circle (or oval) of quilting you are working upon. It is better to leave the basting as long as possible in the beginning of each hoopful for control. Do not *pull* the bastings out; cut only small sections away at a time.

"Medieval" Quilting

"Way back when in days of yore" a tradition was established that every seam demanded quilting on both sides of the seam. Some of the Flower Garden patterns had so much quilting on them (going around all those minute angles) that a quilt was forever being completed. But rules were rules.

Circulating at a quilt show, you may commonly overhear one quilter criticize another quilter's quilting: "Look, she didn't even quilt around that appliqué". . . . "That's terrible, she didn't quilt on her seams, either." The latter statement has some validity: all seams *should* be stitched on both sides if this is practicable. It is beautiful. However, with my technique (adapted from the teachings of Amish quilter Hazel Bellinger), appliqué—if firmly anchored—need not be stitched on top. I do not quilt on the *inside* edge seams of any of my appliqué work. Thus our hypothetical show-viewer is probably right about one thing. At one time, she (or he!) might have been right about both statements. The cotton batts (as we've already mentioned) demanded, and demand, more quilting. Today the great polyester/bonded batts available do not require as much quilting. Moreover, there is such a thing as *too much* quilting. Too much quilting can suppress shadows so that the work resembles nothing so much as a piece of limp cardboard.

Here is the rule of thumb I use: do not quilt on top of appliqué, quilt right next to it, along the line where the two fabrics meet. The traditional ideas about how much quilting to do were established back when women had more time on their hands—in winter—not in today's society. Let's make our quilting simply beautiful and simply done, and concentrate on making stitches that are the best we can do—on quality, not quantity. Remember, as with all things, we improve with age . . . time . . . and experience. No one was born knowing how to quilt!

A final hint for new quilters: "The night has a thousand eyes, and the day has but one" . . . and with the thousands of stitches you have woven, and will weave, into your work of love . . . your eyes during the night might make a misstitch sometimes . . . so quit when you get tired. Your eyes can stand just so much. Work in the early morning.

101

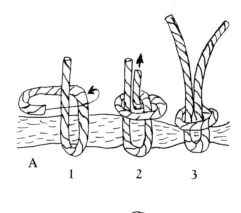

A   1   2   3

B

Figure 48.

A. This is Charlotte's Amish Knot—an overhand slip knot. Another appropriate name might be "the forever knot"; this knot is easily accomplished and it will not untie or unravel easily.

B. Avoid the square knot!

Knotting Appliqué

Amish women are famous for their knotted comforters. The three layers are placed in the frame as a quilt to be quilted would be. If you should wish to knot an entire quilt—top, batting, and bottom (although sometimes a flannel sheet can be used between the top and bottom layers instead of batting)—do *not* finish the edges of your quilt before knotting.

Making the correct kind of knot is important. I feel sorry for those unwary women who purchase darling baby quilts with the usual square knots used to keep them together. They don't! They wash out eventually. *Square knots should be avoided.* On the other hand, the knot shown in Figure 48 will not come out. Once, when I was teaching quilting at an Indiana State Teachers Association seminar in Indianapolis, a woman kissed me on the cheek for teaching her this easy knot. She said, "I knot, I wash, they come out—and now I know how to solve my dilemma."

One or two strands of yarn may be used; use polyester yarn because wool will wash away quite quickly. A large-eyed darning needle will be easiest to handle.

Here's how to make an Amish comforter knot: Thread a needle with either one or two strands of yarn. To make this less difficult, try taking a piece of aluminum foil or waxed paper; fold it around the yarn ends, and slip this through the eye of the needle. Of course, embroidery floss may be used to knot a comforter, too—there is no rule!

Again, refer to Figure 48. Push the needle straight down through all the layers of the quilt or comforter, from the top. Pull all but about two inches of the yarn through; then place the needle ¼- to ⅜-inch from the point where it came down through the bottom and push back through all the layers. This should give you a ¼- to ⅜-inch space between the in and the out of the thread (or floss or yarn). Now take the needle behind the 2 inches of yarn left loose (we'll call this the " soldier") to the left, thence around front and to the right (Diagram A, 1). Follow Step 2 next, which shows you how the yarn should go behind itself and up through a circle opening formed between material and yarn. Pull excess yarn on through until the knot starts to tighten up, as indicated in Step 3. Now grip your fingers around the 2-inch strand while pulling the needle until the knot is tight (Step 3). This is your "forever knot."

Trim both strands to the length desired, usually about 1 inch. This knot will stay perky and stand tall like a soldier: it will *not* mash down with washing and wear. As Hazel Bellinger once said to me, "They're like little soldiers that stand straight up—and stay there!" This Amish woman was a wonder at quilting and a joy to my heart.

Once the knotting is finished, the edges are bound. The next chapter teaches you how to bind a quilt.

CHAPTER 10

THE BIAS THAT BINDS, AND OTHER FINISHING TIPS

o paint the birche's silver rind
And quilt the peach with softer down;
Up with the willow's trailing threads
Off with the sunflower's radiant crown . . .
Oliver Wendell Holmes,
"The Meeting of the Dryads"

The rind on a citrus fruit is its finishing touch; the bark on a tree is its natural protection; and the down on a peach encases the rich nectars inside. So it is with a quilt: the binding is a quilt's protection against fraying.

But what *kind* of binding is the question. Quick bindings are not the answer, not the best! Finishing touches to the handmade article either make or break the final product.

There are various techniques for that final binding of a quilt. There are people who say, "Why bother using a bias binding—I just cut the under-fabric larger than the top and fold it up and over" (or vice versa, over and under). To me this is sloppy quilting . . . and *not* for you, who care about end results. Too much work, time, and money went into the planning and making of your quilt to stoop to the "quick finish." There are those who propound allowing a half-yard of fabric for bias binding. There is no way in the world a large quilt can be bound with a half-yard of anything. There are also those who tell you to "cut the bias 1½ inches wide." This is impossible, especially if your batting has high loft. Not only is it terrible to handle such a wee bit of fabric, but wrapping it around a top-batting-back combination is the downfall of many a quilt—because it never gets finished!

The width of fabric needed to finish a quilt using a fatt batt, or for that matter an average batt, is a *full two-inch measure* of bias. This is narrow enough! Some quilters think that a double bias should be used. This might have been true way back when, in order to get maximum mileage out of a quilt with minimum repair, but with the abundance of fabrics available today it is unnecessary. Extraordinary care once had to be taken to increase

Marsh Marigold (78″ × 100″). Inspired by the beautiful spring-growing flower found along streams in America, this quilt was first introduced to the Eastern Long Island Quilters' Guild. Suggested colors would be a white background, yellow/lemon for flowers, crisp medium bright green for leaves (as nature has chosen). Possibly a dark forest green could be used as well as a "pebble" color for water always nearby; a sharp shade of water blue could be hidden, perhaps, in the slim stripes of bias along the squares. The reverse side should be one of the colors on top.

104

the longevity of utilitarian items, but in today's world of quilting this approach only makes a tough task tougher.

A two-inch bias should be used for binding quilts. Let this statement stand alone!

There is the technique of making a tube and then cutting it around to have a "continuous bias"—many books advocate this idea; however, I do not find it any faster. I recommend cutting the bias and joining the seams one by one. There is certainly less chance this way of the little machine stitches pulling out when you are finally ready to use it.

Allow 1½ yards of fabric for bias binding of an average-sized quilt. Fold a "diaper" triangle from the point of a corner to selvage side; cut this to obtain a true bias. (See Figure 49, Diagram A.) *Remove the selvage before cutting strips* two at a time. Measure the 2 inches all the way across, using a medium pencil to mark the cutting lines. Then cut the strips and join. (This is repetitive but not difficult!)

Press seams open; your seam should be no more than ¼-inch. If you are careful, there will be no need to trim. A simple method of joining these small pieces of fabric is with a continuous sewing machine thread. That is, sew two together, run the machine *a few blank stitches* (leaving a bit of a chain stitch between each section of binding), then sew another set, and so forth. When done, clip the threads and press. (See Figure 49, Diagram B.)

You are now ready to put on the bias. Remember, *bias* means the stretch-and-pull-easily, angle side of the fabric. If you pull the straight of fabric (along the selvage line), there is no stretch. Try it to be sure you understand this statement.

A few more notes about bias. Many of you may recall those 3-yard packages sold to trim pot holders, aprons, and towels, the kind with both sides turned under. This is *not* for quilting. Your quilt bias will be one *flat* piece 2 inches wide, and you do not press in any seam-stitching. Press only the seam where you joined the little strips together.

The less you handle the bias the better; it will stretch and pull out of shape at the slightest provocation. The less basting the better when you're working with bias *anything*.

Don't be deceived into thinking "I can't make bias,"... you can. You will! Take your time. After all, you have come through several "worst" parts of quiltmaking already. Bias binding should not pose any great obstacle.

Removing the Quilt from the Frame

It is a mess, isn't it? All that extra stuff (fabric/batting). But what a glorious feeling to have your quilt free from the wooden monster that has held it captive for weeks. And glory above... to *see* the other wonderful

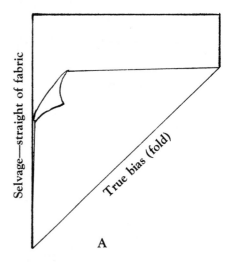

Figure 49.

A. A corner of the fabric is folded to the selvage to create "true bias"—similar to a diaper triangle. Crease with your fingers and cut up the line to separate the two pieces; now you have two pieces of fabric from which to work.

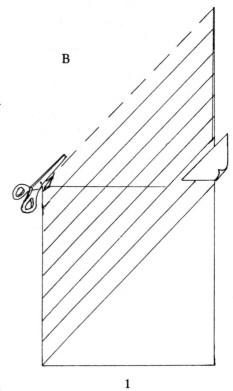

Figure 49 (continued)

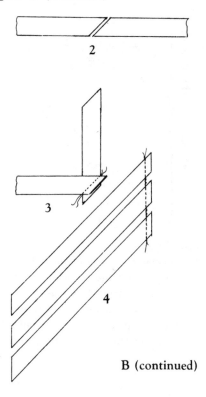

B (continued)

B. 1. With a ruler, and using a medium pencil, measure your bias binding strips (usually 2 inches) all the way up. When you come to a point and the "small triangle" appears, do not use this; otherwise you will have too many seams and they will be too short. 2. This is how the bias should be before joining. 3. Sew the bias strips at an angle, as indicated. 4. To save time you can sew all of your bias strips at one time and cut them apart. The angle in the illustration only shows one side of the bias—to show you the few stitches needed *in between* strips. These will protect the machine stitching from coming apart. Press seams, which were about ¼-inch open. Your bias is done!

side, the one you spent so much time crawling around on the floor looking up at (if you used a floor frame)!

Throw the beautiful quilt on the bed or sofa and enjoy. Relax. Look at it. Call in a neighbor—or ten—to help you admire your masterpiece. Everyone knows a lot of people, and sharing happiness and accomplishment is fun. Especially if this is your first quilt . . . share your glee!

Back to basics! What to do with all of the extra material hanging all around the quilt? *Do not cut it off until you have basted all of those raw ends together.* (This may be done before you remove the quilt from the frame.)

You will have no problem if you baste with quilting thread, leaving no more than a ½-inch seam, all the way around your quilt. Use stitches about ½-inch long, or longer. This is one of the best-kept secrets in the quilting world: you must draw up your basting threads as you baste to match the pulled-together quilting stitches you've used throughout the entire quilt.

Repeat: When the quilt is off the frame, do not trim the edges *until* you have basted all around the edges using quilting thread, and have pulled these basting stitches as you do quilting stitches to bring the edge into the same proportion as the rest of the quilt. The basting seam allowance is no more than ½-inch. (See Figure 50.) Your quilt may have an irregular shape if you leave your edges slack—the binding will follow the meandering edge instead of the firm outline you had planned.

Check to see whether you are satisfied with the look. Perhaps you might want to adjust your gathers here and there: move the fabric along the basting stitches. Do *not* distort the edge too much: this will distort interior design lines of the quilt.

Now you may trim off the excess—using the top, of course, as the guide for cutting, just as you measured the ½-inch seam basting allowance (Figure 50). Hold the three layers firmly between your fingers as you cut. Because of the puckering, you might inadvertently cut too much off the bottom layer; it is very easy to do, so take this precaution. If it would make you feel better—and perhaps it would be advisable for the first quilt—try a second row of basting stitches close to the edge. Then, when it comes to cutting, there is no chance of a mistake. In the meantime, the bias is still waiting to come into play. . . .

It is best never to have a loose bias end on a corner or on the inside edge of a curve—it is too difficult to handle in the finishing process. I usually begin and end a bias binding on the upper end of the quilt, up where the work will be under the pillow, or even at the top, just as a precaution.

I never baste bias! The more it is handled the more difficult it becomes to handle, as I mentioned previously. Begin sewing the bias binding on the top side of the quilt right at the sewing machine: no need to baste. If you have taken the time to make a ½-inch cardboard guide for your machine stitches, or if you have a guide already on your machine, it helps you not only to measure but to keep a straight seam. The time saved is wonderful.

It may make you feel better to pin on the bias binding, but this is basically a waste of time. I place the bias seam side up, the *right side to quilt top*. This is very important. (You are going to have the machine stitching on the right side of your quilt.) Use a medium stitch on your machine and *sew slowly!* Keep feeling underneath carefully before you stitch each few inches; hold down the bias on top. Proceed like this all the way around the quilt. You must move the quilt carefully because it is so large and heavy. Each time you move the quilt, make certain your machine needle is *down* into the machine—this will help you control the next series of stitches.

At some point soon you are going to think, "What is this all about? Quilting was a piece of cake compared to doing this." Just wait, this step only lasts a little while—and you are almost finished!

By going slowly, finger-pressing the top/batt/back plus bias binding carefully just before it moves under the machine needle, you will save yourself a lot of agony later. (Ripping out crooked stitches is a miserable undertaking.) Remember to keep that ½-inch seam at all times. Then your finished product will be excellent.

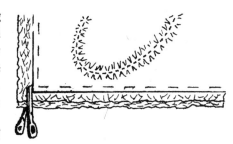

Figure 50. The quilt top edge is the guide to use to give your quilt—just out of the frame and with edges securely basted—its final "haircut."

Going Around Those Corners . . .

Don't be afraid to turn a corner, or a curve, when placing bias on the edge of your quilt. It is not as difficult as you might anticipate. The secret here is to clip off *a little bit only* at the corner. Another valuable hint is to place two dots to follow. (See Figure 51.) Use whichever technique works best for you. Perhaps a practice run on a similar fabric combination will save you trouble.

When the bias is completely on, check to see if you've erred and your seam is more than ½-inch wide. Adjust as necessary; you can trim here and there to even up, but don't become scissor-happy. Then, fold the raw edge around that heavy ½-inch seam, pin, and hand-whip it down. In the original 2-inch width you cut, you have allowed about a ½-inch seam allowance front and back and about ½-inch of finished binding front and back. Lap the bias binding over the raw edge of your quilt to cover the raw edge. (Again, see Figure 51.) If your seam is a little more than ½-inch wide, don't panic: simply trim it gently. Be frugal! You *need* that ½-inch seam to give the edge of your quilt character.

About turning a corner: do not be too particular. It is almost impossible to have a perfectly sharp turn because there is too much bulk. There are, however, a couple of ways to handle going around a corner. When you get close to that area, take a needle and thread and run a few tiny stitches on the ½-inch seam line of the binding; draw it up so that it will "ease" around the corner without pulling or distorting the quilt's shape. Another suggestion: when you are almost to the corner, the edge of the binding can be

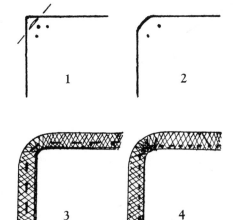

Figure 51.
1. Gently clip the corner.
2. Your clipped corner should look like this.
3. Machine-stitch the bias to the right side (½-inch seam allowance).
4. Here is the bias curve beautifully covered and hand-whipped down with appliqué stitch.

carefully pleated on both sides of the corner and stitched down to ease around the corner.

A final thought about bias finishing: rather than basting, pinning, gathering, or tucking, I sometimes just take a pin and push extra fabric up for that "ease" needed. Experiment first; you'll be glad you did.

Final Finish of Bias Edging

At last, the final statement to your quilt: *the end*! The bias binding is almost on; there should be no reaeon to do any further trimming. As you sew your final seam, finishing your binding, it is important to hide your stitches. Use an invisible stitch, my Amish backstitch, the satin stitch or the feather stitch. Use short matching lengths of thread; a regular spit knot will do to begin, but hide it. Stitch in place several times to end the thread when you have gone as far as possible, and then run the needle and thread into the quilt to hide as before, leaving a tail of about 1 inch inside. Take your time finishing the quilt . . . .at this point, haste does make waste. There is no need to remove the basting stitches you put on the quilt edge before sewing on the bias—unless you can see them. Remove only what you can see by cutting, *not* pulling. When hand-whipping the binding edge down, you can cover up any visible machine stitches to give your quilt a more professional look.

"But must I pull out all those quilt-edge basting stitches?" you ask. No, you need not! After all, fifty years from now, who will know they're in there?

Is Garnish Necessary?

Now is the time to decide whether the quilt needs a tassel (or four tassels). Stand back and look. Is there something missing? Would a brightly colored tassel add a dimension and really set off the work?

If so, making a tassel is very easy. Don't be too skimpy in the length or fullness. (I have been known to put 9-inch tassels on a baby quilt.) A tassel is a strong statement; using one that is too short and too thin is not much better than nothing! (Note, though, that tassels take quite a bit of yarn.) As almost everyone knows, you should always remove the tassels before washing. Tassels for show are fun. Who needs to be practical all the time, anyway?

How to Make a Tassel

Refer to Figure 52.

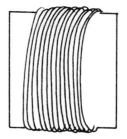

1. Determine the length needed. For a 9-inch tassel, take a piece of stout cardboard (I often use a book) of the desired length. Begin to wrap the yarn around it, counting turns so that your tassels will be the same thickness.
2. Tie at least two pieces of yarn about 10 inches long around and through one end of the cardboard-wrapped yarn. Tie firmly.
3. Cut the other end of yarn, being certain to take a firm grasp of the end already tied; there is a tendency for the yarn to become taut in wrapping and it will very likely spring loose when you snip.
4. Wind more yarn around the "neck" of the tassel-to-be; use two 15-inch lengths. Tie tightly. Let the remaining length on these 15-inch pieces fall down to become part of the tail.
5. The bottom of the tassel will look unkempt. Take your scissors and shape it evenly.
6. Sew the tassels to the corners of your quilt, or pin them if the quilt is not for an infant or young child and there is no danger of a pin being swallowed. Then the tassel can easily be removed for washing. If the quilt *is* for a young child, you might include a hanger of yarn and attach your tassel with buttons.

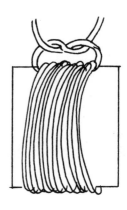

NOTE: This same technique can be used to make pom-poms. It is the length of the yarn that determines size. Use steps 1, 2, and 3.

Buttons and Bows . . .

Here is another idea for quilts: buttons and bows add a touch of *savoir faire*. Whether the quilt is to be given away, kept for posterity, framed, or just hung for your family enjoyment, do something different!

Perhaps a perky bow . . . a big one. If you do not wish to use satin, make a tube of one of the fabrics used in the quilt and create the bow. If you have enough bias left, use two strips of the 2-inch bias binding. Seam, turn, press, and you have a bow. "But what about the ends?" Simple! Knot them. Knots do take up a lot of fabric, so consider this ahead of time. Then trim off the ends. It is very posh and professional.

Figure 52.

Another wonderful decoration for a quilt is a button—or four—on the corners. Buttons can hide a mitre that you aren't quite delighted with (so can bows, for that matter). Buttons of pearl for "heirloom" appeal can be added if sewn securely, particularly on baby quilts. You might want to do this with monofilament thread. CAUTION: do not sew all the way through to the back of your quilt; this could distort a design that you worked hard to create.

Bias with a Ruffle

Rather than encumber you earlier on, I decided I would save this complicated-sounding idea for last. A truly lovely way to finish a quilt if you've used an appropriate design, such as a floral design, is to use a bias ruffle. Making a ruffle for a quilt takes a lot of fabric. For a 3-inch ruffle on an average twin-sized coverlet you will need another 2½ yards of fabric. According to the formula we've already established, a 3-inch ruffle showing takes a 7-inch piece of bias; 3 inches on each side (finished) and a ½-inch seam allowance turned under on each side.

Those of you looking for a real challenge might think about using two different colors of ruffle and bias binding, one for each side (back and front). (See Figure 53.) This method of using two colors for the ruffle makes it possible to add lace for another dimension of luxury to your quilt, no matter what size it is. You will need to use 1½-inch bias strips to hold that ruffle, not the usual 2-inch bias. This is simply because that extra ½-inch has nowhere to go and nothing to wrap around when this finishing technique is used. Always remember to allow a ½-inch seam on whichever side you want showing on a finish. It is the "stuff" in between that gives a quilt that finished, full look on the edges (not skimpy and washed out).

There is nothing worse than putting your time and effort into making something and then skimping at the end. If you are going to do it up, wonderful, then *do it*. A woman who puts beading on a dress and skimps on that last ½-inch or so makes it look like she ran out of money instead of beading! Don't do that to yourself. Be generous in finishing your quilt.

Using Lace

Should you desire to edge your work with lace, be aware that at the bottom of most lace there is usually a little built-in thread for gathering! Use a straight pin to locate and, if you *carefully* pull this thread, all the gathers you need will appear. This is a jewel of a secret not often shared. There is no need to spend hours hand-basting to gather. However, many of the new laces today do not have this feature, more's the pity; I then resort to the ruffler attachment on my sewing machine. It saves a great deal of time; I also use it to make my quilt ruffles. Look at the Heather Rose quilt (Chapter 2 opening, page 10). There are 25 yards of lace on this work!

Finishing Wall Hangings

What to do with wall hangings? How do you mount them? Should you use tassels or not? Cover them with glass? Put them in a frame? Time will ravage needlework unless it is protected.

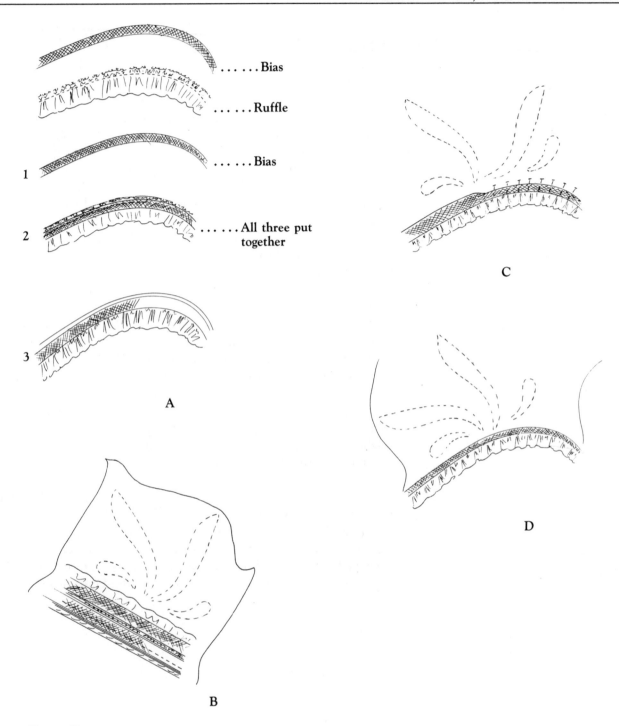

......Bias

......Ruffle

......Bias

......All three put together

1

2

3

A

C

B

D

Figure 53.
A. 1. Two pieces of bias, plus ruffle . . . 2. Are all put together and stitched. 3. This is how the three pieces look from outside.
B. Here is one side of the bias to be stitched to the quilt (off frame), that is, to all three layers.
C. The wrong side of the quilt is shown here, with the other side and bias turned down ½-inch, pin-basted and being whipped down with the Amish backstitch.
D. This is the finished bias with a ruffle on the right side.

Cleaning an old piece? Use white cornmeal. Brush it on, let it sit overnight, and shake it off the next morning. It is at least a bit cleaner.

If you insist on framing, do not allow glass immediately next to the work. Do not use sponge rubber to give it puff—it will draw in moisture and mildew, and your work will be ruined before its time. There must also be breathing room. Therefore, a pegboard is imperative on all work with glass on the front; otherwise the work can be stretched on canvas.

Tailor's weights are great additions to small, quilted wall hangings. They come in various weights and sizes, similar to the "drapery" weights. Or, if all else is unavailable, you can even use some heavy plumber's washers (but placed in a plastic bag, lest they rust) and attach them to the back corners until you can obtain the real weights. This will help the piece keep better balance and eliminates gaping sides. Tassels, too, often help with the weight problem. Tassels at the top and bottom are not gauche if they suit your design.

Using an antique picture frame is wonderful for displaying an antique quilt, but these frames are seldom large enough. Remember, too, that quilts being made now will be antiques in 100 years, according to auctioneers. If you have enough money to frame that "wonder of wonders" quilt to make it a permanent part of your art collection—just do it. If you like this alternative, I recommend that the quilt be hand-whipped onto a canvas frame, similar to an oil-painting frame, and then simply framed—taking care that the glass (or plexiglass) is *not* next to the work. This is all that is necessary. I designed and made a quilt for the Sesquicentennial celebration of the La Porte Presbyterian Church in La Porte, Indiana, and it is framed in this manner. It took a good eleven hours to hand-whip the work to the canvas frame, using quilting thread. The quilt contains 359 signatures; it took me five full months of "free" time to embroider. Many of the church symbols were quilted into the 74″ × 84″ work. This quilt was then framed by Thanhardt-Burger Corporation of La Porte, Indiana, in a large oak/gold-touched frame. Just in case the gold lamé cross that I appliquéd to the quilt should decay with time, beneath it I appliquéd an off-white cross as a replacement. I call this "thinking ahead"!

CHAPTER 11

THE CARE AND FEEDING
OF QUILTS AND QUILTERS
— Tips and Tales

here is so much good in the worst of us, and so much bad in the best of us, that it should remind all of us, not to criticize the rest of us.

Unpolished pearls never shine.

—Anon. Folk Sayings

Smiles come to your faces to think you have actually read through to the final chapter of this book. Quilting at its best is yours if you will but *think positive*. You should simply live up to your very own fine capabilities, *not* those of this particular book or of any instructor. It hardly matters how quickly you can understand a chapter; you must keep your own pace. It is your quilt! Best of all, you will complete your project because I have shared many secrets with you and actually taken you to that small town instead of letting you "flounder" on the highroads looking around for that final—detailed—direction.

Do complete your work: never begin something and not finish it. If it doesn't turn out as you pictured it, be of good heart and try again—something else, another project. Do not make the same item twice . . . . it is boring! Do something different.

The poetic offerings I have used throughout this book have been borrowed to make your reading light. And should you find yourself teaching someone, someday . . . do it in a lighthearted manner. Do not demand perfection: remember, once even *you* didn't know how to quilt.

Always remember it is *your* quilt, *your* wall hanging, *your* work, and *you* can do anything *you* want. Do not be entrapped by conventional ideas! Explore them if you like—your own way. Color is the first key to originality, then line and design—imagination, even vision. And if the work is not perfect (here I bring out one of my favorite classroom statements) fifty years from now, who will know the difference? Give whatever you decide to make your very best effort. "Though the rain it raineth, every day," you can quilt on "rainy" days! When the sun doth shine, be in your garden

Hollyhock Heaven (79″ × 79″). *Colors:* The background is white with a large hollyhock blossom in the center and five tall plants emanating from the center. The flowers are azalea pink and the leaves a bright forest green. The reverse side of the quilt is all azalea pink. A double ruffle is pink covered with white chantilly lace. To add drama, although not shown in the line drawing, tassels of silk were added to each flower anchored with a black satin antique button—and each indented petal has a small black velvet bow to make an "ending statement."

getting some exercise—and really look at those flower colors, the green of the leaves, and colors of the sunset.

Even though your heart might be at your quilting while doing household or other chores, you can be designing more quilts and truly looking at colors. Scratch any ideas you might garner down on a piece of paper, lest you forget. Then, on the next rainy day, reflect on your "gardening" time, and do the thing you thought of. Everything you do will get going easier, better, faster, for the experience of having done it once.

Sitting at a quilting frame for hours on end is not good. You do need exercise. Using a poor light is even worse . . . on your eyes and the quilt!

Having your fingers pricked, growing callousy pads on your otherwise beautiful hands, is a price you may have to pay for the satisfactions of quilting. I can only recommend that you rub any hard skin that develops on your fingers with a lubricating salve or oil every night. When you are not quilting, itching may bother you: peel off the mess if you can do so easily. Of course, you will have sore fingers for a few days, but they will soon feel better. I have even seen quilters with fingers that look like those of mill hands, with callouses so thick I cannot fathom how the needle point can be felt on the "under" hand while quilting. Amish women who spend months and months quilting have tremendous stamina . . . but their fingers suffer for the pricking. There is one other tip I can share here. When you have used a needle too long, it becomes sharper—believe it or not. The point might even develop a little barb on it. It then pricks your finger even deeper. Throw the needle away and break out a new needle. Also, a needle often becomes bent; discard this needle. Your stitches will be the better for it, as will your fingers.

I do not recommend some of the techniques I've heard mentioned to preserve the "under" hand fingers, such as using corn-removing medicines to make a "thick skin." Too much of this might deteriorate skin tissues. It is not worth injuring your body, is it?!

Your back can suffer from "hunching" over too much; stretching will help enormously. Touch your toes a few times between hours at the quilt. Take care of yourself.

Rules of Thumb

Washing

Remember: grandmother didn't have a local dry-cleaning establishment to care for her quilts. She didn't even have polyester batting, which dries so quickly. You have both, most likely. But dry cleaners are not for quilters if their work has a polyester batting of any kind. There is something about those chemicals that does not agree with the batt. I would never send one

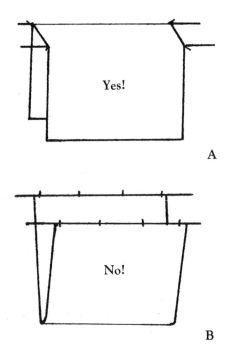

A

B

Figure 54.
A. Hang your quilt over two lines; this prevent fading due to moist colors rubbing each other. If your quilt is properly spun off in the washing machine, there should not be too much excess water. Use pinch-type clothespins, set at an angle on all four ends of the quilt.
B. Never hang a quilt from its ends—either together or separated—in the way shown. This arrangement puts too much stress on the quilt.

of my quilts to a dry cleaner. And even if the cleaner is not sure about using the chemicals, the establishment might "wash" (heaven forbid) your work with a lot of other things; then you may really have trouble. To add insult to injury, the next step for your poor quilt is into the dryer!

Professional washing is another thing to avoid. The cleaners do not acknowledge the hundreds of hours you have put into that quilt, nor the love, nor the money. Impersonal feelings are not for quilts. They truly need tender loving care.

Do you have a washing machine at home? Use it. Gentle, warm wash, gentle spin only (half the normal speed, and you can regulate this with the dial). Most important: do not let too much water remain in the quilt when you hang it. Hanging on the clothesline will put too much stress on some of those precious threads. They may pop out—it *is* possible, no matter how much care you took anchoring knots and endings.

Balance in the washing machine is important also. Your quilt might become wrapped around the center post if the wash load is not properly balanced, and damage can be done. If you are worried about a dye running, you might try adding about ¼-cup of table salt to a machine half-filled with cold water; let the quilt soak before washing. This will have a dye-setting effect. No need to be too delicate, on the other hand. Remember the hard washings that quilts received years ago, being pounded on rocks and hand-wrung by two people?

Too much care in washing is not good for quilts. If you have a clothes dryer, keep it turned off. If you have a clothesline, use it. Pick a cloudy day; sun will bleach those tender colors. But hang the quilt outdoors if you can. (See Figure 54.) If you have a basement, hang it down there in the same fashion. You might want to put a piece of white tissue paper between each clothespin and the fabric to keep the quilt clean; or, use new clothespins. Too much wind is no good, but some won't hurt. Just don't let the poor quilt be beaten to death by Mother Nature.

Keep these few points in mind, and you'll find that it is really fairly easy to wash and dry a quilt!

Storage

I have looked over many of the books I reviewed years back for my "Renaissance of Stitchery" column in the Washington, D.C., area, as well as newer books now on the market, to find out what other teachers recommend about quilt storage. After considering these printed instructions and comparing them to today's "Amish wisdom", which is garnered from years of hand-me-down sayings, I've concluded that the care of quilts today is often treated in an overcomplicated way. The business of folding and unfolding quilts on a time schedule is rather overstimulated, in my opinion. If you have made a quilt correctly in the first place, you should

Charlotte's Clematis Quilt. This unusual appliqué layout has been balanced with the pillow in mind. The book jacket provides a close-up of the appliqué designs and the embroidery on the flower stamens.

Charlotte's Clematis Quilt, detail. Stuffed clematis flowers and leaves stand out from the lower corners of the quilt.

Heather Rose Quilt. The quilt has been wound onto the frame using the under-and-over technique preferred by the author. Notice the side straps of waste cloth attaching the quilt to the sides of the frame.

Heather Rose Quilt. This quilt has a very unusual hexagonal shape.

Heather Rose Quilt, detail. Bias binding, a generous ruffle, and lace have been used to finish the quilt.

Hollyhock Heaven Throw. The throw has been quilted and trimmed and is now ready to be bound and finished. Notice how well the quilting design and trapunto work carries over to the back side of the throw.

Hollyhock Heaven Throw. A ruffle and lace have been used with bias binding to finish the throw, but in a different arrangement than that used for Heather Rose.

Hollyhock Heaven Throw. The Hollyhock Heaven Quilt has been adapted from this throw.

Hollyhock Heaven Throw, detail. The large center flower has been trimmed with a lace doily, a button, and a tassel.

Hollyhock Heaven Throw, detail. Stamens and pistils are represented by buttons and tassels.

Les Fleurettes Violetta Quilt. This is an exercise in cross-stitch embroidery and appliqué. The center panel is framed by two mitred borders.

Sunbonnet Sue Quilt. Batting and backing cloth are substantially larger all around than the quilt top. The quilt backing is attached to the frame by means of a sleeve of waste cloth on the frame cross-bar (not to be confused with the quilt's own sleeve, which will be fashioned from the "extra" backing material on the top side of the quilt).

Sunbonnet Sue Quilt. The appliqué work was done by the author at age 10. The top was constructed and the quilt completed in 1983.

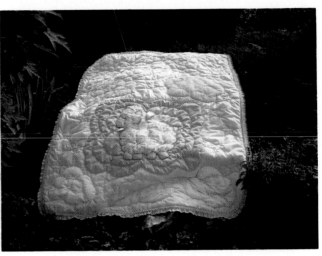

9 (Cloud 9) Baby Quilt. This appliqué quilt incorporates a prestamped lamb needlework pattern of the kind available at most fabric counters.

Big Top Child's Quilt. Shapes from fabric with a very large print have been used with other circus motifs devised by the author.

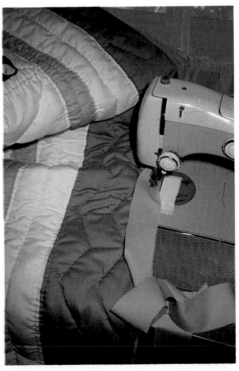

Adding bias binding to a quilt, using a sewing machine. The quilt edge has been basted and then trimmed carefully before binding. Notice the paper guide next to the throat plate of the machine: it helps to keep those ½-inch seams straight.

Ronald's Jelly Beans Throw. This piece combines reverse appliqué with appliqué. The ground fabric is the golden yellow; the multi-colored "jelly beans" have been appliquéd using the more common method.

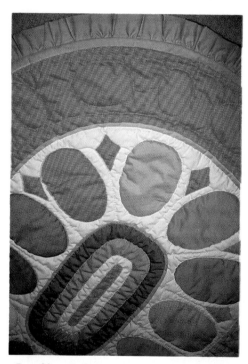

Ronald's Jelly Beans Throw, detail. The juxtaposition of the reverse-appliqué center of the oval and the brightly colored appliqué rings surrounding it gives this throw extra dimension.

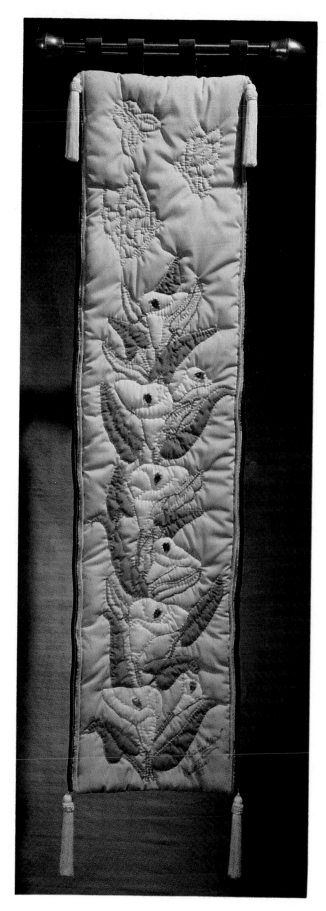

Katherine's Callas Wall Hanging. This wall hanging (or wide bell pull) is named for Katherine Hepburn. The trimming makes this piece sparkle: antique leaf sequins for the calla stamens, gold lamé edged with black on the long sides, silken tassels. Photograph by Edward Weiss, Slidecraft, Inc.

Marigold Quilt. This quilt is featured in the July/August 1980 issue of DECORATING & CRAFT IDEAS magazine.

Calendula Mosaic Quilt. The appliqué design for this quilt is adapted from a black-and-white oil painting. This is lattice stripping with a difference.

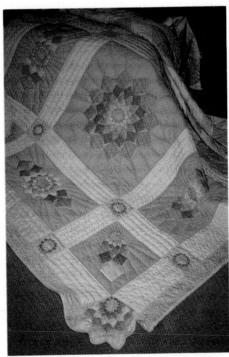

Calendula Mosaic Quilt, detail. Notice the adjustment of the radiating quilting lines to each block and oblong shape. Corners are given particular flourish.

Rhondora Rosemaling Quilt. Rosemaling painting (and sometimes carving) is a traditional Scandinavian peasant craft. The quilting motifs in this counterpane are reminiscent of typical rosemaling designs.

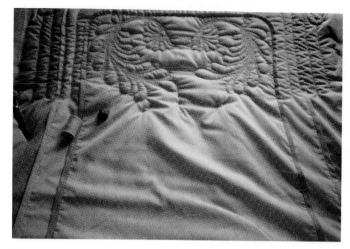

Heirborne II Baby Quilt (Courtesy of Dr. and Mrs. Clement Elshout). A counterpane-in-progress is shown on the quilting frame. Notice that several needles are being used as the quilting proceeds. This quilt has a top that was actually appliquéd one layer to the next: to prepare the top for the frame, the extra fabric was trimmed away from the back.

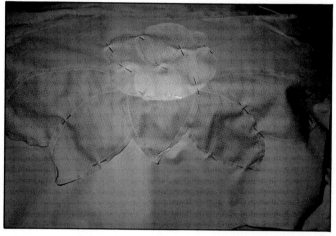

Magnolia Elizabeth Infant's Quilt. Appliqué pieces have been pin-basted in place following the template guide (which is given with the quilt pattern) for placement and sequence. Further basting is unnecessary.

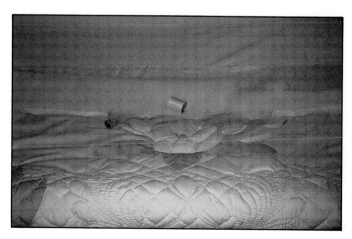

Magnolia Elizabeth Infant's Quilt. The quilt is shown on the frame. This is the top edge: notice that the curved, aqua flap is turned in toward the center of the quilt. Batting and backing extend well beyond the quilt-top edge. The author's leather thimble appears at center left!

Magnolia Elizabeth Infant's Quilt. The unusual shape of this quilt actually makes for easier "tucking in." Elaborate quilting provides drama for the center portion of the quilt. Photograph by Edward Weiss, Slidecraft, Inc.

Magnolia Elizabeth Infant's Quilt, detail. Finishing has been handled with bias binding, a bias ruffle, and lace. Notice the French knots embroidered for the flower stamen.

Iris Trilogy Quilt. This close-up shows how to position the three-dimensional "beards."

Iris Trilogy Quilt Top. Iris flowers and buds have been cut from three fabric colors (hence "trilogy"). The right side (not shown) has a roughly symmetrical arrangement of appliqués.

Iris Trilogy Quilt. Sign, date, and name your quilts for posterity, as shown, with embroidery stitches or indelible ink. Do this before quilting.

Picotee Lace Daylily Quilt, detail. The lace edging for the fancy daylilies is gathered beforehand. Notice that parts of the familiar orange daylilies are sometimes tucked behind leaf blades and stems, as in nature. The lace-edged daylilies, however, are left free.

Picotee Lace Daylily Quilt. The appliqué work is shown in progress. Flower and leaf units to the right are complete, including lace edging; those to the left are only pin-basted. Leaves, stems, flowers, and buds are appliquéd together in units rather than one item at a time (all the leaves, then all the buds, etc.). The fabric has been left a little bit loose in the hoop to allow for easier stitching.

Picotee Lace Daylily Quilt Top. This is only one of many possible layouts for the appliqué. All appliqué could, for example, be placed on the overhanging portions of the quilt for a very dramatic effect. This quilt has a rough symmetrical arrangement of appliqués on the left side as well (not shown).

Hmong Tulip Circle Wall Hanging. This sequence of photographs illustrates in detail how to do the appliques for this hanging.

Size and rough layout of appliqués are settled and tried out against the background cloth before appliqué work begins.

Concentric circles (adapted from the Hmong "snail" motif) are stay-stitched by machine before cutting; when the circle is cut out, an extra ¼-inch is allowed around the outside line of stay-stitching on the circle.

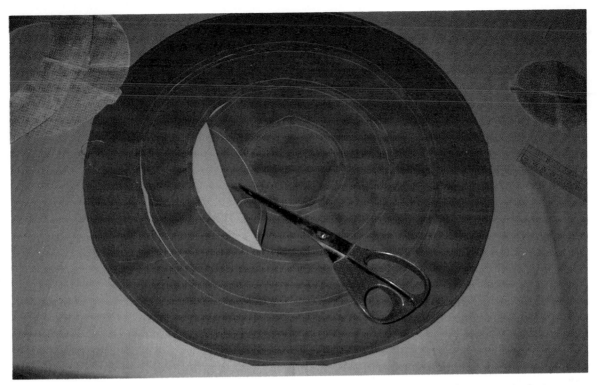

Once stay-stitching is complete, the inner circles are cut, leaving small segments attached to keep the circle shape. These little bridges are later snipped one at a time, as they are reached in the process of appliquéing (which begins at the innermost circle). Notice the brown paper patterns. (The Hmong, however, do not use patterns as such.)

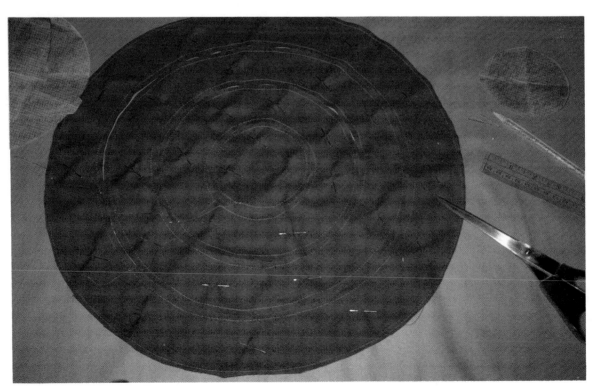

The clipped concentric circles (with bridges still intact) are next pin-basted to the background cloth.

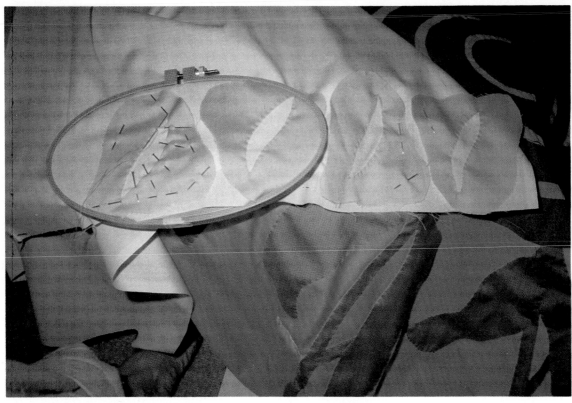

The circle appliqué is complete, as is the leaf, stem, and bud appliqué. Tulip flowers are next reverse-appliquéd to the underlining cloth—the four of one color at once, before the lining cloth is cut out at all. This makes the reverse work easier and the finished tulips more accurate in size and shape.

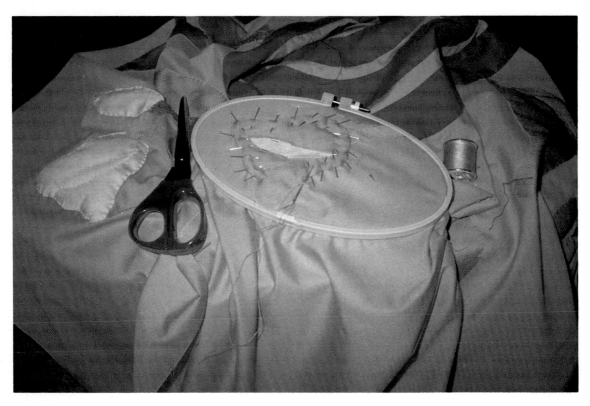

The tulip flowers are stuffed lightly, then pin-basted into place.

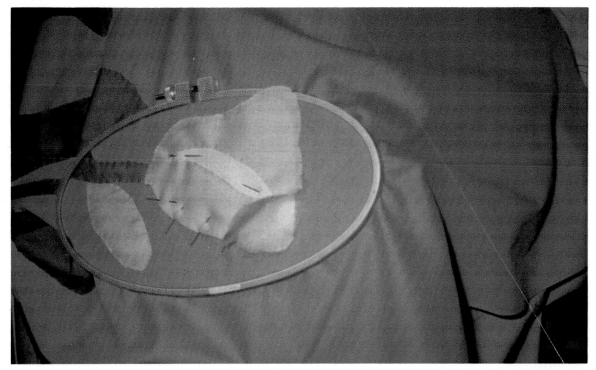

The same procedure is used for the second batch of tulips. Appliqué the tulips into place, finally, either all at once or one batch at a time for quicker gratification!

Hmong Tulip Circle Wall Hanging. The hanging is shown wound around the quilt-frame arms (or poles) ready to be put on the frame. Again, backing and batting extend beyond the quilt top; a quilt sleeve is provided for. (The Hmong, however, do not quilt their work.)

Hmong Tulip Circle Wall Hanging. A simple design of radiating lines and concentric circles has been chosen for the quilting. Edges are simply bound; corners are decorated with bows and large tassels. Photograph by Edward Weiss, Slidecraft, Inc.

have no problem. Of course, extra care should be taken if the house is invaded by silverfish, moths, and so forth; and an occasional airing is helpful. Don't store quilts in a plastic bag. Plastic bags are for garbage cans, not quilts. Static electricity draws moisture, dirt, mildew, and silverfish. The only place you need silver fish (the kind that swim) is in the frying pan in the form of trout! Old (clean) sheets are the answer. If you don't have any, ask your mother-in-law. Take that old sheet and make a sack for the quilt. Some folks have rug-rollers recommended to them; however, I think that tends to crush the quilts.

Always fold your quilts right side *in*, usually in thirds, because this puts less stress on the threads.

One continually reads a fair amount of useless advice: "Only have a quilt on a bed for three weeks," for example. What folly! Have more faith that today's textile industry does think about deterioration of colors! How on earth did some of our heritage from the past survive? Three weeks on? Three weeks off? Pilgrim women were lucky to have *one* quilt!

What do I do with all my quilts? I keep wishing I had more space! They are folded kindly in sheets, or moved around the house to different beds to air out—and be shown off. The season of the year decides which quilt is out—that is really old-fashioned, isn't it? But *do* use your quilts. Share them (and share your quilting secrets, as I have).

It is all well and good for me to give advice about the care and feeding of quilts. However, you made them, and, by golly, do with them as you will. But share them. Use them. If the quilt does fade a bit, well, you may find that the wear makes the quilt all the more special to you. Use another one, give it away to someone, or sell it at auction as an heirloom!

Pièce de Résistance

When all is said and done and the last man is counted, who will know you made that quilt? "My children saw me working on it and they know." Did you sign it? "Me sign my quilt? Why, that is foolishness. That is egotistical," you say. *Do* sign your quilt. Your name in full, not just your initials. In your own handwriting. Include your maiden name also, if you're married. Location, date, and—if you feel like it—to whom it is being given. Best of all, give the quilt a name.

Many quilts do take years to complete for one reason or another. It has taken on your sparkling personality; even if you selected a kit to make (heaven forbid), the work might be identifiable by your own personal technique. "My technique? I don't have such a thing," you're thinking. *Wrong.* No two quilters or needleworkers on earth do things exactly alike, no person's stitch is identical to another person's. Quilting is almost like a fingerprint or handwriting; it is individual. Bet you never thought about it that way . . . .

It is truly unfortunate that some experienced quilters look at beginners' quilts and make caustic, unkind, or degrading remarks. Unkind words do more to dampen enthusiasm than this world dreams of. Kind words, laced with encouragement, are imperative. After all: wisdom is affection nurtured with direction! Amish women were taught by their grandmothers and great-grandmothers when they were girls—are you teaching your children? Do you let them thread a few needles, throw a few stitches? You don't? Shame on you!

Amish ladies can be unsophisticated in the ways of the outside world; they have often been sheltered even from sewing on an electric sewing machine. (Some have no electricity in their homes.) But they have been sewing since they were "so high." They let their children begin early. I am of Norwegian descent; I was born here in America (Chicago), yet I had a needle in my hand at age five. I made my doll clothes, and my first quilt top was completed when I was ten—a Sunbonnet Sue that appears in Dolores A. Hinson's *The Sunbonnet Family of Quilt Patterns*. There is nothing the matter with putting a sewing needle, knitting needles, or even a crochet hook in the hands of a five-year-old boy or girl! You must show them how to use them—and supervise them, of course. But children *can* use these implements. The striking use of color in Amish quilts suggests that early work with fabrics, needles, and so forth instills a feeling of confidence about colors, line, and design.

The Amish do not sign their quilts! Their identity is lost, because pride in one's creations is considered a sin by some. However, you can sign your name. Embroider it with a complementary single strand of embroidery floss; or, if the work is of a muted, delicate color, a perfectly matched floss should be used. Sign on the front your name and the date; on a back corner, put in location and anything else you wish to record in stitchery.

Another idea, once shared with me by Mrs. Arthur Seippel of Winchester, Virginia, is to stitch a tiny pocket on the backside of a quilt with a closing—a tiny baby button, or perhaps snaps. Write or type a little history of the quilt and enclose this document—it is a document—with the quilt when giving it away. *You* know the history, but who else knows it?

Tips and Tales

There are tips and tales here that will follow you in your quilting forever. Perhaps another of my favorite classroom statements, "Quilting is making shadows of love," best explains my personal feeling for this form of expressive stitchery.

- Always begin to quilt at the bottom (using a floor frame), because if you make a mistake it can always be hidden "under the pillow."
- "Bring along your thimble—you'll find something to do with it."
- "Crooked as a dog's hind leg" seaming is what happens when you haven't used that ½-inch marker taped to the right side of the sewing machine needle on the throat plate.
- Don't run out and purchase a fortune's worth of templates when all along you have some wonderful cardboard just waiting to be used "someday."
- If you have some patchwork completed and you know it will never be a quilt, appliqué it to a solid, complementary backing: there is the beginning of a new quilt.
- If you insist on using a metal thimble, try "slipcovering" it with the finger of an old leather glove. Better traction will be the result.
- Use a deflated or burst balloon to help pull that needle through the quilting fabrics.
- Learn to "wiggle-quilt" instead of quilting one stitch at a time.
- Don't shy away from counterpane work. It is nothing more than pure quilting.
- If you are a beginner, go with appliqué. The work grows faster and you will not be so bedeviled by "matching points."
- Never give away your first quilt—keep it in the family.
- Keep a record of all your quilts. In fact, number them.
- Avoid kits like the plague unless you *must* go this route. Originality is more rewarding.
- Should you get a spot of blood on your work, do not panic. Take a few inches of quilting thread, white or off-white, put it in your mouth, and saturate it with saliva. Take the thread and rub it on the blood spot and it will disappear forever. Magic. Do not use water or have someone else do it for you; it must be your saliva to remove your blood. And, do this at once!
- Remember that "expensive" does not necessarily mean "best" when purchasing fabric. Broadcloth should be used for most quilts, but do not hesitate to experiment with other fabrics. Be daring.
- If you insist on using calico prints in your quilts, do not be surprised if they fade more quickly than solids—because they do, especially if they are all cotton.
- Always cut off the selvage before quilting fabrics; it is impossible to quilt through. Selvage leftovers make great cords to tie things together with.
- Plan your quilt on paper first. It is easier to change pencil lines than seam lines.
- Use a yardstick to measure; in fact, two yardsticks are better for all that fabric. Use a yardstick to "even" the grain when you're getting your quilt ready for the frame—when it is still on the floor.
- If you get stuck on a project and don't know what to do next, do nothing. Let it alone, do something else, and *then* come back. Problems

sometimes solve themselves when left in peace. Or they at least look better in the morning!

- Never press appliqué pieces before sewing them onto a background. Hand-turn as you go. Do not baste those ¼-inch seams down unless you absolutely have to. Pins are much easier and less work.
- Set pins vertical to a horizontal line, never with the same line as the piece you are sewing down.
- When doing appliqué or quilting on a hoop, do not have fabric too taut; keep it "loose as a goose in flight" and floppy. You then have a better chance of manipulating your needle and making a hill with your finger underneath for the needle to pierce.
- Do not tackle too large a project for your first quilt, yet do not undertake anything too small and lacking challenge. You are better than you think, and you do not want to be bored, do you?
- Use those ½-inch marking dots on corners. They save time. Ripping is usually unnecessary when the dots are followed.
- Never *cut* batting; always tear it gently. Cut batt doesn't "butt" smoothly. "Tearing butts the batt—keep that under your hat!"
- Save old sheets to make "headers" (sleeves) for quilts going on floor frames; old sheets also make sacks for your pillows and side straps for the sides of your quilting frame (to hold the quilt taut).
- Do not be afraid of color . . . use it. "Use color when you are alive—when you are dead, there is no color." (Charlotte Bass)
- Enter as many quilt shows as possible. The more you enter, the better you get from seeing other work and being in competition. Judges in most competitions will critique your work on the other side of your entry form.
- There should be three judges in a quilt show—with any luck, one knowledgeable about color, one about line, and the other about design! "Because they own a quilt shop" does not make them an expert!
- If you do piece quilts and want to teach this skill to children, pick the central piece and call it the "mother," to which the "father" will join, to which the "children" will join, and so forth. Making a game out of it makes it easier for them to understand and more fun.
- My sincere apologies to anyone called Aunt Hattie, whose name I have used throughout this book . . . . it is an expression of love!

Quilting Is an Expression of Emotion

There isn't a quilter alive who cannot testify to the satisfaction, relaxation, emotional release, and gratification garnered from having quilted anything! A quilt does not have to be judged to render these rewards. I don't like to be criticized . . . neither do you. If you can't say something constructive about someone else's quilt, it is better to say nothing, unless you are a teacher who can help the quilter do better. Don't hurt the feelings of a new quilter—put yourself in his or her place. You were "new" once. Everyone needs praise and encouragement.

A Few Notes About Quilting Competitions and Judges

Owning a shop for quilters does not make one expert. Shop owners are just good businesspeople in a good business—and may be excellent judges of quilting too, but this comes separately. Home economics teachers are not always best, either; their world has been limited primarily to home-sewing. A good judge might be someone in fashion, an artist, a couturier (if you can find one), someone in the engineering or architectural world, even a builder—perhaps an author of a book who is a quilter. Try to find judges with an open mind and an open eye for line or design. A florist would be a great person to judge color sense in quilts if you judge on this—which you should.

And . . . if nothing else, in doing a quilt show, do have a section for kits only, a section for original work only, a section for "This is my first quilt" only. Professionals should never compete with amateurs; it is simply not fair. (A professional is one who accepts money on a regular basis to do anything in quilting: line, design, piecing, quilting, and so forth.) A special exhibit for "invited" pieces might be included. And appliqué should stand alone. It should not be judged with pieced work; there is no similarity.

A work that has won a first-prize ribbon within the previous three years should not be eligible for competition. This rule gives newcomers more opportunity and keeps Aunt Hattie from cleaning up the ribbons year after year! These quilts should be exhibited, though, for their inspiration to others. Their makers deserve praise . . . not more ribbons.

Without the benefit of a peer to help you in quilting, to encourage you and guide you, the next best thing is a good book. I hope you feel that this one falls into that category. Appliqué is my passion in stitchery, and I certainly hope my words have been beneficial to you. Proceed at your own pace. Try some of the projects I have suggested. Adapt them to suit your own needs. Appliqué, quilt, stitch. Share what you have learned with your children, or someone else's children, so that the wonderful world of quilting will not disappear—as it almost did after the Industrial Revolution in 1850.

Your original ideas expressed in quilting will last longer, be worth more to your family, become the heritage for your children and their children. You are making memories; that is what needlework is all about. I say to my students, "Quilting is making shadows of love—so go make some shadows!"

AUTHOR'S FOOTNOTE:

No one is perfect! Ideas you would like to share, suggestions about improvement of appliqué techniques, and anything else related to quilting— send them along either to the publisher (Arco Publishing, Inc., 215 Park Avenue South, New York, NY 10003) or directly to me: Charlotte Bass, Lilac Manor Farm, 5013 East—450 South, La Porte, Indiana 46350.

SOURCES FOR QUILTING SUPPLIES AND RELATED ITEMS

INDIANA

Gohn's, Main Street, Middlebury, IN 46540

Haarer's Antique Shop, Shipshewana, IN 46565

Lolly's Fabrics, 301 E. Washington St., Millersburg, IN 46543

Mabel's Patchwork Quilts, 108 No. Monroe St., Millersburg, IN 46543

Calicoe Quilts, Metzler's Dept. Store, Topeka, IN

Martin's Quilt Shop, County Road 11 and County Road 46, Nappanee, IN 46550

Oppenheim's, North Manchester, IN 46962

Spector's, Nappannee, IN 46550

Spector's, Shipshewana, IN 46565

Yoder's Department Store, Shipshewana, IN 46565

OHIO

Helping Hands Quilt Shop, Box 183, Berlin, OH 44610

Lone Star Quilt Shop, Box 32, Mount Hope, OH 44660

Patchwork Place, 105 W. Jackson Street, Millersburg, OH 44564

Schlabach's Store, Walnut Creek, OH 44687

Spector's, Middlefield, OH 44062

Spector's, Millersburg, OH 44654

Spector's, Mount Eaton, OH 44659

Spector's, Sugarcreek, OH 44681

Sugarcreek Quilt Shop, S. Broadway, Sugarcreek, OH 44681

PENNSYLVANIA

Ephrata East End Mart, 711 East Main Street, Ephrata, PA 17522-2598

Samuel Greenberg Co., 6626 McCallum Street, Philadelphia, PA 19119

ILLINOIS

Marshall Field's, 111 N. State Street, Chicago, IL 60609

DISTRICT OF COLUMBIA

G Street Couture Fabrics, 11852 Rockville Pike, Rockville, MD 20850 (formerly Washington, DC)

"Finger's Friend" Leather Thimble by Dritz is available from:
  The Risdon Corporation
  P.O. Box 5028
  Spartanburg, South Carolina 29304

PART II

PROJECTS

CHARLOTTE'S CLEMATIS QUILT
(76″ × 112″) Clematis
(Ranunculaceae)

(Shown on book jacket and Chapter 1 opening page)

NOTE: This is not an inexpensive quilt to make, but the final product is worth the money and the effort.

Materials:

6½ yards light sky-blue (almost white) for quilt top background
9 yards bright white (6¾ yards for back, 2 yards for bias, ¼-yard for flowers)
⅓-yard deep clematis purple
⅓-yard hot pink
⅓-yard lavender
1 yard very dark green
1 yard very bright green
7 yards gray/beige for side strippings and 7-inch ruffle (Should you not want to make a ruffle and wish to bind the quilt in white only, you will need only 1½ yards for bias stripping to avoid too many seams.)
20 yards chantilly lace, about 3 inches wide
1 fatt batt, 90″ × 108″, plus 10″ (buy two)
quilting thread, off-white
colored mercerized thread for flowers

Instructions:

Cut:

On the width of fabric: Blue
    1 piece 43″ × 81″ (background for appliqué work)
    2 pieces 13″ × 43″ (top and bottom of main piece)
On the length of fabric: Blue
    2 pieces 13″ × 81″
    4 pieces 13″ × 13″ (curve off one corner of each piece for corners)

Cut: Gray/Beige

On the length of fabric, cut about 10 yards of 2-inch fabric, joined together for stripping up the sides and bottom of the quilt where appliqué work will be executed.

Should you decide to make the 7-inch bias ruffle, be ready to do a lot of piecing, gathering, pinning, stitching, and so forth—but it is worth the effort.

Cut: All flower colors and leaf colors

Draw the patterns onto cardboard: use these templates to draw on fabric. You will need:

Flowers
(vary flower patterns in different colors)
6 white
10 hot pink
11 deep purple
8 lavender

Leaves
17 dark green large A
14 dark green medium B
5 dark green small C
10 bright green A
14 bright green B
5 bright green C

Buds
19 buds, gray/beige

Stamens
35 stamens (to prepare,
see Chapter 6)

Quilt Backing: Prepare the quilt back as directed in Chapter 10.

1. Appliqué flowers and leaves to the 43″ × 81″ blue section. Some of the flowers and leaves may have trapunto . . . "careful, not too much." Add stamens as directed in Chapter 6.
2. Join each of the 13″ × 43″ sections, with a 2-inch strip in between, to the top appliquéd piece. Be certain to leave a tail of about 15 inches on each side for joining the side strips. Sew to the dot. Then sew the 13″ × 81″ strips in the same manner, matching dots. Finally, sew the remaining 2-inch strips to the edge of the quilt.
3. Using dots, join your corner blocks—with 2-inch strips already attached to the other parts of your quilt top.
4. Press as directed in Chapter 10. If you are satisfied that the entire top lies well, then trim seams and finish as directed; trim seams again.
5. Prepare the quilt back.
6. Making a sandwich—back/batt/top—prepare as directed. Quilt, and finish as you like. *Enjoy!*

Add ¼-inch seam allowance.

Bud

Butterfly quilting patterns

1

A

Add ¼-inch seam allowance.

3

B

C

2

Stamen

129

HOLLYHOCK HEAVEN QUILT
(78″ × 99″)
Althaea rosea (Malvaceae)

(Adapted from the Hollyhock Heaven Throw, shown on Chapter 11 opening page.)

NOTE: Colors of this quilt can be of your choosing, but select colors true to the hollyhock . . . and complement with stark white.

Materials:

12 yards bright white broadcloth, 44″ wide (6½ yards for backing, 2 yards for center front, 3½ yards for side bars)
5 yards azalea pink broadcloth (3¼ yards for side bars, 1½ yards for center hollyhock and flowers)
5 yards muted forest green (2½ yards for 2-inch bias binding, 2½ yards for side bars; leaves to be cut out of remainder)
1 6-inch lace doily (hand crocheted, pure white)
¼-yard sheer white fabric to cover doily for appliqué
quilting thread, pure white
1 fatt batt, 90″ × 108″
colored thread to match fabrics to be appliquéd

Cut: Forest Green	Cut: Azalea Pink
4 leaf A	12 hollyhock flowers
4 leaf B	12 blossom tops (to be gathered at the bottom and joined to the bud base)
8 leaf C	20 bud bases
8 leaf D	8 tiny blossoms

Each bud base should be hand-sewn to the blossom where "x x x" indicates gathers. The tiny blossom is "x x x" gathered and stuffed and joined to the bud base. Large blossoms may also be stuffed *very slightly* to accentuate the gathers only.

Instructions:

Cut out flowers and leaves. Cut one 20-inch circle and scallop its edges. (To make a newspaper pattern, fold a square of newspaper in half to form an oblong, then in half again to form a square. Open back up to the oblong shape. Have the folded edge toward you. Then take the right-hand folded edge and fold it upward from the center point—marked from your second fold—so that the edge is placed about two-thirds of the way to the center of the top edge of the oblong. Fold over again three times, so that your oblong is divided into five roughly equal cone shapes. Then use a dinner plate to make a curve about 10 inches across: you can angle the plate a bit to give the curves more definition. When you open out your paper, you'll have a pattern for a five-petaled hollyhock.) Appliqué the large hollyhock to "dead center" of the white background fabric. Appliqué the sheer fabric-covered doily (cut the fabric ¼-inch larger than the doily, baste around the edges, then use my appliqué stitch and attach it to "dead center" of the large hollyhock already in place.)

Allowing about 18 inches for clusters of hollyhock stems (radiating out of the center hollyhock toward each of the four corners), place the leaves and flowers to please you. Keep them as close to "nature's own" as possible. Remove all but one cornerful. Pin this corner into position and begin to appliqué *from the first blossom up.* This pattern works well with the leaves tucked under the blossoms here and there; do not be afraid to trim a little off leaves to make them appear more life-like beneath the blossoms.

When the first full stem is completed, do not hesitate to add an extra tiny blossom here and there. Repeat this on all four corners.

Follow the directions on mitring and the use of bias binding. Complete the quilt.

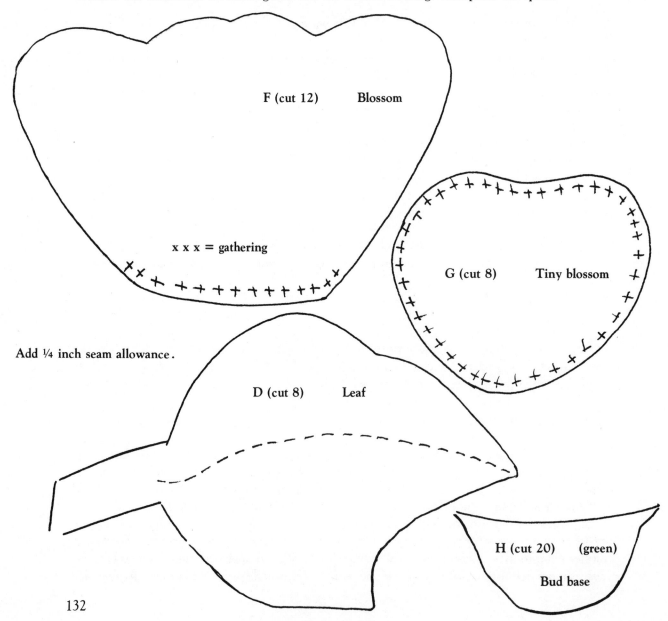

F (cut 12)   Blossom

x x x = gathering

G (cut 8)   Tiny blossom

Add ¼ inch seam allowance.

D (cut 8)   Leaf

H (cut 20)   (green)

Bud base

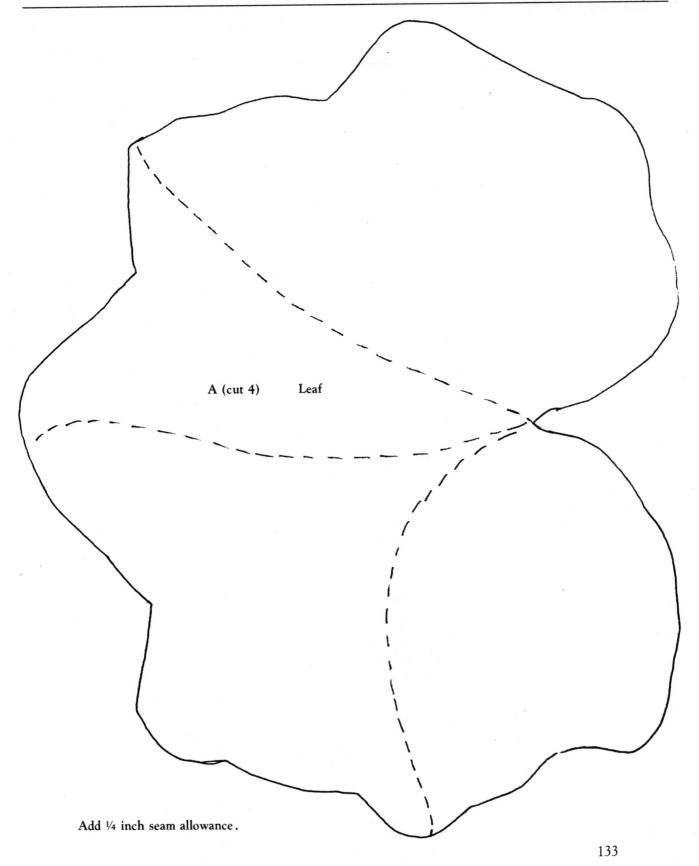

A (cut 4)   Leaf

Add ¼ inch seam allowance.

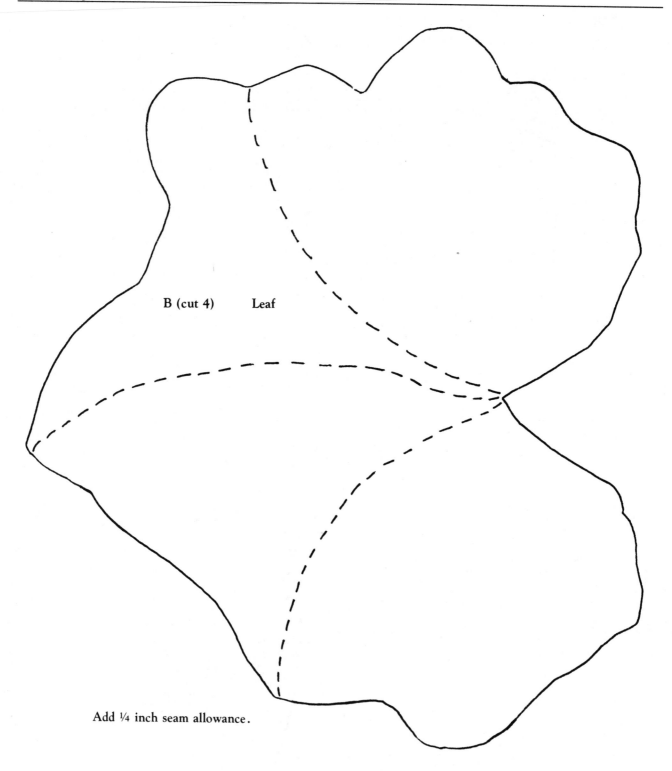

B (cut 4)   Leaf

Add ¼ inch seam allowance.

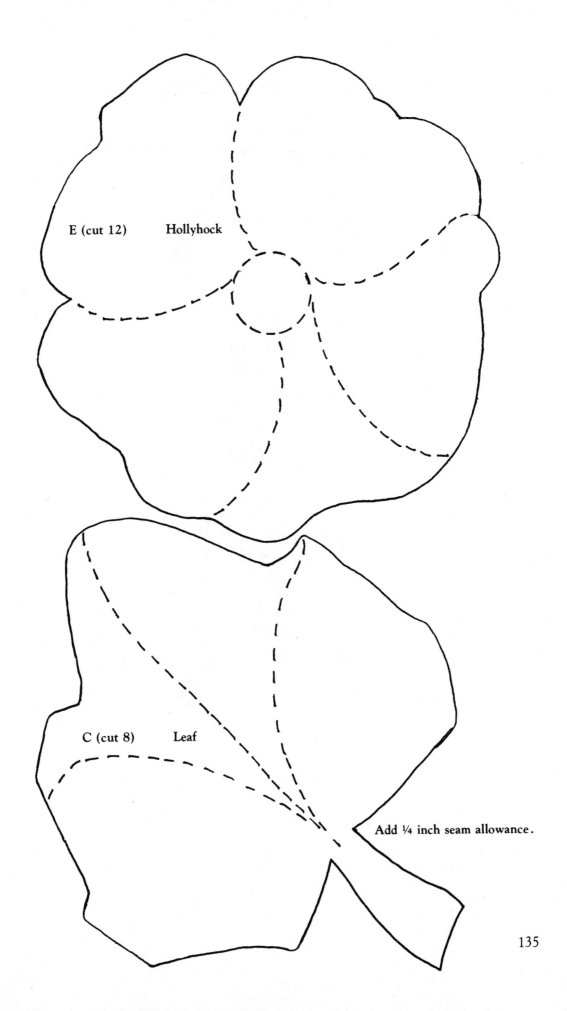

E (cut 12)   Hollyhock

C (cut 8)   Leaf

Add ¼ inch seam allowance.

135

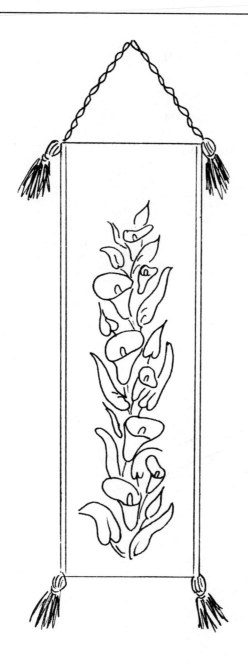

KATHARINE'S CALLAS
(16″ × 48″)
Zantedeschia aethiopica (Araceae)
(Bell-pull or wall hanging)

Materials:

1⅓ yards misty-green broadcloth
¼-yard white broadcloth
½-yard muted forest green broadcloth
3½ yards of 2-inch bias binding (*your* color choice)
1 skein embroidery floss, forest green
1 skein embroidery floss, bright yellow
quilting thread
batting
No. 7 or No. 8 crewel embroidery needle
3 yards black velvet ribbon
3 yards gold cording or braiding
2 10-inch wooden dowels (or 12-inch for a wall hanging)
4 decorator-type tassels in white
8 large gold sequins in half-moon or teardrop shape

CUT: White

4 Calla Flowers A
2 Calla Flowers B
2 Calla Flowers C

CUT: Forest Green

4 Leaves D
4 Leaves E
2 Leaves F
2 Leaves G
1 Leaf H

CUT: Misty Green

Two 16-inch wide lengths of your 1⅓ yard piece, for top background and back. (For a piece this size, it is not really necessary to allow extra backing fabric for crawl: cut the back a bit larger if you want to be extra-cautious.

Instructions:

1. Using templates for the calla lilly and leaves, draw on your fabric with pencil. Allow ¼-inch extra for seam allowance. Cut the pieces out.

137

2. Cut *two* 16-inch-wide lengths of fabric from your 1⅓-yard piece. One will be the front of your work and the other the back.

3. Follow the layout pattern for placing your flowers and leaves. Be certain to note areas where I have recommended that an embroidered leaf be used: use only an outline stitch here, as quilting will give the leave the "vein."

4. Cut out your flowers and leaves and place them on the fabric. It is best not to plan embroidered leaves until after you have appliquéd all the pieces down. Then, if a place needs filling, fill it. Begin about 4 inches from the bottom.

5. Plan on doing trapunto with your lilies, but not with the leaves. You will do this as you appliqué up the work . . . begin at the bottom.

6. After all leaves and flowers have been appliquéd down, add stems to the leaves and flowers with embroidery floss. Use two strands only with a topside backstitch. Press on the wrong side very carefully; use a towel beneath.

7. Place your sequins, if you decide to use them, in position where the stamen of the flower will be. Otherwise, you can embroider a stamen in, in the form of a teardrop. I used sequins and made yellow French knots around them for color. (Sequins may be added last; however, if you plan on using French knots, they must be done now.)

8. Place the other half of the main fabric on the floor. Tear a fatt batt to the same size and add this to the backing. Then, carefully lay your pressed top onto this. Pin around the edges, then baste with broad stitches.

9. Begin quilting at the bottom of your work in a medium, broadsided hoop. Delineate your flower curves and leaf veins with quilting. Even though you would like to, *do not overquilt.*

10. Remove the quilt from the frame. Trim the edges, deciding if you will have a bell-pull or a wall hanging. Add bias down both sides. Turn the quilt bottom side up in back, forming a space for a dowel to fit through. If you wish, a gold button can be put at each corner on which a tassel will be hung, or, you can use brass rods with decorator ends. Hang the quilt with satin cord.

11. Should you decide to make a bell-pull instead of a wall hanging, trim the sides in to about 10 inches (total width) and finish with bias. Then, hand-whip—*over the bias*—velvet ribbon and gold braid. NOTE: If the pull does not hang right, try using drapery weights on the lower corners.

AUTHOR'S NOTE: This entire pattern would adapt itself beautifully to a full-size quilt, with the callas radiating toward the center or up the side.

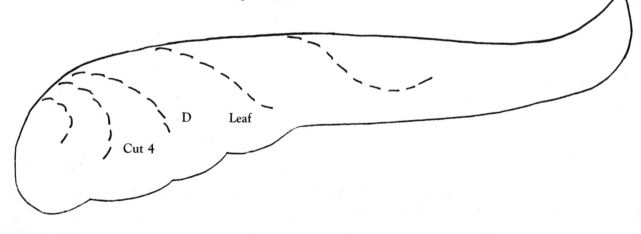

D   Leaf

Cut 4

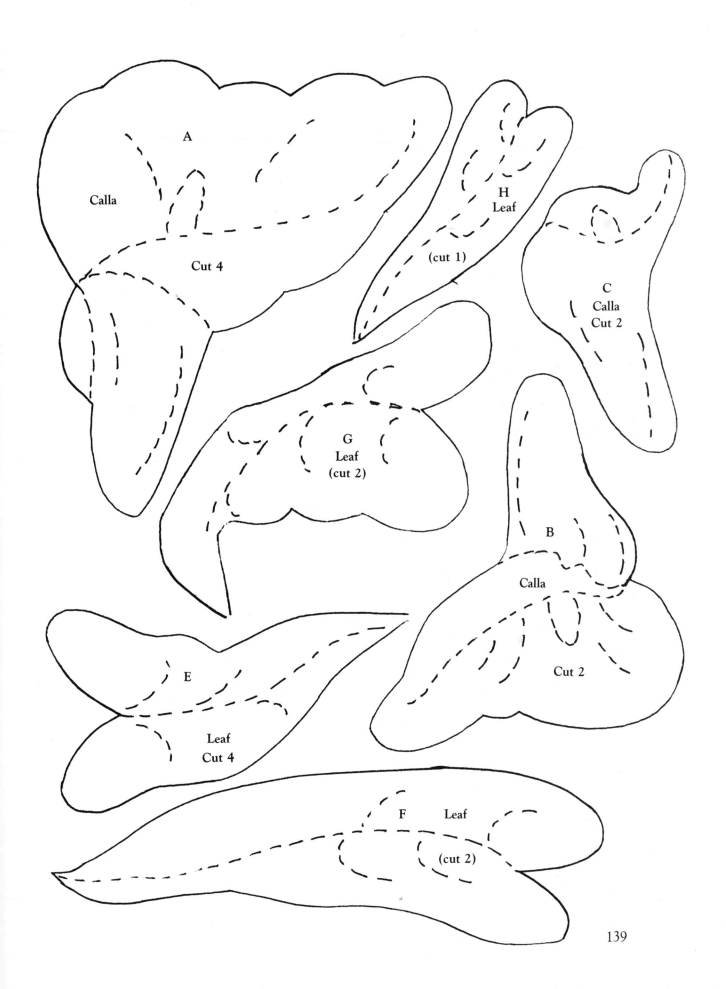

A
Calla
Cut 4

H
Leaf
(cut 1)

C
Calla
Cut 2

G
Leaf
(cut 2)

B
Calla
Cut 2

E
Leaf
Cut 4

F   Leaf
(cut 2)

139

MAGNOLIA ELIZABETH
CRIB QUILT

(46½'' × 48½'' plus lace or ruffle)
M. *heptapeta (Magnoliaceae)*

NOTE: Thanks to the Brooklyn Botanic Garden's Director of Education, Doris Stone, for suggesting the name of this new magnolia for my infant's quilt.

The shape of this magnolia is important, so I have provided a template (pattern) simply as a guide to help you get the proper roundness. I find the template invaluable in placing the petals. (Consistent order in this and other flower patterns can easily be lost without such a guide.) Cut this template out in cardboard—and remember, it is only a guide.

Materials:

The colors in this quilt should be very delicate. The color of Magnolia Elizabeth is actually a soft, soft, yellow, almost cream-yellow. But other colors may be used; in fact, multiple shades of white could be fantastic.

1⅓ yards soft, dusty pink for quilt top background
1 yard soft aqua for curved side strips
⅓ yard soft, ice yellow for magnolia petals
1½ yards light, fern green for leaves (This amount includes sufficient material for a bias binding of fern green on the *top side only*. Back bias binding should match backing.)
3¼ yards backing fabric, the color of your choice (White, dusty pink, or ice yellow would all be good choices. This seems like a lot of fabric, but I prefer no seaming or piecing on the backing of this quilt except what is necessary to join side bars.)
1 skein embroidery floss (or silk thread if desired) to accent leaves and flowers (Use a shade of yellow stronger than the ice yellow if you choose to embroider stamens and pistils. If you prefer to appliqué these, use a scrap of yellow, again stronger than ice yellow.)
quilting thread
batting
No. 7 or No. 8 crewel embroidery needle

NOTE: If you prefer not to trapunto the magnolias, use two layers of fabric for the petals, treating the two layers as one throughout. This will give the flowers more substance and prevent a shadow from the seam allowance. Increase the amount of ice-yellow fabric you buy accordingly.

Instructions:

Silk embroidery thread might be used to finish the center of the flowers with stamen and pistil: French knots would be appropriate. See the discussion of the Clematis quilt in Chapter 5 and Figure 20 on page 47. Also, consider a touch of silk embroidery thread along the lines to be quilted on the flowers and leaves. (Quilt alongside these lines in the final quilting.) If you plan to use embroidery, I recommend that you do it after you have drawn your patterns on fabric, but *before* you have cut them out—for easier handling.

In fact, I recommend laying this entire quilt out in newspaper before cutting fabric. The pattern is complicated, and the fabric work will be easier if you have first experimented with paper patterns.

When you are ready,

CUT: Soft, Dusty Pink

On the width of the fabric, cut the center piece, 35″ × 43″; fold this piece into quarters and mark the edge at the folds (four marks in all). This will be the background piece for your appliqué work. The measurement for this piece includes seam allowance.

CUT: Soft Aqua

On the width of the fabric, cut two each of the two curved side bars (add seam allowance of ½-inch to the patterns given). (Be sure to join the two pieces of the long side bar at the dash lines to make one pattern piece, matching V's *but not clipping them, before* you cut.) Mark O's ½-inch in from points of side bars, on seam lines. Match quarter marks on background piece with center marks on side bars; sew together up to O marks. There should be ½-inch left open to the ends of the side bars. This ½-inch gap will become important when it is time to bind your quilt. The unusual shape of this quilt will, believe it or not, make tucking-in easier. Note that in my layout the top side bar is turned so that it curves in. If you follow this layout, bind the curved edge, or appliqué a bias strip over the curved edge once you have appliquéd the top bar down to the quilt top.

CUT: Light Fern Green

12 leaves, as follows:
Leaf C Cut 8
Leaf D Cut 8
Leaf E Cut 4

CUT: Soft, Ice Yellow

For the flowers, 24 pieces, as follows:
4 each of petals, F through K

CUT: Deep Yellow (unless you choose to embroider)

Stamen L Cut 4
Pistil M Cut 4

CUT: Backing Fabric

To accommodate the width of the side bars, you'll probably have to piece your backing. See Figure 40 on page 90 for the best method of doing this.

1. Appliqué leaves and flowers to your quilt top, either as shown in the quilt layout given or to your own taste. In any case, follow the template given carefully for order of appliqué and placement of petals. Stuff the flowers *lightly* as you go, if you wish: it will add a beautiful softness to the design.
2. Press as directed in Chapter 8. If you are satisfied with the way the top lies, trim seams and prepare as directed.
3. The quilting design should be simple: perhaps a 2-inch diamond design, or small 1½-inch squares with a beautiful feather design for the corners. For the ambitious, the template provides another possibility for a quilting design. Transfer the design you choose to your top using one of the methods suggested in Chapter 10.
4. Make a top-batting-backing sandwich, and prepare for the frame as directed.
5. Finish as you like; I find that lace and/or ruffles complement this light, graceful design well—especially if the quilting design is not too fussy. Refer to Chapter 10 for binding instructions.

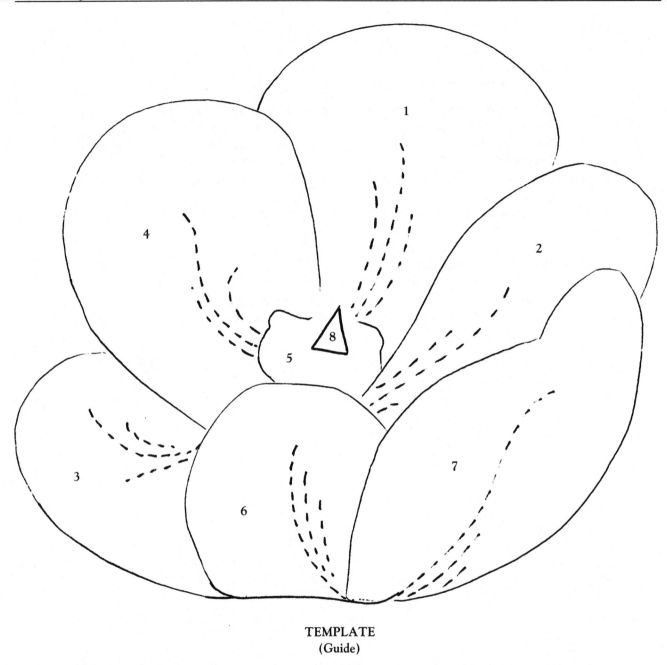

TEMPLATE
(Guide)

This is a guide for placing Magnolia Elizabeth petals in proper sequence to make your fabric flowers look "natural." This is *not* a pattern for appliqué. However, it can be used as a template for a quilting design, and you may also like to add the leaves in your quilting lines. Be careful to preserve the roundness of this flower (thus the template); if you don't, it could turn out looking like yesterday's magnolia instead of this lovely new variety.

144

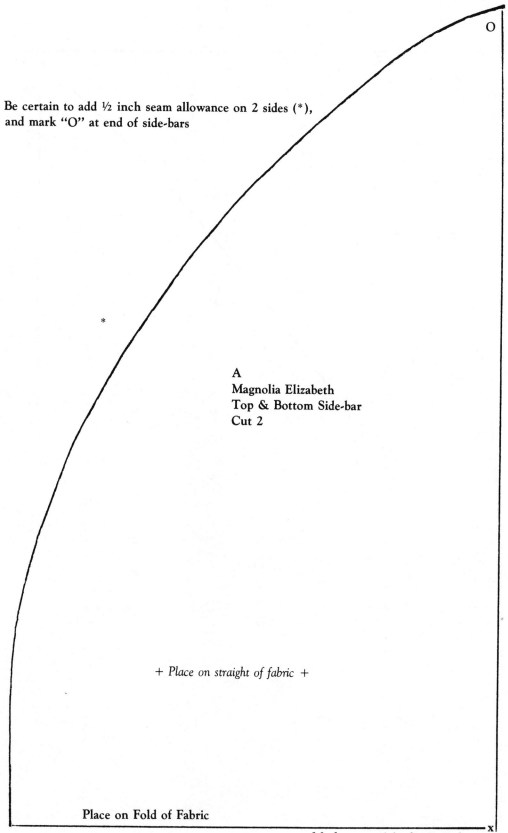

Be certain to add ½ inch seam allowance on 2 sides (*),
and mark "O" at end of side-bars

O

*

A
Magnolia Elizabeth
Top & Bottom Side-bar
Cut 2

*

+ Place on straight of fabric +

Place on Fold of Fabric

Mark center 'x', clip ⅛ inch.

Be certain to add ½ inch seam allowance on 2 sides (*)

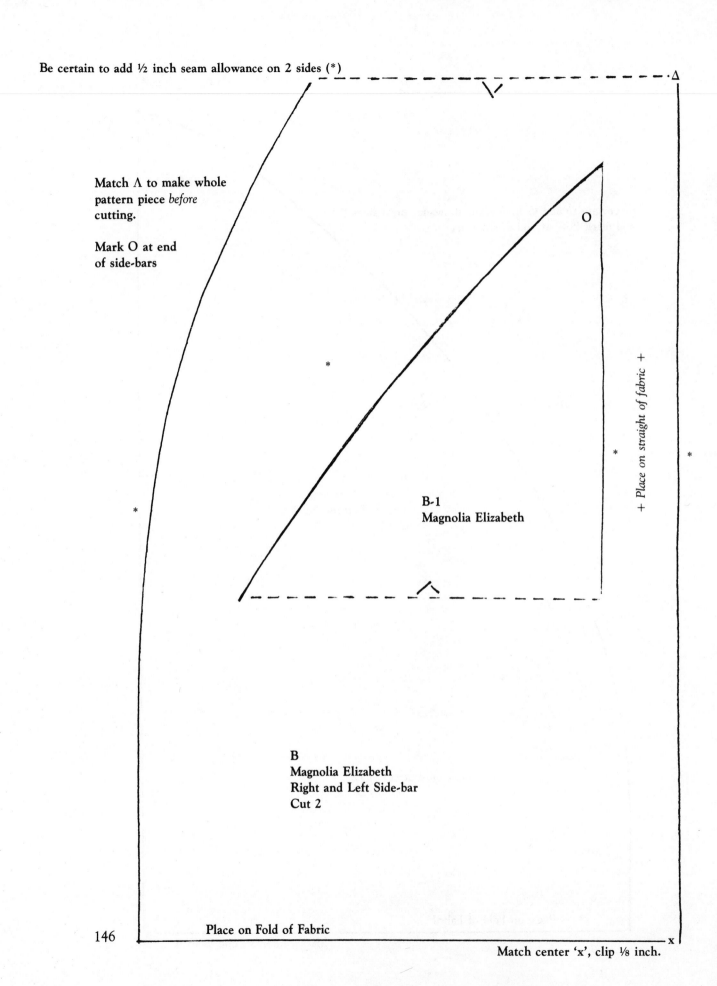

Match Λ to make whole
pattern piece *before*
cutting.

Mark O at end
of side-bars

*

O

*

+ Place on straight of fabric +

*

B-1
Magnolia Elizabeth

*

*

B
Magnolia Elizabeth
Right and Left Side-bar
Cut 2

Place on Fold of Fabric

x

Match center 'x', clip ⅛ inch.

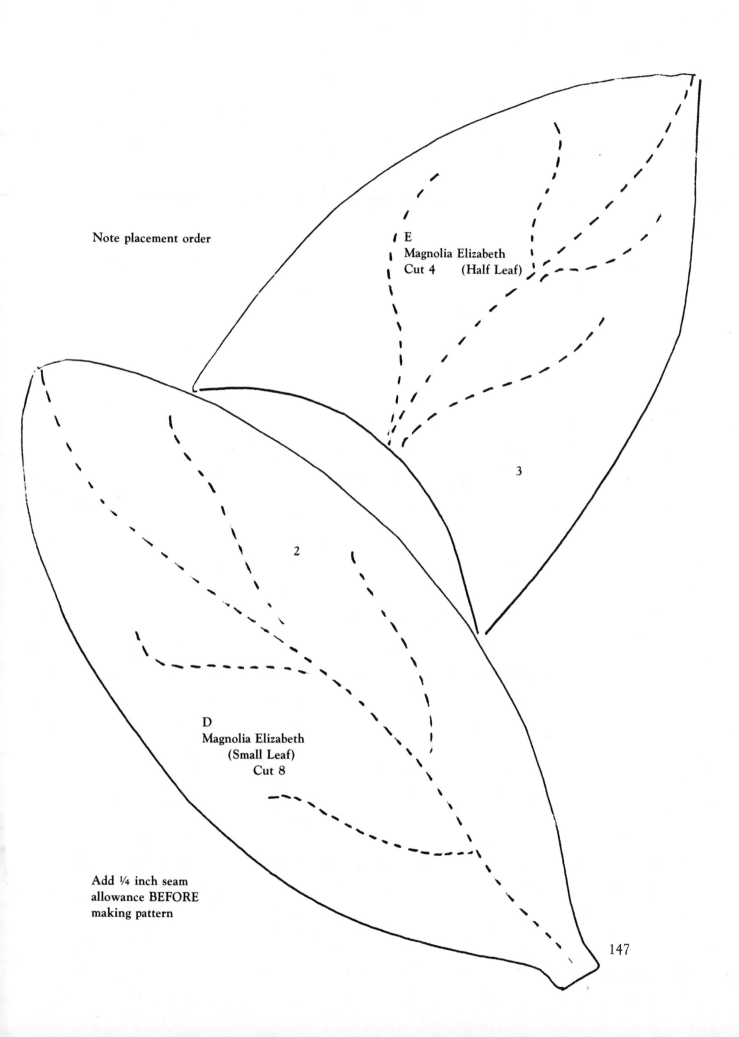

Note placement order

E
Magnolia Elizabeth
Cut 4   (Half Leaf)

3

2

D
Magnolia Elizabeth
(Small Leaf)
Cut 8

Add ¼ inch seam
allowance BEFORE
making pattern

147

Add ¼ inch seam allowance

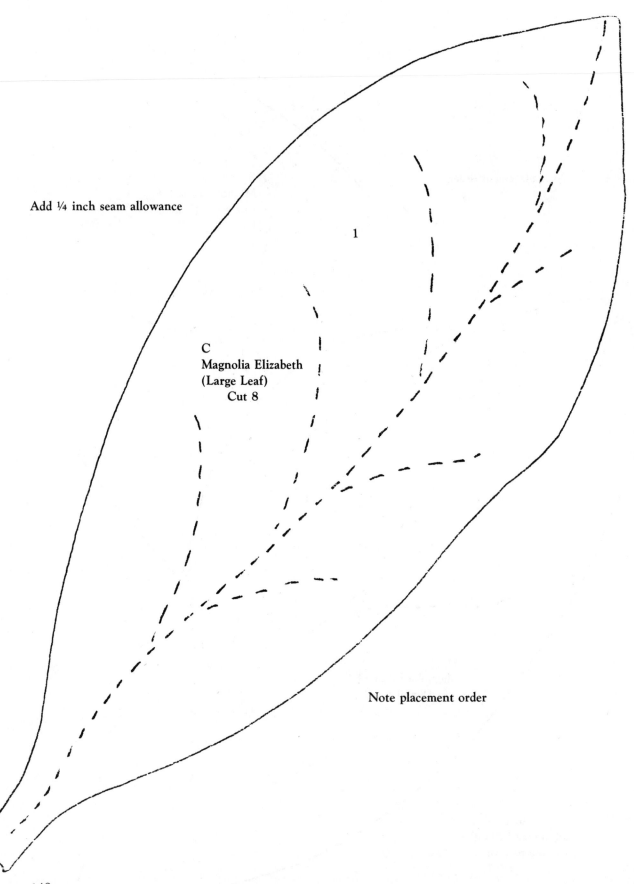

1

C
Magnolia Elizabeth
(Large Leaf)
Cut 8

Note placement order

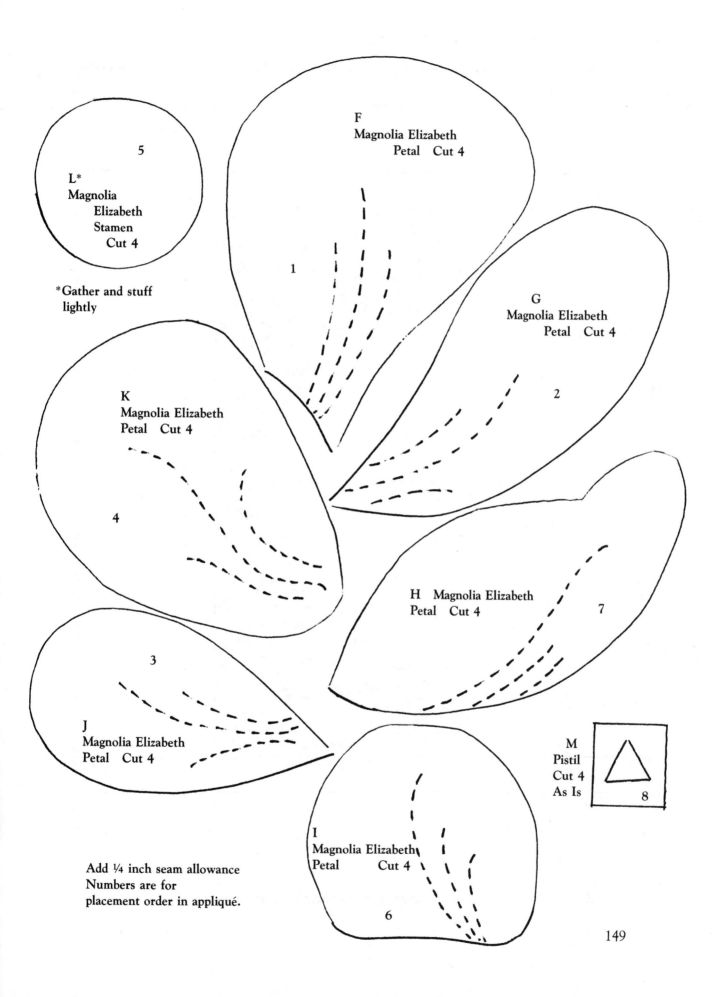

5

L*
Magnolia
Elizabeth
Stamen
Cut 4

*Gather and stuff
lightly

F
Magnolia Elizabeth
Petal   Cut 4

1

G
Magnolia Elizabeth
Petal   Cut 4

2

K
Magnolia Elizabeth
Petal   Cut 4

4

H   Magnolia Elizabeth
Petal   Cut 4

7

3

J
Magnolia Elizabeth
Petal   Cut 4

M
Pistil
Cut 4
As Is

8

I
Magnolia Elizabeth
Petal   Cut 4

6

Add ¼ inch seam allowance
Numbers are for
placement order in appliqué.

149

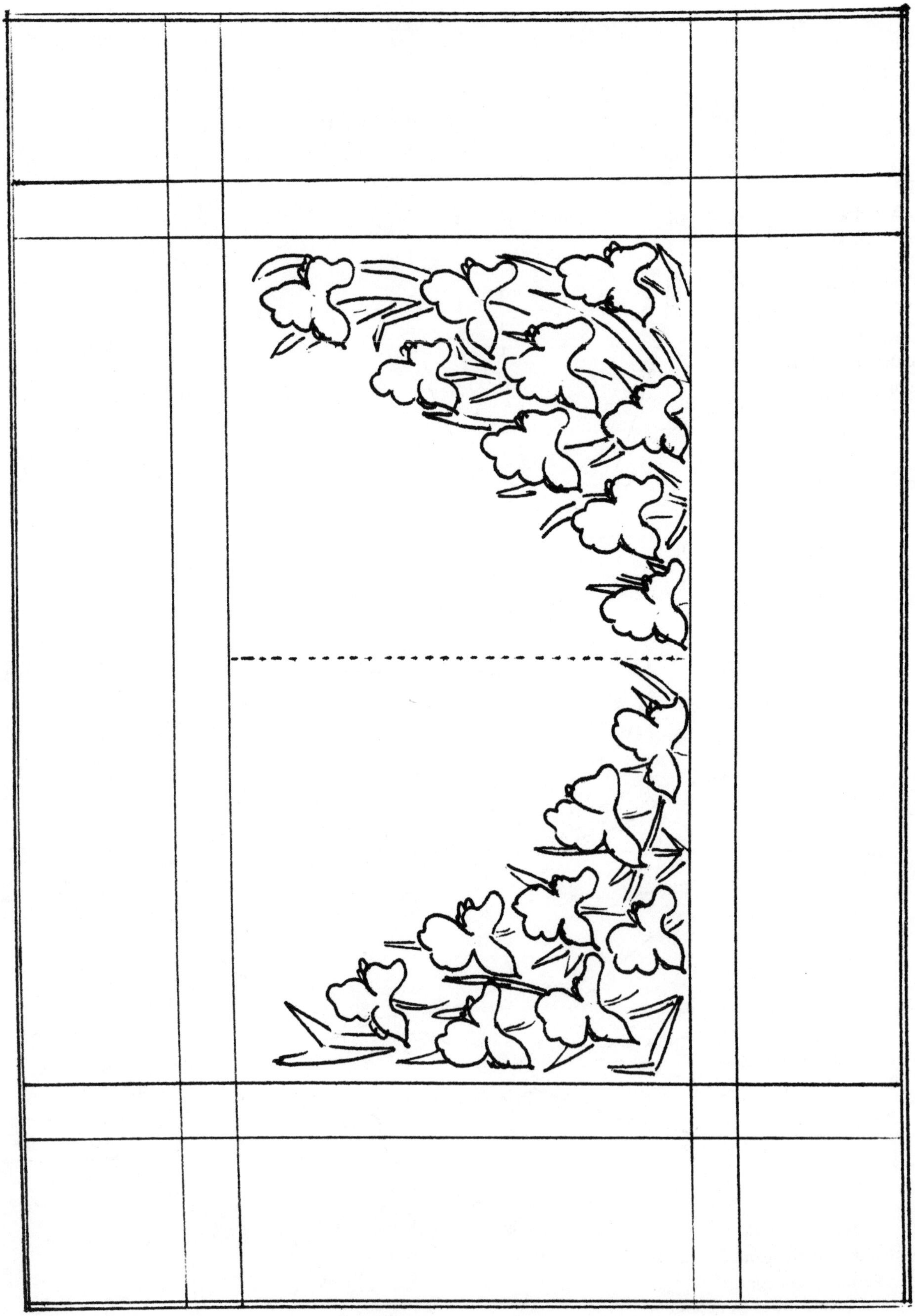

IRIS TRILOGY

(100″ × 104″)
I. germanica (Iridaceae)

Make your quilt any size you desire. The "recipe" for a quilt top below should be enough for a quilt that fits a double-sized bed. Only flower and leaf yardages are given.

The broken line down the center of the quilt layout shown indicates where I seamed my top background to make the quilt wide enough to cover a double bed. Any seam joining is up to you, however, as are all other decisions: how many flowers are to be used, how to handle your border, etc. (See Step 5 below on the subject of borders *before* purchasing material.)

Choose colors to suit your decor. The original of this quilt has a dusty pink background with strips and bars in pure white. The binding is the same muted, dusty orange as the iris "beards." Flower colors are heather lilac (a gray lilac), bright, snowy white, and soft, light gold (hence "Trilogy"). The leaves (of various sizes) may be all one color green or various shades. Try taking a blade of iris with you when you select fabric.

Materials (excluding any border appliqué):

¾ yard heather lilac (for iris flowers and buds)
⅔ yard bright white (for iris flowers and buds)
⅛ yard dusty orange (for iris beards)
⅔ yard light gold (for iris flowers and buds)
1½ yards forest green (for leaf blades)
batting
quilting thread
backing material
No. 8 crewel needle
binding material

There are three stems from which the buds will come, in addition to the iris flower head. These should be used in various places: suit *your* eye, *your* design. For my double-bed sized quilt, I used the pieces and color distribution given below; I give these numbers to help you figure out numbers and proportions for *your* design. Mix sizes and colors around. I recommend that you cut out the number of iris you think you will need in newspaper and the number of stems in brown paper and lay them out on the floor. Make adjustments *before* you cut fabric. You may want to consider reverse appliqué for the flowers: if so, remember that you'll be cutting top fabric instead of flower shapes.

NOTE: Make whole pattern pieces by joining patterns where indicated, matching V's. Do *not* cut notches!

CUT: Heather Lilac

9 iris flowers A
3 iris buds J

CUT: Bright White

7 iris flowers A
3 iris buds J

CUT: Light Gold

7 iris flowers A
3 iris buds J

CUT: Dusty Orange

46 iris beards (two for each full-sized flower) G

CUT: Forest Green

9 long blades B
7 each blades D, E, F
23 stems, total, from C, H, I (mix sizes to suit your design)

Instructions:

1. After experimenting with newspaper and brown paper, cut desired appliqué pieces. Lay out the entire quilt against the background fabric, and pin appliqués in place to suit your fancy.
2. The iris beard is easy to make. See Figure A. Take the cut pieces and lay them out with a bit of batting—no larger than an elbow macaroni—then fold in half lengthwise. Sew raw edges together with basting stitches. Then pull up the stitches a bit to create a bit of gather, which will add dimension to your quilt design. The beard should be no more than 1½ inches in length after it has been gathered. Hide the raw edges of the beard under the top edges of the left and right petals, keeping the beard as close to the middle of the iris flower as possible.
3. Appliqué the leaves and flowers down. If you wish, stuff the full flowers and perhaps the buds, *lightly*. Various leaves may also be stuffed for a dimensional look.
4. Finish preparing your top: add borders and strips as instructed in Chapter 5.
5. Mark your quilting lines. I have used fan-shaped arrangements of iris (as found in nature) for the quilting design in my borders, thinking that more appliqué would look too fussy. If the idea of appliqué pleases you, however, plan for it when buying fabric and lay it out in newspaper and brown paper as suggested for the appliqué above *before* working with fabric. For the rest of the quilt, I used rectangles about 2 inches by 4 inches because they suited the dimensions of my quilt better than squares. Please yourself.
6. Prepare for frame, quilt, and bind as described in Chapters 8 to 10.

Figure A. Iris Trilogy beard

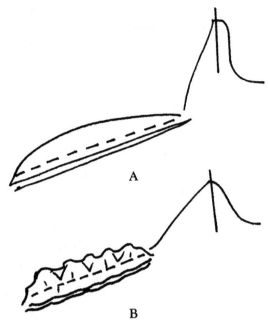

A

B

A. Place small amount of batting in beard pattern, fold fabric over, and baste close to the edge.
B. Pull basting thread up to make a beard about 1½ inches long. Knot thread so the beard holds its shape.

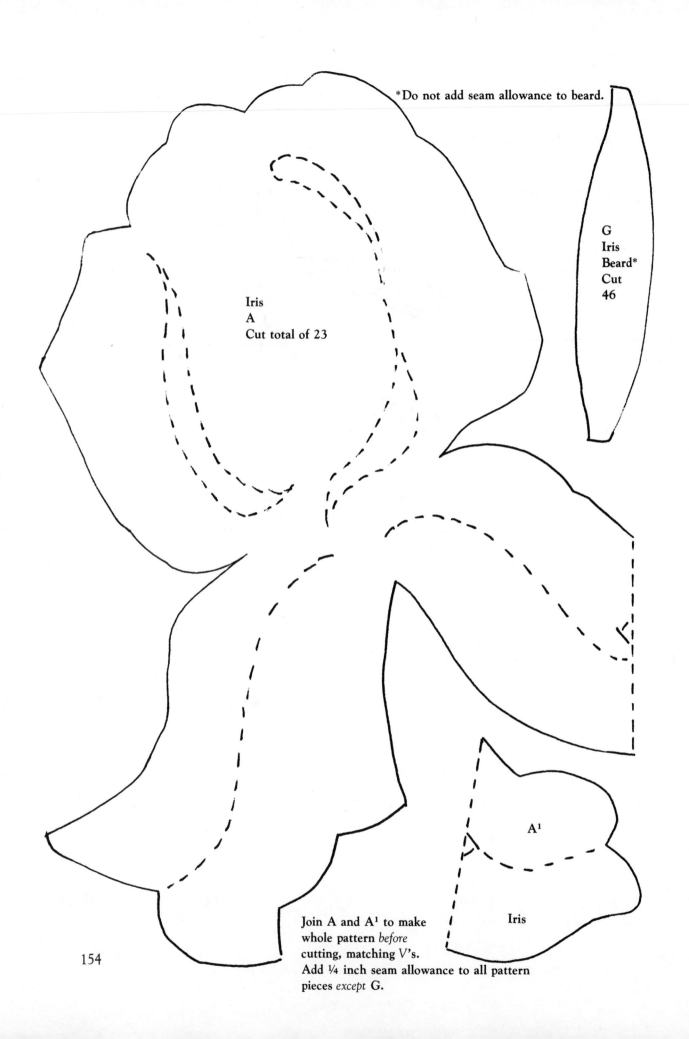

*Do not add seam allowance to beard.

G
Iris
Beard*
Cut
46

Iris
A
Cut total of 23

A¹

Iris

Join A and A¹ to make
whole pattern *before*
cutting, matching *V*'s.
Add ¼ inch seam allowance to all pattern
pieces *except* G.

154

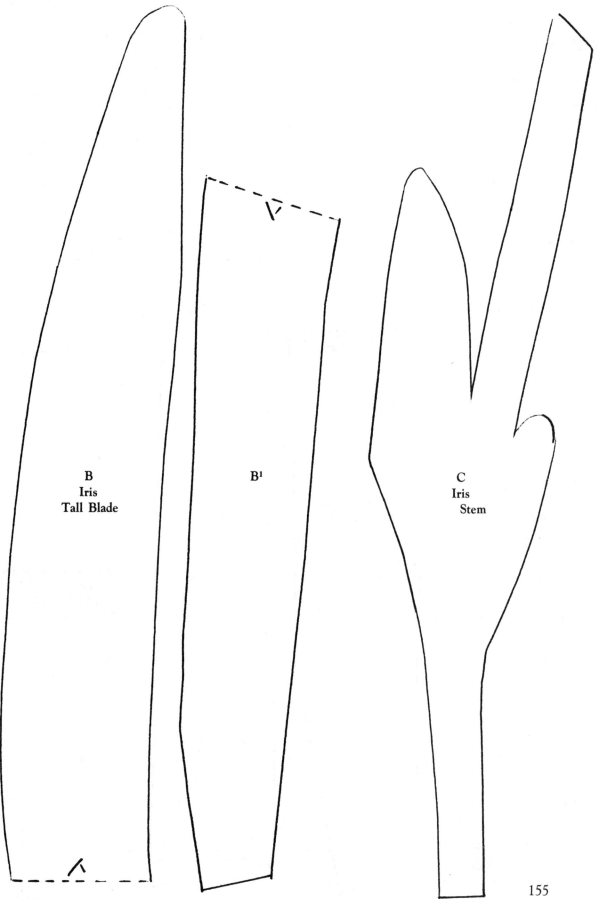

B
Iris
Tall Blade

B¹

C
Iris
Stem

Add ¼ inch seam allowance to all pattern pieces. Join B and B¹ to make a whole pattern *before* **cutting, matching** *V*'s.

155

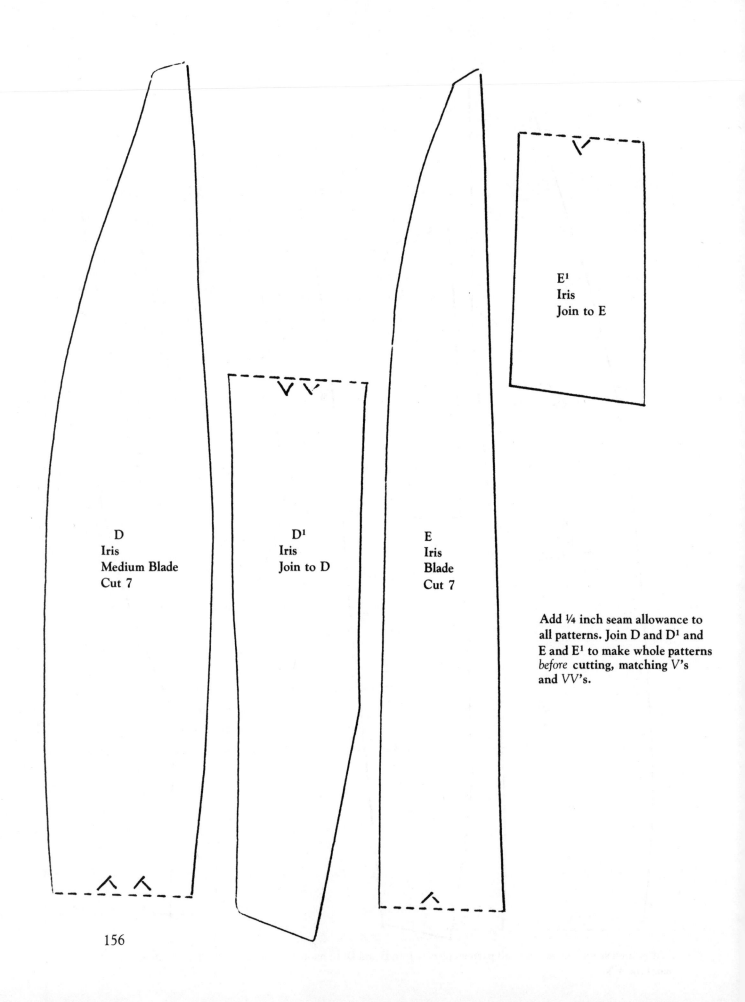

D
Iris
Medium Blade
Cut 7

D¹
Iris
Join to D

E
Iris
Blade
Cut 7

E¹
Iris
Join to E

Add ¼ inch seam allowance to
all patterns. Join D and D¹ and
E and E¹ to make whole patterns
before cutting, matching *V*'s
and *VV*'s.

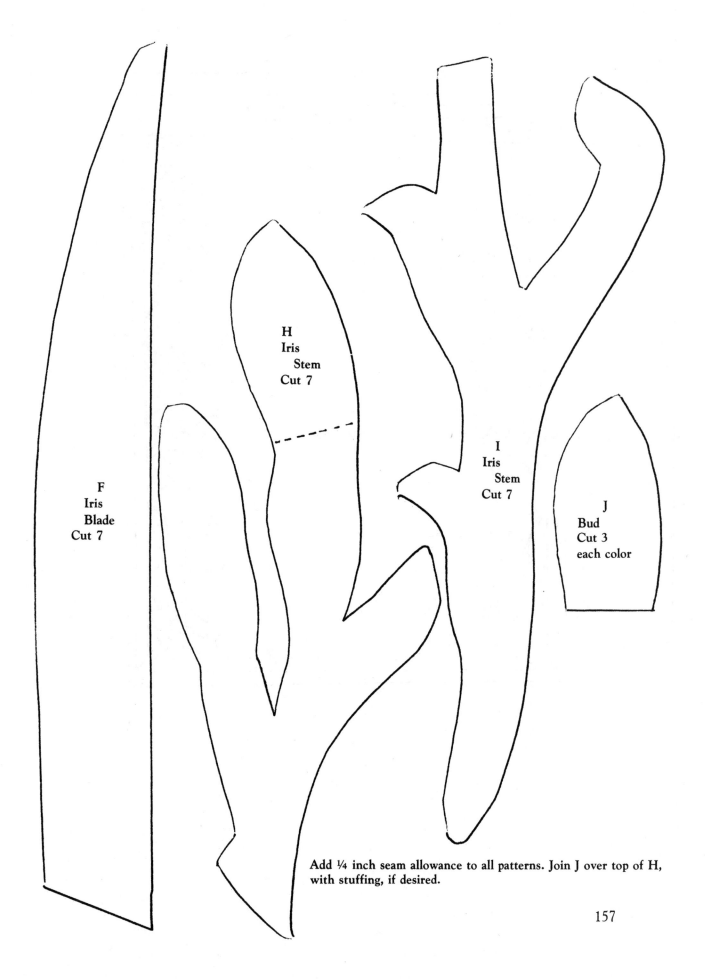

F
Iris
Blade
Cut 7

H
Iris
Stem
Cut 7

I
Iris
Stem
Cut 7

J
Bud
Cut 3
each color

Add ¼ inch seam allowance to all patterns. Join J over top of H, with stuffing, if desired.

157

PICOTEE LACE DAYLILY

(100'' × 104'')
Lilium (Liliaceae)

The name of this quilt may seem unusual, but the flower depicted is actually named Chicago Picotee Lace Daylily.[1] The flower name derives from a kind of lace known as "picotee"—"points and pricks." Often, this lace is called "Brides Picotees"—"bride" having to do not with a groom but with the kind of bar used by French lacemakers to create crocheted lace as early as the 17th century. Interestingly, "picotee" also refers to flowers: flowers having one base color with a small amount of another color along petal margins. Every quilt needs a name, and this is how my Picotee Lace Daylily came to have its identity. Wanting to express the lace part in my quilt, I placed gathered polyester lace around the large petals, where nature's "ruffle" is, and I let the three star-like side petals stand alone.

This is another quilt for which all the important decisions are left to you: what size, what color, how to arrange the appliqué, how to handle the border. Should you use lace? Should you try some reverse appliqué? Trapunto? What about using the flowers in another way, perhaps as part of a Baltimore-style Bride's Quilt? (For those of you new to the world of quilting, this is not just one quilt made for a bride in Baltimore, as it sounds. The Baltimore Bride's Quilt is a sort of sampler quilt featuring fancy flower baskets or vases full of various blooms. Often a horn of plenty is included, a depiction of home or church, a flag, some hearts, birds, a bible, etc. For more information about this fascinating quilt genre, see Dolores A. Hinson's *American Graphic Quilt Designs* [Arco, 1983].)

Follow "Planning Your Masterpiece," Chapter 3, to help carry through your decisions.

I used a 44-inch wide fabric and added enough on either side to fit a king-sized bed—see Chapter 3. As with Iris Trilogy, I suggest that you cut everything out in newspaper (flowers) and brown paper (leaves) and fiddle with the paper patterns before you cut fabric—maybe even before you buy fabric.

Materials:

I have used very dramatic colors for the original quilt. Color combinations can be thrilling if you let your imagination fly. I selected a strong, green-black background, reminiscent of the garden at daybreak and sunset, color and shadow. I was careful to test my background for color-fastness before I proceeded. Luckily, my fabric came through beautifully.

½-yard soft peach (for daylilies)
½-yard soft pink (for daylilies)
½-yard soft orange (for solid daylilies)
1 yard forest green (for leaf blades)
12 yards ⅔-inch width delicate *polyester* lace
12 small white tassels for stamens and pistils
batting

[1]Courtesy of the Wayside Gardens Co., Hodges, SC.

quilting thread
backing material
No. 8 crewel needle
binding material

For my layout, there should be a color repeat in the narrow borders around the appliquéd top—perhaps two or three. Side drops should be the same color as the top. Top background fabric will, of course, depend on the dimensions you choose for your quilt; see Chapter 3. The appliqué fabric measurements above will do for a twin-sized bedspread as well as a coverlet-style king-sized quilt *if* you lay out your flowers on the "to the floor" or overhang portions of your quilt. The flowers and leaf stems would fall right into the borders in this arrangement. This makes a very dramatic quilt, especially in strong colors. The top of the quilt would be best left plain, but beautifully quilted.

If you choose to reverse appliqué, cut background fabric (not flower fabrics) following the instructions in Chapter 7. For regular appliqué, when you are ready:

CUT: Soft Peach

6 picotee daylilies A
6 each side petals D, E, F
6 daylily buds I

CUT: Soft Pink

6 picotee daylilies A
6 each side petals D, E, F
6 each daylily buds I

CUT: Soft Orange

10 daylily blossoms C

CUT: Forest Green *and* Fern Green

In each color:
    6 double leaves H
    6 tall leaves J
    6 stems G
    5 medium leaves B
    10 small leaves F

Try to keep the leaves on the straight of the fabric as much as possible: this will make appliqué work easier. You may wish to have a denser leaf population. Play with paper *before* you cut.

Instructions:

1. Plan *everything* out on paper—measurements and all.
2. Prepare your top background fabric: seam as necessary. I added side strips, pressed, and then trimmed my seams to ¼-inch. This is one of the few quilts I have *ever* trimmed seams on

before completing the top. But with appliqué to be done in some places over the seam lines, I thought it best to work over as little seam as possible. Press carefully and trim even more carefully than usual, as instructed in Chapter 8.

3. Machine-gather lace. I recommend polyester lace for its springiness, which is essential for the effect needed here.

4. After you've arrived at a satisfactory layout, pin, then appliqué whole flowers "as you go." See Figure A for procedure. There is a lot of appliqué required for this quilt—but completing whole flowers "as you go" makes it fun. I like a little stuffing in all the petals of the picotee daylily and also in the solid daylilies and the buds. Use your imagination. Don't be afraid to lap part of a leaf over an orange daylily: nature does—it will give your fabric garden depth!

5. Especially if you've chosen a layout featuring all appliqué on the overhang, choose a quilting design carefully: the quilting will be the drama on top of the bed! Perhaps leaves and flowers could be repeated in the open; perhaps 2-inch squares would be more to your taste . . . don't forget butterflies. The appliqué can be outline-quilted and quilted "in the ditch." Mark the design you choose on your top.

6. Prepare for frame, quilt, and finish as instructed in Chapters 8 to 10.

7. Add small tassels for stamen and pistil of picotee flowers (you could also embroider these or quilt them in).

This flower design may be adapted to a block pattern; consider appliquéing flowers to clothing or using the design for other decorative purposes.

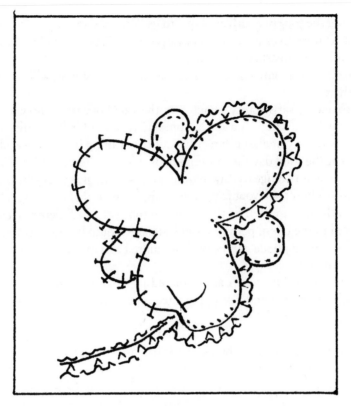

Figure A. Picotee Lace Daylily. Lace is sewn on at same time appliqué work is done, including petals. If you wish, the small petals can be appliquéd down first and then the main portion of flower laid down on top. Be certain to sew the small petals in far enough so that raw ends will be *under* the main blossom.

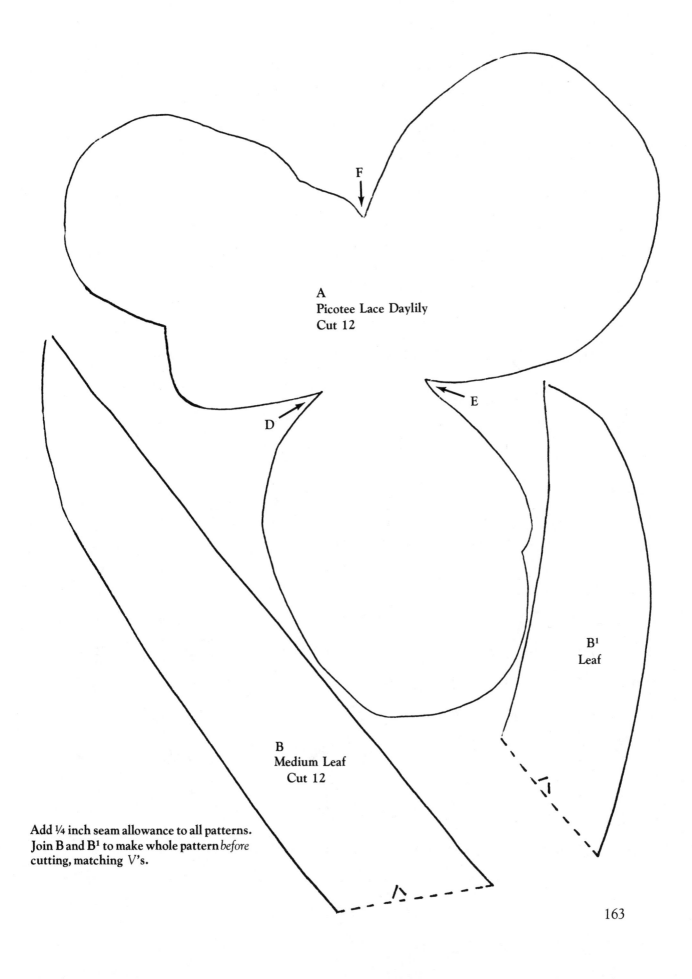

F

A
Picotee Lace Daylily
Cut 12

D

E

B¹
Leaf

B
Medium Leaf
Cut 12

Add ¼ inch seam allowance to all patterns.
Join B and B¹ to make whole pattern *before*
cutting, matching *V*'s.

163

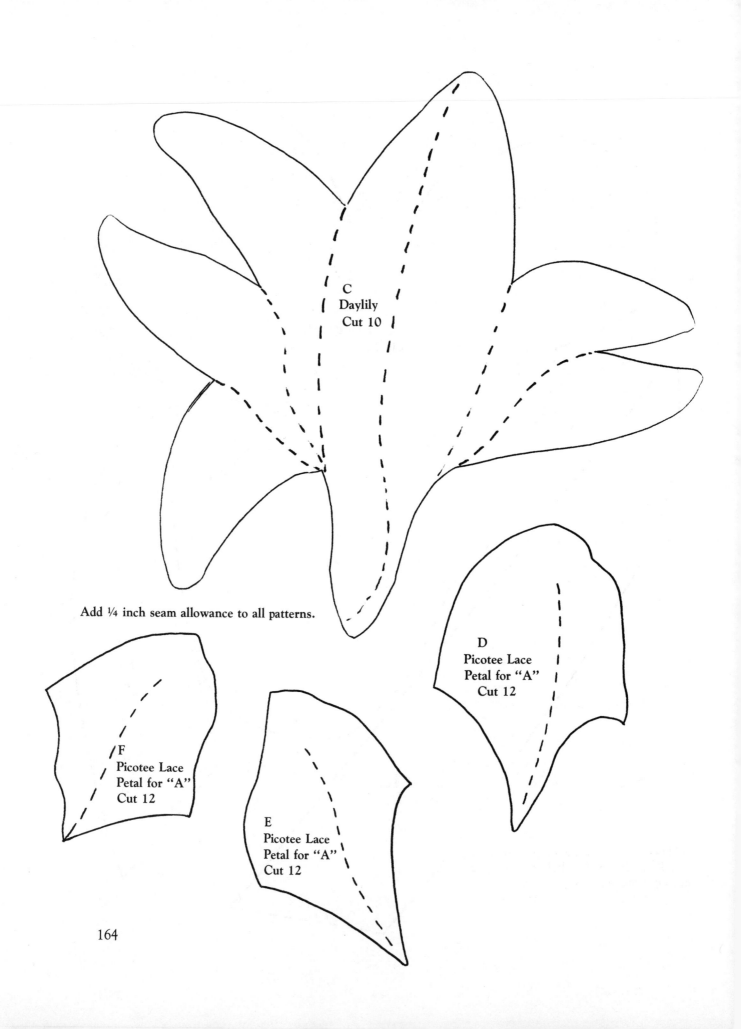

C
Daylily
Cut 10

Add ¼ inch seam allowance to all patterns.

D
Picotee Lace
Petal for "A"
Cut 12

F
Picotee Lace
Petal for "A"
Cut 12

E
Picotee Lace
Petal for "A"
Cut 12

164

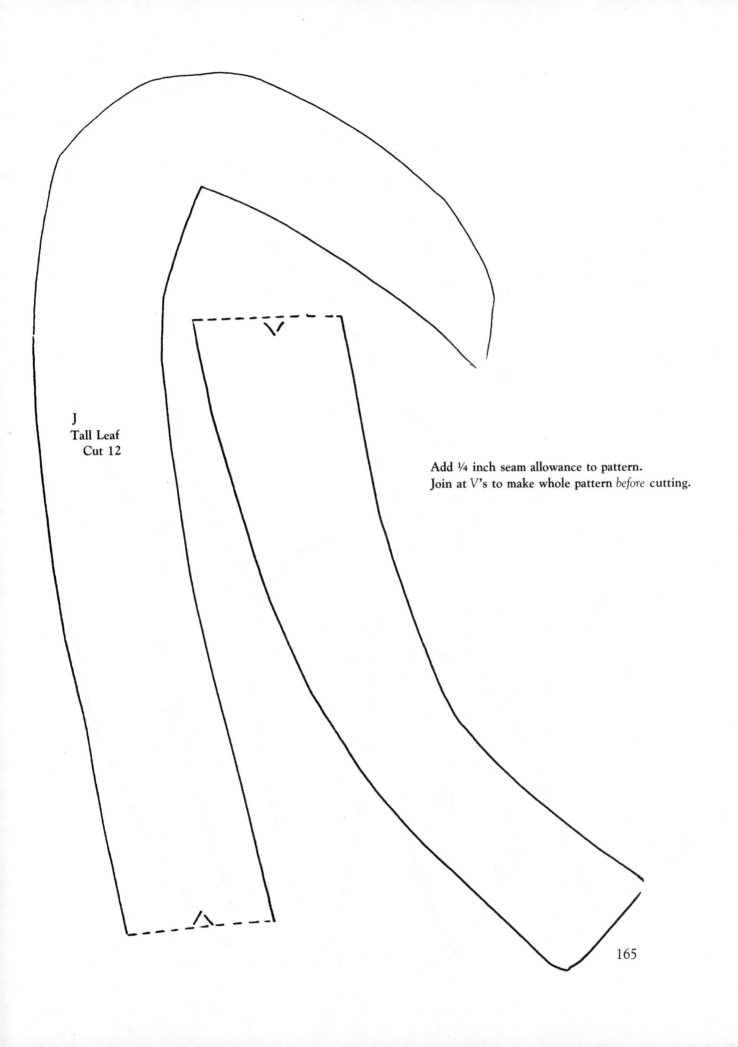

J
Tall Leaf
Cut 12

Add ¼ inch seam allowance to pattern.
Join at V's to make whole pattern *before* cutting.

165

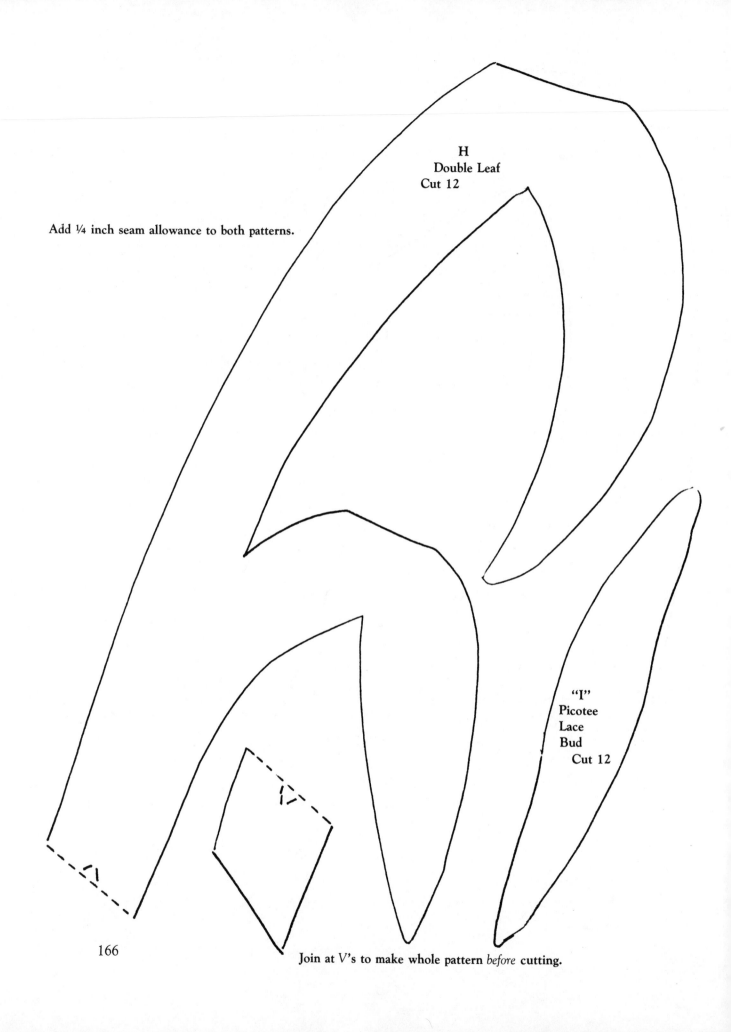

H
Double Leaf
Cut 12

Add ¼ inch seam allowance to both patterns.

"I"
Picotee
Lace
Bud
Cut 12

166

Join at *V*'s to make whole pattern *before* cutting.

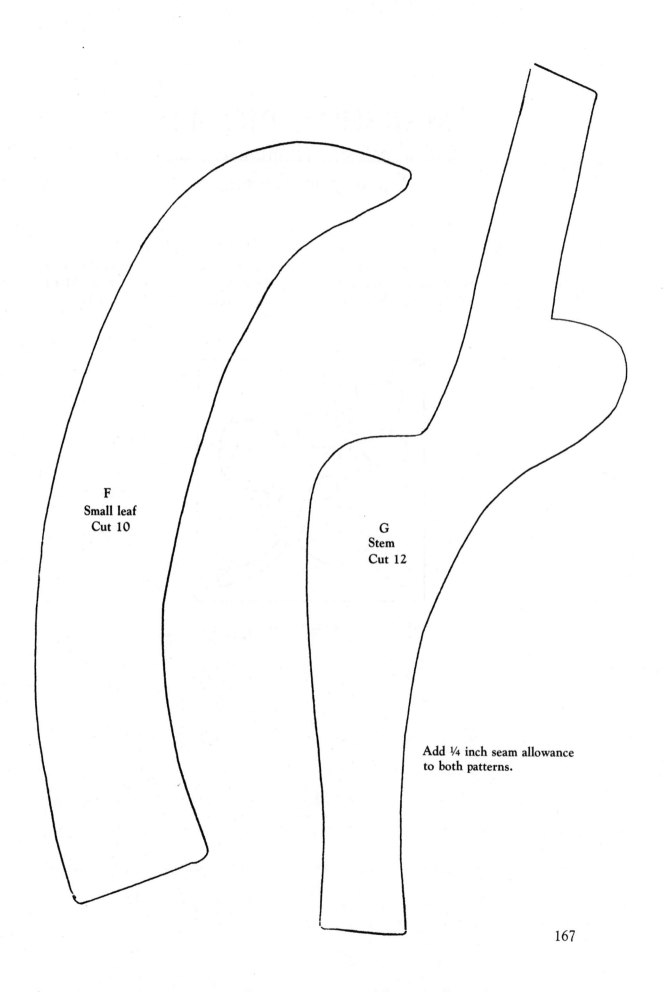

F
Small leaf
Cut 10

G
Stem
Cut 12

Add ¼ inch seam allowance
to both patterns.

167

MARSH MARIGOLD
Caltha palustris (Ranunculaceae)
(Size to your choosing.)

There are no specific instructions for building this quilt. The Chapter 10 opening page shows a possible layout, which is basically traditional—and should be to your liking. Now is the time for you to use your newly gained expertise and your trained imagination: go build yourself a Marsh Marigold quilt or wall hanging. Or, adapt the pattern to aprons, skirts, shirts—anything you desire!

(NOTE: Seam allowance is already included.)

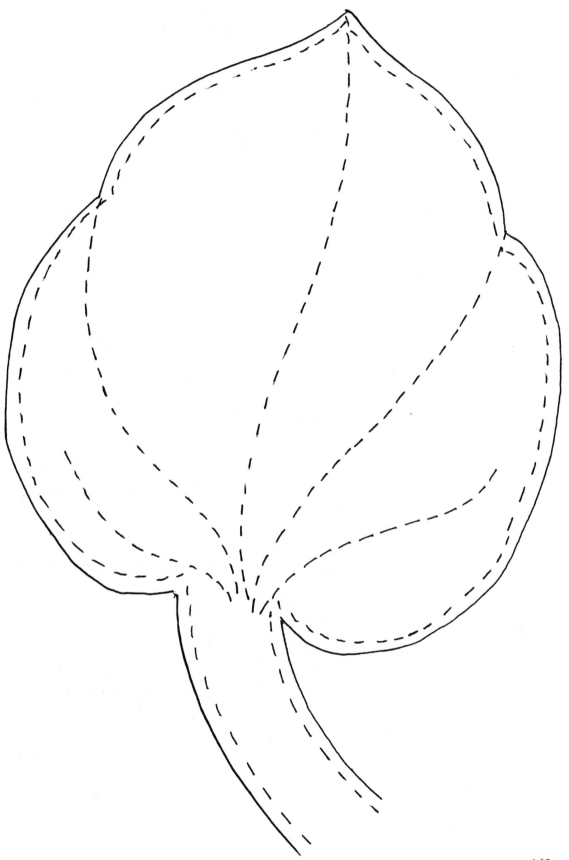

169

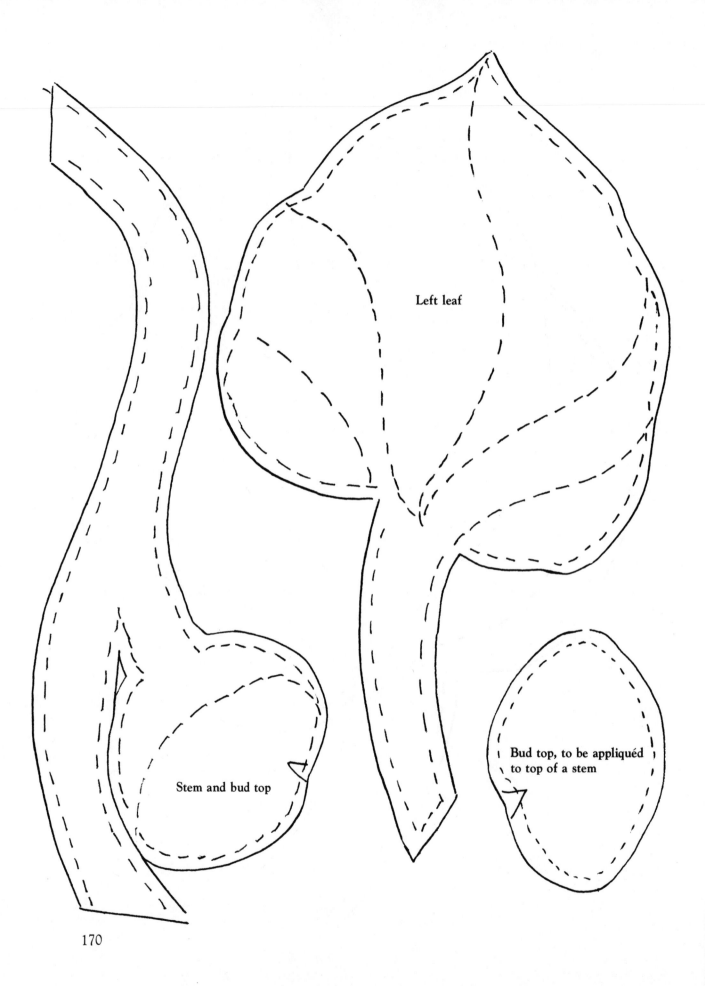

Left leaf

Stem and bud top

Bud top, to be appliquéd
to top of a stem

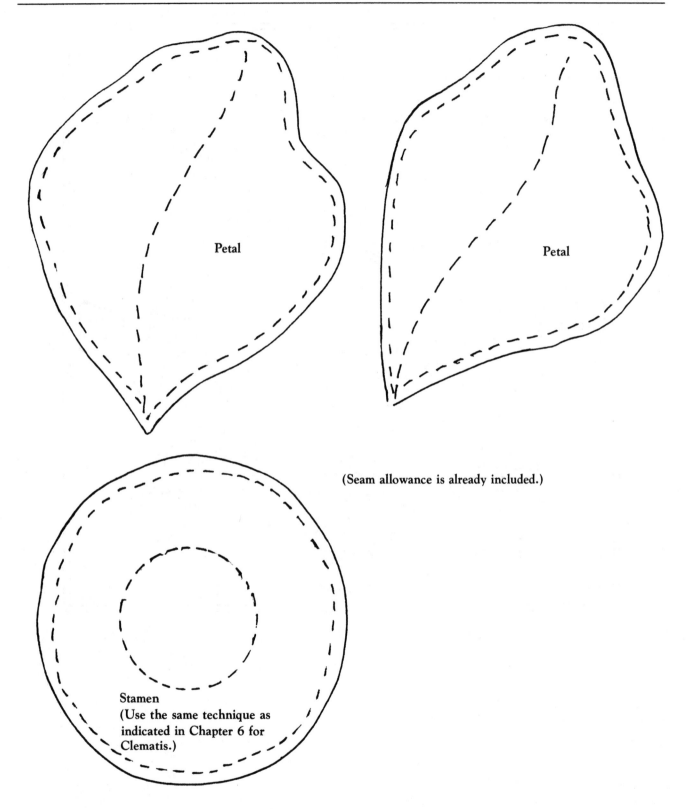

Petal

Petal

(Seam allowance is already included.)

Stamen
(Use the same technique as
indicated in Chapter 6 for
Clematis.)

171

HMONG TULIP CIRCLE

(44'' × 44'')
Tulipa (Liliaceae)

This study in circle appliqué and reverse appliqué is given in wall-hanging size but can, of course, be made in any size you desire. If you make a double- or twin-sized quilt, place the design toward the bottom so that the appliqué is not lost under the pillow.

Most tulip patterns use fabrics piled on top of one another to show nature's variations. However, I have used reverse appliqué for my tulips, which gives a new dimension to an otherwise familiar subject in quilts. Think about adapting the technique to other flower designs. The bud of the tulip asks to be stuffed just a little, as does the flower itself.

Materials:

Please use bright, vivid, extravagant colors for this design. The Hmong love color.
3¾ yards teal blue (for background fabric and backing)
1½ yards deep purple (for Hmong Circle [16 inches diameter] and bias binding)
¼ yard soft fuschia (rose red) (for tulips and buds)
¼-yard sunset violet (for tulips and buds)
1 yard forest green (for bias stems and tulip leaves, 8 of each pattern)
¼-yard light purple (for underlining of tulips—reverse appliqué)
¼-yard soft pink (for underlining of tulips—reverse appliqué)
Batting
Quilting thread
No. 8 crewel needle
Thread to use for appliqué (*exact* match to fabric colors)
(See page 65 about using batiste with reverse appliqué to give stability.)

Instructions for cutting the Hmong Circle are given below. Before proceeding to the circle, whether you intend to do just regular appliqué on your tulips, or both regular and reverse,

CUT: Soft Fuschia

4 Tulips A
4 Tulip Buds B

CUT: Sunset Violet

4 Tulips A
4 Tulip Buds B

CUT: Forest Green

8 Tulip Leaves E   8 Tulip Stems C
8 Tulip Leaves F   8 Tulip Bud Stems D

Do *not* cut the tulip reverse-appliqué lining fabrics yet.

Instructions:

1. Just thinking about how to appliqué a circle is enough to make you not want to complete it—but I have discovered a very easy way to use this magnificent Hmong idea in contemporary quiltmaking. (This same technique can be used to make squares, diamonds, or whatever.)

    First, decide what size your circle will be (my layout calls for a circle 16 inches in diameter). Divide your circle into four rings of various widths. Please use a newspaper to make your pattern; make the circle with a compass or some circular object. Cut out the newspaper rings so that you can see exactly where you are. I recommend that you make a second pattern of your circle out of brown paper before cutting out the rings, to serve as a check on shape later on.

    So, what you have is four newspaper rings—what next? Find the center of the piece of fabric you intend to use as your circle, following Figure 25 on page 56. Insert a pin in the center of the newspaper middle circle; match it to the center of the fabric (which you have finger-creased). There, you have center to center. Now, using white pencil if you've used dark fabric and lead pencil if you've used light, mark the center circle on your fabric, *lightly*. Take the next-sized ring, fit it up to the center circle, and pencil in this next ring, and so forth to your outer circle. (The solid lines in Figure A indicate these drawing lines.)

    Using your sewing machine, stay-stitch about ¼-inch on each side of your ring lines. If you use the measure on your sewing machine plate as a guide, you will have an even stitch-line. You have not yet cut the circle; you are still working on one solid piece of fabric. Once you have drawn and stay-stitched the inner circles, do the same stay-stitching outside the outermost circle. If you began with a circle 16 inches across, you now have a circle 16¼ inches across, because of that line of stay-stitching.

    After you have carefully pressed the piece, cut along the solid lines exactly between the stay-stitched lines on each side. You will want to leave the circles joined here and there, as shown in Figure A, so that you have control of the circle when you lay it on the top background fabric for appliqué. While actually doing the appliqué, you can snip the little pieces of fabric left joined to separate them. This control is important and will ultimately save time in layout and appliqué.

    Pin the circles in place (see Figure B) and begin to appliqué. *Begin in the center* and work out. Check your work against your brown paper circle occasionally to be sure you are keeping the circular shape. Do not plan on going around each ring on one hoop setting (unless this seems easier to you). I move my oblong hoop around the work so that I have control of the whole circle at all times. If it makes you feel more secure about doing this appliqué work, draw lines on the top fabric as a guide; I find it does help.

    The stay-stitching is the answer to turning a smooth circle. I find that if I clip in to (but *not* through) the stay-stitch line as I go, this works fine. I clip and turn under and pin a few inches, then stitch, and I often have two needles going at one time in my hoop area. (This is a working method I've already described for quilting, but I frequently use it while I'm appliqué-ing, as well.)

Try to use as exact a thread-to-fabric match as you can for the circle appliqué work and for the other appliqué work on this piece.

2. Before you get to the outermost edge, the tulip leaves and stems must be in place. Tulips do not grow in air, and the stems should be anchored (that is, hidden) under the outer ring. You might want to pin the tulips in place after you've pinned the third ring of the circle, before you begin to appliqué. When I made this hanging, I actually had everything pinned in place before I began the appliqué, flowers, stems, leaves, and all. Once the stems are positioned, complete the circle appliqué and the stem appliqué: obviously, stems must have their raw edges turned under before the circle is closed up, so you may find it easier to appliqué the stems before you complete the circle.

3. For the innermost ring of your Hmong Circle, you may want to open up the background fabric and put in a little stuffing to give the dimension of the cap of a wheel. Follow the technique I used with the lamb in "9" (see pages 58– 59), closing up with a widespread "turkey" stitch. Do not stuff while appliquéing the inner circle down — this will distort the inner ring and your entire circle will look out of proportion!

4. If you have decided not to do any reverse appliqué, simply pin the tulips in place in the color order desired and appliqué them down, stuffing them as desired.

5. If you *do* want to use reverse appliqué—and I advise you to try: the effect is stunning—trace the ZZZ shape in place on the A tulips, following the placement lines on the A pattern. (The other dash lines are quilting lines.) Working on whole pieces of fabric, reverse appliqué all four fuschia tulips to the pink fabric, and all four violet tulips to the light purple fabric. Press carefully on the wrong side, and just a bit on the right side. Then cut out the whole A tulip shape from the lining fabrics, following the darker whole tulips on top as your guide. You will have whole flowers, each with two layers of fabric. Do not follow the usual procedure of trimming "excess" lining fabric: here, the lining fabric will provide you with little pockets into which you can put stuffing—just a little!—as you appliqué the whole tulips onto the background fabric. This will give you a flat area where you've reverse appliquéd and an undulating curve on each side of this spot—a very unusual effect.

6. For a quilting design, I suggest a set of radiating lines coming from the outer of perhaps three concentric circles in the area where the leaves appear. Quilting "in the ditch"—right where appliqué and background meet—around the center circles and around the flower appliqués is particularly effective with this design. Don't forget the dash lines on the tulip flowers. Mark this or another design of your choice on your quilt top. (The Hmong do not quilt their pieces, but this design is an adaptation of Hmong ideas, not a replication.)

7. Prepare for the frame, quilt, and bind following the instructions in Chapters 8 to 10. The tulip designs can be adapted to skirts, jackets, and other items. One other idea I'd like to share: an entire square of cloth can have the circle cut out and be reverse appliquéd to another fabric, and the procedure can be repeated to show several layers of fabric underneath! The dimensional effect would be totally different. Try it on an experimental piece: it is difficult to execute.

Figure A. Solid lines represent the cutting lines after the machine stay-stitch lines—shown as dashes—have been set in place.

Note the 000 sections. These will stay in place until you come to them in appliqué . . . *then* clip them. They hold fabric together for placement and control.

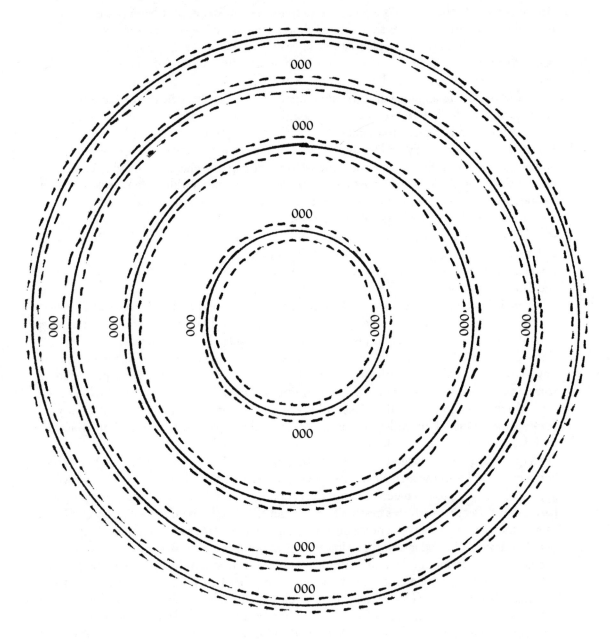

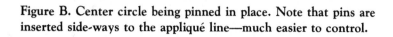

Figure B. Center circle being pinned in place. Note that pins are inserted side-ways to the appliqué line—much easier to control.

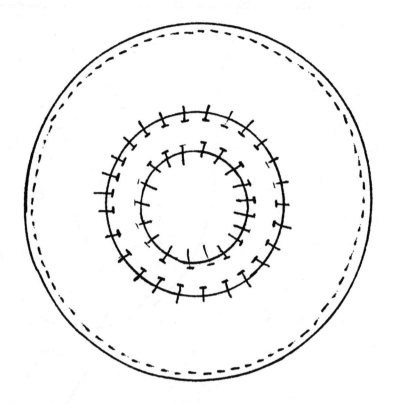

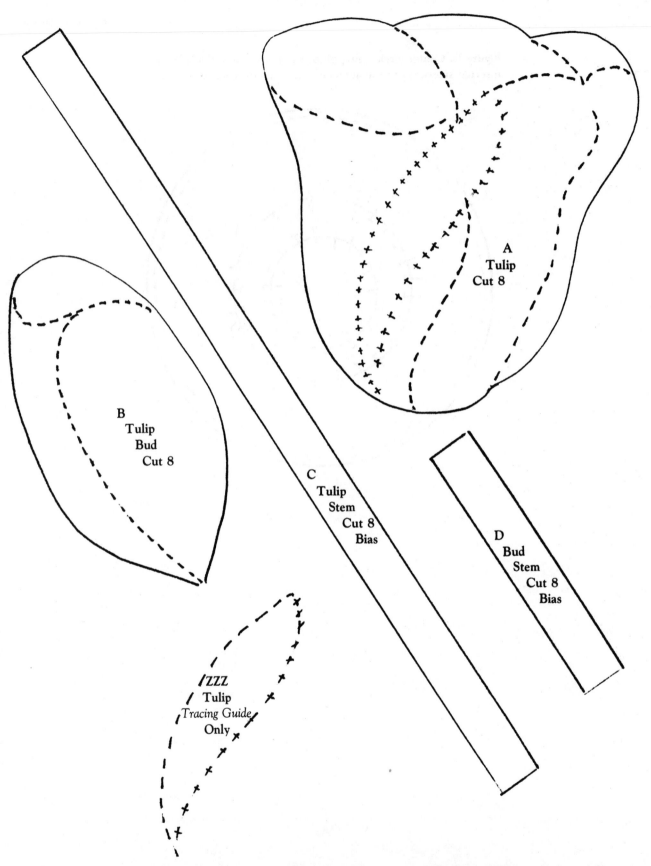

A
Tulip
Cut 8

B
Tulip
Bud
Cut 8

C
Tulip
Stem
Cut 8
Bias

D
Bud
Stem
Cut 8
Bias

ZZZ
Tulip
Tracing Guide
Only

178   Add ¼ inch seam allowance to all pattern pieces *except* ZZZ. Piece ZZZ is to be traced for reverse appliqué only: do *not* cut out. Tulip A shows a +++ line for placing ZZZ.

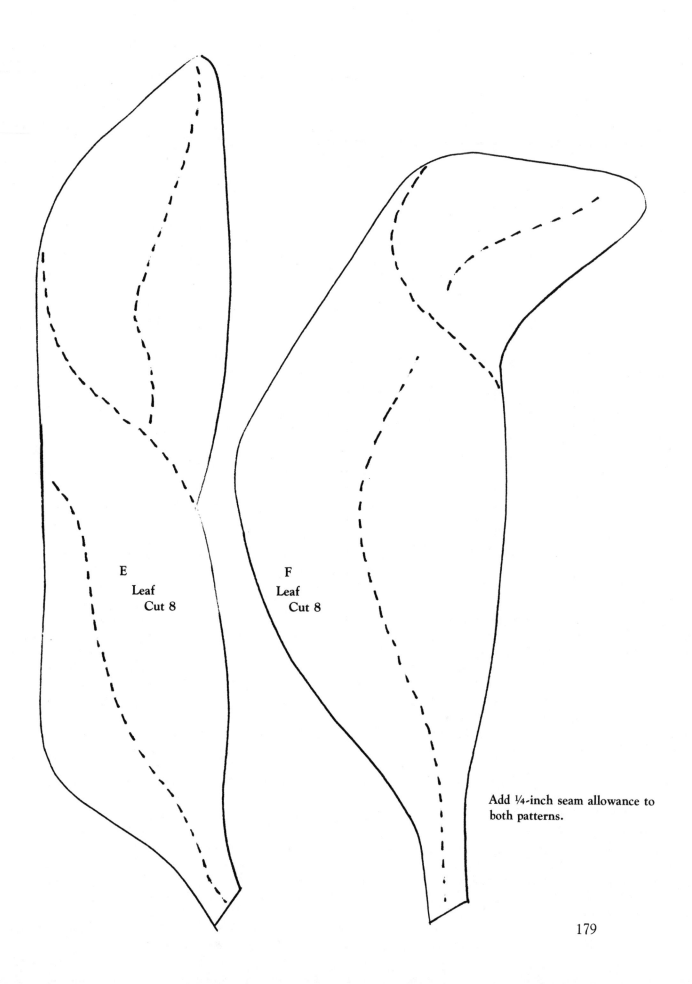

E
Leaf
Cut 8

F
Leaf
Cut 8

Add ¼-inch seam allowance to both patterns.

179